Anyone who has ever taken a shower has had a thought or idea—

Our Thoughts and Ideas...bring about action.

Our Actions...practiced long enough...become habits.

Our Habits...at first become cobwebs...then cables.

Cables are the strands of life that build character

...and it's character that drives us to success!

—Rodney R. Weckworth

PONDERS
PROVERBS &
PRINCIPLES

Inspiring...Motivating...Character Building...
Interesting and Fun!

by RODNEY R. WECKWORTH

illustrations by Tania von Allmen
foreword by Zig Ziglar

Contents

CHAPTERS

Foreword

"A number of years ago I read in a long-forgotten magazine an insert of approximately three paragraphs identifying the "heart of the sale." Several years later when I wrote my book, *Secrets of Closing the Sale*, I had expanded those three paragraphs to seventy-two pages. Admittedly, that might be an unusual example, but imagination—according to Einstein–is more important than facts. One reason I have so thoroughly enjoyed these past four years of reading Rod Weckworth's *Ponders, Proverbs and Principles*, is because of what they do to my imagination.

I'm excited about these proverbs and principles being put into a book form. Not only do you learn some great truths of life and acquire some of the fine principles for living and being successful in every realm of life, but you are entertained as you're being informed. The humor often contains data and tidbits of information which make for interesting conversation, enabling you to effectively communicate with people from every walk of life as a result.

The book will provide a rich mother lode of material for those who on occasion have to make a public presentation. It contains some proverbs that will enrich any preacher's sermon. It has practical applications that would enable any teacher to be more effective in dealing with the students in the classroom. It contains wisdom and common sense that will help employers to deal more effectively with employees and merchants to build better customer relationships. It contains some wit and wisdom that will enable the parent to do a better job of relating to, understanding and loving their children enough to give them a solid direction in life.

The book will be helpful to the discouraged who seek a word of hope and encouragement. It will bring laughter—or at least a smile—to the person who is looking for, on the day he or she reads this one, a reason to smile when the need is great. In short, here's a book that truly is designed to benefit the reader, whoever that reader might be. The messages are so universal they transcend race, creed, color, sex, ethnic origin, corporate position, celebrity status, political persuasion, financial worth (or lack of same), geographical location or any other perceived barrier, whether mythical and non-existent or real and highly visible.

I highly encourage you to read this book and keep it within easy reach so you can pick it up on a moment's notice and get a message that will make you feel better about life in general and your future in particular."

—Zig Ziglar

Acknowledgements

For encouragement and inspiration, my wife and best friend of forty one years, Helena. To my son Jason and daughters Shannon and Angie. Great, longtime friends Mike and Linda Willis, Lonnie and Sue Parsons, and Jim and Sharon Lott. Steven and Kathleen Moore, longtime business partners of 30 years, and the many others who have made a difference in my life.

For help in compiling many of the life principles found throughout this book, Reverend Dan Hill.

For their creative help in the design of this book, Tania and Alex von Allmen. Thanks also to the proofreading and editing assistance of Marty Maskall and Michelle Ulrich.

Thanks also to attorney Jerry Kuperstein for his legal advice when Rod's Ponders was in the early stages.

I want to thank the rest of my extended family who have helped me to know that the principles found in real life situations always help to build our character. Stephanie, Jessica, Sierra and Laurie Weckworth, Amanda and Tony Winn, Jeff, Grant, Jenny, Lauren and Noah Baggaley, Andee Melendez, Desi Averitt, Kristen Weckworth, Tony and Cyndi Nelson and many others.

This book is dedicated to the memories of my late grandparents, Harvey and Hazel Fraser who instilled in me character and integrity that will last a lifetime.

Finally, a special thanks to all the surgeons and medical staff at University of California Davis Transplant Center, and our son Jason Weckworth, who as a living donor of his kidney gave me a second chance at life. Without your gifts, this book wouldn't be possible.

About the Illustrator

Tania von Allmen discovered a love of art early in life. She often utilized her cartooning skills to earn extra credit and boost her GPA in math, science and history courses. She is the author and illustrator of How to Massacre the Art of Selling Anything, a humorous cartoon guide to the profession of selling. In addition to cartooning, Tania's diverse talents include unicycle riding, saxophone playing, mixed media painting, and graphic design. Tania would like to dedicate this book to Mr. Bill Hill —teacher, leader, mentor, and friend.

Preface

Inspiring...Motivating...Character-Building...Interesting and Fun! *Ponders, Proverbs and Principles* is a collection of quotes, stories, anecdotes, insights and more. Many of the stories are true, some are fictional, but all of them will move the reader to achieve his or her potential for life's best.

We hope our readers have fun with *Ponders, Proverbs and Principles*, and at the same time, it is our hope that this volume will challenge readers to develop character. (They say ability will take you to the top...but it takes character to keep you there.) The emphasis is on practicality through timeless insights from the world's great personalities. We believe readers will find this book instantly useful as they travel the road to success.

As the reader meditates on...thinks through...and then applies the material in this book, positive results can be expected! Individuals, and both corporate and office staff will be motivated by the inspiring and positive insights.

The Author

A native of Sacramento, California, Rodney Weckworth likes to give people something to think about. *Ponders & Principles* is an outgrowth of a hobby taken to its extreme. For 40 years, he's had a "thought for the day". Now, that collection is at least in the 500,000 range.

Rod did not keep these thoughts to himself, however. As a partner in the 82-year-old company, Rex Moore Electrical Contractors and Engineers, he shared his daily proverb first with the staff of the company and then with the firm's clients.

Mr. Weckworth said he discovered the impact of his folk wisdom while trying to collect an overdue bill from a client. He told the debtor, who was making the customary excuses about the late payment, "Mere talk don't cook the rice." The phrase so moved the client that he asked for a written copy and, more importantly, forwarded a check by the end of that week. "The guy really liked it," remembered Mr. Weckworth, "so I thought I'd send him the next week's thoughts in the mail too."

Within the month he was sending 10 sets of weekly thoughts off to other clients of the contracting firm, with plenty of positive response. Those were the days, 18 years ago, when the emerging author hand wrote his thoughts.

However, it wasn't long before the weekly mailing list had expanded to hundreds of names and had become a major marketing tool for the company. "You can bet people who received the 'Ponders' thought of Rex Moore before they thought of our competition," said Mr. Weckworth.

But, he didn't stop there. People who made unlikely potential customers also received his weekly wisdom. President George H. W. Bush, Vice President Dan Quayle, Gen. Norman Schwarzkopf, and Paul Harvey are among the list of notables who have personally thanked the Sacramento businessman for putting them on his mailing list.

Rod also wrote a daily column for the *Sacramento Union* newspaper between 1991 and 1995 called Rod's Ponders.

In 1999, Rod retired from the electrical contracting business, and had a kidney transplant in 2003 thanks to his donor, son Jason. With a new lease on life, Rod has reinvented his old business venture known as Rod's Ponders into Ponders and Principles.

1 – Wishes, Fools and Facts

– Ponder –

"Do not wish to be anything but what you are and try to be that perfectly."

—St. Francis De Sales

– Proverb –

"The fool attempts to fool himself and won't face facts."

—Proverbs 14:8, The Living Bible

– Principle –

Our culture says, "change your image." Therefore, plastic surgeons and plastic surgery centers have become fashionably acceptable. However, plastic surgeons report that many people are still dissatisfied with themselves after nose jobs, facelifts, tummy tucks, and a plethora of other cosmetic treatments all over the body. Why? Because cosmetic surgery cannot change self-perception. If a person still perceives themselves as they did in the past, the procedure was useless.

Every human life is a treasure chest of fulfillment and satisfaction. The trick is to find the key to the chest, and that . . . is the pursuit of life.

– Baffler –

Why is one side of aluminum foil shiny and the other side dull?
(Which side retains more heat?)

Did you know...

The familiar lanky Yankee, goateed figure of Uncle Sam was based on a circus clown character created by Dan Rice, a star clown of the 1840s!

-Ponder-

"Small opportunities are often the beginning of great enterprises."

—Demosthenes

-Proverb-

"The intelligent man is always open to new ideas. In fact he looks for them."

—Proverbs 18:15, The Living Bible

-Principle-

The single most important daily decision is the choice we make about our own attitude. Few people have choices over circumstances and opportunities, but all have a choice concerning attitudes.

F.W. Woolworth was given the insignificant job of gathering remnants from all the shelves in his employers store and selling them for what he could. The rapidity with which the remnants sold gave him the idea for a five-and ten-cent store. The result was a chain of stores across the country and a fortune of some forty million dollars.

-Baffler-

When a fly lands on a ceiling, how does he fly in:
A. Upside Down?
B. Does a roll over?
C. Does a flip?

Did you know...

In Tibet, it is a sign of respect to stick out your tongue at guests.

3 – Defeat and Hope

-Ponder-

"Defeat should never be a source of discouragement…but rather a fresh stimulus."

—Robert South

-Proverb-

"Hope deferred makes the heart sick; but when dreams come true, there's life and joy."

—Proverbs 13:12, The Living Bible

-Principle-

Consider the life of this man who refused to quit. Here is his record:
At age 22- he failed in his business.
At age 23- he was defeated for the Legislature.
At age 24- he failed in his business again.
At age 25- he was elected to the Legislature.
At age 26- his sweetheart died, leaving him heartbroken.
At age 27- he suffered a nervous breakdown.
At age 29- he was defeated for Speaker of the House.
At age 31- he was defeated for elector.
At age 34- he was defeated for Congress.
At age 37- he was elected to Congress.
At age 39- he was defeated for Congress.
At age 46- he was defeated for the Senate.
At age 47- he was defeated for Vice President.
At age 49- he was defeated for the Senate.
At age 51- he was elected President of the U.S.
Who was this man who refused to quit? This is the record of Abraham Lincoln!

-Baffler-

What's the average amount of money left by the tooth fairy:
(A) In 1950? (B) In 1989? Which one has greater value today?

Did you know....

Just before you get struck by lightning, all the hair on your head will stand on end!

-Ponder-

"Leadership is the art of getting someone else to do something
that you want done because he wants to do it."

—Dwight D. Eisenhower

-Proverb-

"The master may get better work from an untrained
apprentice than from a skilled rebel."

—Proverbs 26:10, The Living Bible

-Principle-

Inherent within all human beings is the desire to be valued as a person more than
a commodity. People will respond to leadership if leadership will give them love, dignity and respect.

One of the most successful retailers in the country is also one of the most successful people developers. In their 1988 Annual Report, the Chief Operating Officer of
Wal Mart, Don Soderquist, said this:

"Every associate is an individual with certain God-given talents and abilities. If
they are allowed to use their talents and abilities, we can accomplish far more together than any of us could if left alone to develop and operate our own store. Although
we fail many times, it's so important that we work together, that we treat each other
like we would like to be treated, that we really care about each other."

1988 Annual report of Wal Mart (Bentonville, AK)

-Baffler-

Alfred always tells the truth…Bernie seldom does…Charlie never does. The first
person says that the second person is Alfred…The second person says, "No, I'm
Bernie."…The third person says that the second person is Charlie.

Who's Charlie?

Did you know....

The highest recorded speed of fluid expelled by a
sneeze has been measured as 103.6 mph.

5 – Thoughts and Knowledge

-Ponder-

"Some people drink at the fountain of knowledge...others just gargle."

—Unknown

-Proverb-

"Above all else guard your thoughts, for they influence everything else in your life."

—Proverbs 4:23, The Living Bible

-Principle-

Fifteen prominent college professors took this challenge: "If all the books on the art of moving human beings into action were condensed into one brief statement, what would that statement be?" The result of their deliberation was:

What the mind attends to, it considers.
What the mind does not attend to, it dismisses.
What the mind attends to continually, it believes.
What the mind believes, it eventually does.

-Baffler-

Where does the speed limit start?
(A) When you can see the sign...(B) At the sign...(C) 250' past the sign

Did you know....

Chewing gum while peeling onions will keep you from crying.

-Ponder-

"You're getting over the hill when most of your dreams are re-runs."

—Sunshine Magazine

-Proverb-

"The wicked man's fears will all come true, and so will the good man's hopes."

—Proverbs 10:24, The Living Bible

-Principle-

Everybody ought to be a dreamer! Everybody ought to have goals and dreams for their lives, their business and their families. Dreaming is the first step in a long journey toward maximizing our potential.

This country exists today because those who have gone before us dared to dream. Every significant technological breakthrough is the finished product of a dream. Never, never, never stop dreaming!

-Baffler-

Why do ranchers hang old boots on fence posts?

Did you know....

Abraham Lincoln has been the subject of over 8,600 books,
a distinction ranking second only to Jesus.

7 – Life in a Forward Motion

-Ponder-

"Life can only be understood backwards, but it must be lived forward."
—Soren Kierkegaard

-Proverb-

"We all have happy memories of good men gone to their reward,
but the names of wicked men stink after them."
—Proverbs 10:7, The Living Bible

-Principle-

Swedish chemist Alfred Nobel awoke one morning to read his own obituary in the local newspaper. The obituary notice read: "Alfred Nobel, the inventor of dynamite, died yesterday. He devised a way for more people to be killed in a war than ever before. He died a very rich man."

Actually, it was Alfred's older brother who had died; a newspaper reporter had bungled the epitaph.

The bogus obituary had a profound effect on Nobel. He decided he wanted to be known for something other than developing the means to kill people efficiently and for amassing a fortune in the process. So, Alfred initiated the Nobel Prize, the award for scientists and writers who foster peace! He said, "Every man ought to have the chance to correct his epitaph in midstream and write a new one."

-Baffler-

Why do firehouses have Dalmatians?

Did you know....

It is illegal to leave a naked dummy in a store window in New York City.

8 – Pursuit and Wants

-Ponder-

"Be careful of what you become in pursuit of what you want."

—Stephen Nogleberg

-Proverb-

"Have two goals; wisdom—that is, knowing and doing right—and common sense. Don't let them slip away, for they fill you with living energy, and are a feather in your cap."

—Proverbs 3:21-22, The Living Bible

-Principle-

When Apple Computer fell on difficult days in the 1990s, Apple's young chairman, Stephen Jobs, traveled from the Silicon Valley to New York City. His purpose was to convince PepsiCo's John Scully to move west and run his struggling company.

"Financially," Scully said, "You would have to give me a million-dollar salary, a million-dollar bonus, and a million-dollar severance."

Flabbergasted, Jobs gulped and agreed, if Scully would move to California. But Scully would only commit to being a consultant from New York. At that Jobs issued a challenge to Scully: "Do you want to spend the rest of your life selling sugared water, or do you want to change the world?" That question knocked the wind out of Scully, and he agreed to move to California!

-Baffler-

What is a timber doodle?

Did you know....

The dollar sign is a modification of the figure eight as it appeared on the old Spanish "pieces of eight."

9 – Secrets to Long Life

-Ponder-

"Every man desires to live long; yet no man desires to be old."

—Jonathan Swift

-Proverb-

"White hair is a crown of glory and is seen most among the godly."

—Proverbs 16:31, The Living Bible

-Principle-

The question is: Is age a state of mind or body? That's a question everyone can relate to because all of us are getting older.

Dr. Kenneth Pelletier, Professor of Internal Medicine at the University of California at San Francisco says that the latest scientific research indicates aging is a state of mind. Oh, not that the mind can prevent the body from the ravages of time, but Dr. Pelletier's studies concluded that attitude and lifestyle are the elements to staying young. All of the studies point to an "aging set point" as the key. The set point is governed by how old you "think" you are and by what you consider middle age.

-Baffler-

Of your 5 senses, which develops first? Hearing, Touch, Sight, Smell or Taste.

Did you know....

It takes about four hours to hard-boil an ostrich egg.

-Ponder-

"You develop men like you mine for gold.
You gotta move tons of dirt to find the gold
...but you don't go in looking for the dirt
...you go in looking for the gold!"

—Andrew Carnegie

-Proverb-

"Now your attitudes and thoughts must
all be constantly changing for the better."

—Ephesians 4:23, The Living Bible

-Principle-

How important to remember that in developing people it is necessary to consider their natural instincts, appetites and ambitions. If these factors are not taken into consideration, you will fail to create the changes in mind, heart and attitude necessary for people to succeed. Success, it seems...is a product of 80% attitude and 20% talent.

-Baffler-

What did Sherlock Holmes keep in the toe of his slippers?

Did you know....

There are twice as many left-handed men as left-handed women. For some unknown reason, left-handedness generally tends to be a male characteristic.

11 – Accomplishment, Success and Greatness

-Ponder-

"Man was designed for accomplishment, engineered for
success…and endowed with the seeds of greatness."

—Zig Ziglar

-Proverb-

"Those who plot evil shall wander away and be lost, but those
who plan good shall be granted mercy and quietness."

—Proverbs 14:22, The Living Bible

-Principle-

Your life message can have tremendous influence and impact on others. When
hope and purpose have been personally discovered, life takes on a fresh new meaning. You have a life message worth sharing, but more importantly, you have a life
worth living. With all of this in mind, we should continually ask ourselves, "Are we
too busy making a living instead of a life?"

-Baffler-

What does the male praying mantis lose after
mating with the female praying mantis?

Did you know....

The most widely played card game in the world is Solitaire.

12 – Speed and Leadership

-Ponder-

"The speed of the leader determines the rate of the pack."

—Unknown

-Proverb-

"Do you know a hard-working man? He shall
be successful and stand before kings!"

—Proverbs 22:29, The Living Bible

-Principle-

Evidence of breakdowns in leadership are in abundance. Things may often appear to be smooth and stable on the surface, but many times this is only a thin veneer. Internal strife, organizational confusion; whatever the symptoms may be, the root cause is lack of leadership.

Leadership can be defined in one word…"influence." It is rare for subordinates to rise above the pace set by leadership.

Dr. Warren Bennis, Professor of Management at the School of Business Administration, University of Southern California, identifies five traits that "super leaders" have in common: Vision…Communication…Persistence…Empowerment… Organizational…Ability.

-Baffler-

What part of your body is most commonly bitten by insects?

Did you know....

The guppy is named after Reverend R. J. Lechmere Guppy of Trinidad, who presented the British Museum with its first specimens of the fish in the late 19th century.

13 – Nothing Beats Hard Work

-Ponder-

"Genius is one percent inspiration and ninety-nine percent perspiration."

—Thomas A. Edison

-Proverb-

"Work hard and become a leader; be lazy and never succeed."

—Proverbs 12:24, The Living Bible

-Principle-

When Thomas A. Edison died on October 18, 1931, President Herbert Hoover suggested that all the lights in America be turned off for one minute in honor of the noted inventor. It was when he was only thirty-two that the youthful inventor, after thirteen months of repeated failure, had developed the first incandescent light. It was, in his words, the "most difficult" of all his inventions.

But President Hoover's proposal was never carried out, because responsible leaders decided that too much risk would be involved if all lights were suddenly extinguished at the same time.

Edison designed a product that proved indispensable. Even at his death, the world could not do without it for a single minute. A good test of any person's life is whether they make even a small contribution which just one person cannot do without.

-Baffler-

How many minutes does it take the average person to fall asleep?

Did you know....

A study at the University of Iowa has discovered that looking at nude people can stop you from coughing.

14 – Wisdom for All Ages

-Ponder-

"Where God has put a period…don't try to change it to a question mark."

—T. J. Bach

-Proverb-

"Wisdom is a tree of life to those who eat her fruit;
happy is the man who keeps on eating it."

—Proverbs 3:18, The Living Bible

-Principle-

Without proper punctuation, words can be meaningless. Take these fourteen as an example: then that is is that that is not is not that it it is.

Now punctuate them, and they read: That that is, is that that is not. Is not that it? It is.

The significance of fourteen unpunctuated words is not what they say, but what they don't say. They say nothing because they are not punctuated.

Life is that way. Unpunctuated, it is monotonous and meaningless. It takes exclamation points, question marks, periods, and the dashes to make life relevant and rich. Life without punctuation is like a piano with only one note, a phone book with one number, a thermostat with one degree, or a highway with one sign.

The question marks of life perplex us, the commas try our patience, and the periods bring rebellion at man's immortality. But otherwise life is only a riddle, a monotonous succession of unbroken days.

-Baffler-

What season of the year is statistically the most hazardous?

Did you know....

It is illegal to fall asleep under a hair dryer in Florida.

15 – Problems and Opportunities

-Ponder-

"Problems are only opportunities with thorns on them."

—Hugh Miller

-Proverb-

"A wise youth makes hay while the sun shines, but what a shame
to see a lad who sleeps away his hour of opportunity."

—Proverbs 10:5, The Living Bible

-Principle-

Many years ago a new teacher was assigned to a one-room school in Indiana. As was customary, the school bullies tried to bluff him the first day. The ring leader, Jim, drew a comic picture of the new teacher, wrote a few lines under it, and created quite a stir by passing it around the class. Seeing it, the teacher said, "Jim, will you please stay after school a few minutes. I want to talk to you."

Jim's friends hung around outside to see what happened. Could the new teacher stand up to the bully? To their surprise Jim soon emerged with a book under his arm and went whistling on his way.

The new teacher disarmed him by saying, "Jim, you have a rare talent. Your ability to write and draw pictures should be developed. I have a book of stories and poems. Would you like to take it home and draw me some pictures to illustrate the stories?"

Thus he fanned to life a spark of latent genius within the overgrown bully, resulting in the turning point of the beloved Hoosier poet, James Whitcomb Riley.

-Baffler-

What is the most widely talked about subject in the world?

Did you know....

Female giraffes are so disinterested in sex that they occasionally just walk away during the sex act, allowing the male to crash to the ground.

-Ponder-

"Parents who are afraid to put their foot down usually
have children who step on toes."

—Chinese Proverb

-Proverb-

"It's no fun being a rebel's father."

—Proverbs 17:21, The Living Bible

-Principle-

A child psychologist was asked, "If you had one rule for fathers, what would it be?" In reply, the psychologist gave what he called the ABC's of discipline.

"A"…he said, "stands for always. Always be consistent. Maintain a reasonable level of discipline with your child. If you blow your stack because he leaves the cap off the toothpaste today and then say nothing when he damages the neighbor's property tomorrow, you confuse him."

"B"…he said, "stands for busy. But not too busy. Some of the worst jobs of fatherhood are by men of good reputation who copped out under the guise of 'too busy'. If you're not too busy to have a child, then don't alibi out of giving him the time and friendship he rightly expects. If you allow yourself to be too preoccupied, your youngster will read it as rejection."

"C"…he said, "stands for caring. Men are equal partners in parenting. It's not woman's work to rear the young. A major peril to children in America is the bad parenthood of good men."

-Baffler-

What percent of the earth's total water supply is drinkable?

Did you know....

Until the early 19th century, burning at the stake was a legal form
of execution in many parts of the United States.

17 – Kindness and Goodness

-Ponder-

"When you are good to others you are best to yourself."

—American Proverb

-Proverb-

"Kindness makes a man attractive."

—Proverbs 19:22, The Living Bible

-Principle-

What is the best way to destroy a garden? You could drown it with too much water, or burn it up with too much fertilizer. You could plow it, chop it, burn it, or pull up all the plants by the roots. But why all the sweat? Just leave it alone, and the weeds and insects will do it for you.

What is the best way to ruin a friendship? You could telephone everyone you know and spread malicious rumors about your friend. You could make false accusations directly to your friend. You could borrow from him and fail to repay. You could write him insulting letters. But why all the sweat? Just leave him alone, and neglect will kill the friendship. Act as if he doesn't exist. Forget his telephone number. Look the other way when you meet him.

Destructive persons are not necessarily violent, some are merely neutral.

-Baffler-

What do Indianapolis 500 winners drink in the Winners' Circle?

Did you know....

According to the laws of California, it's illegal to set a mousetrap without first obtaining a hunting license.

18 – True Greatness

-Ponder-

"One of the marks of true greatness is the ability to develop greatness in others."

—J. C. Macanlay

-Proverb-

"A prudent man forsees the difficulties ahead and prepares for them;
the simpleton goes blindly on and suffers the consequences."

—Proverbs 22:3, The Living Bible

-Principle-

"If you don't let me run, I'll tear the gym apart brick by brick," threatened Jim Borden when he was a student at State University of New York. Borden, who broke the two-mile school record during his senior year in 1969-70, made the threat to the University's physician who didn't want to clear him for varsity sports.

The reason? Borden was born with a disease called Ichthyosis (from the Greek, "fish" disease). His body overproduced keratin, which gives the skin a dry, scaly appearance. In severe cases sweat and oil glands are often missing, meaning the body can't readily disperse excess heat through perspiration.

Because of Borden's inability to sweat, his doctor warned him not to take part in sports. But Borden was so insistent that his teammates found a way to help him. During a track meet, they simply stationed themselves along the route with buckets of water. When Jim passed, they doused him with cool water. The bucket brigade substituted for the sweat glands.

The will to achieve may be the most important ingredient to success but many times, we need the aid of others also.

-Baffler-

What fruit is known as the "love apple?"

Did you know....

According to the law in Pocatello, Idaho, it is illegal to look unhappy!

19 – Confidence and Understanding

-Ponder-

"Confidence is the feeling you sometimes have before
you fully understand the situation."

—Banking

-Proverb-

"What a shame—yes, how stupid!…to decide before knowing the facts!"

—Proverbs 18:13, The Living Bible

-Principle-

Far in the backwoods lived an elderly couple, Tom and Ella, who had never seen a mirror. One day Tom stumbled onto one in an old trunk in the barn loft. Looking at it, he thought the image was a picture of his father, since it so closely resembled him. Day after day Tom would return to the barn loft to gaze at this father's likeness. His wife, Ella, suspicious of his long absences made a search of the barn loft too. When she held the mirror before her face, she also thought is was a picture, but certainly not of her father-in-law!

So that night she greeted her husband with the words, "Tom, while you were at work I opened the trunk and found that picture. I never saw such a homely old woman in my life. If you're going to waste your time looking at a woman like that, I'm through with you!"

The argument was not settled until they got the mirror and looked at it together.

-Baffler-

What did the early Romans use for mouthwash?

Did you know....

The hood ornament on BMW automobiles doesn't have anything to do with automobiles. It's a stylized airplane propeller. BMW was originally an aircraft manufacturer, and when it stopped making planes and started making cars, it kept the old company symbol.

-Ponder-

"If you have a job without aggravations—you don't have a job."

—Malcolm S. Forbes

-Proverb-

"Sometimes mere words are not enough—discipline is needed.
For the words may not be heeded."

—Proverbs 29:19, The Living Bible

-Principle-

A sheep rancher in Indiana was troubled by his neighbors' dogs who were killing his sheep. He considered a number of possibilities, such as a lawsuit, a new barbed-wire fence, or even the use of a shotgun.

Finally, he settled on a better idea. He gave to every neighbor child a lamb as a pet. In due time, when all his neighbors had their own small flocks they began to tie up their dogs, and that solved the problem.

-Baffler-

What was Elvis Presley's first number one hit?

Did you know....

The famous gambling center, Las Vegas, claims to have the highest number of churches per capita in the entire world.

21 – Ability...the art of giving credit

-Ponder-

"Ability is the art of getting credit for all the homeruns somebody else hits."

—Casey Stengel

-Proverb-

"A faithful employee is as refreshing as a cool day in the hot summertime."

—Proverbs 25:13, The Living Bible

-Principle-

Looking for a sure-fire formula for success, in almost any field? Here it is, in eight simple words: "Surround yourself with people smarter than you are."

Compare this spirit with the individual who can never stand to work around anyone who knows more than he does. The inability to recognize excellence in others can creep into every area of life.

Writing in *Forbes* magazine, H. S. Burns said, "A good manager is a person who isn't worried about his own career but rather the careers of those who work for him. Take care of those who work for you, and you'll float to greatness on their achievements."

-Baffler-

When meat is stamped "USDA" at the supermarket, what is the dye made from?

Did you know....

There are virtually no birds that sing while they are on the ground. Birds typically sing only when they are on a tree branch or on some other spot off the ground.

-Ponder-

"Life begins when you get out of the grandstands and into the game."

—P. L. DeBevoise

-Proverb-

"A lazy man won't even dress the game he gets while hunting, but the diligent man makes good use of everything he finds."

—Proverbs 12:27, The Living Bible

-Principle-

Everyone has his share of disappointments. And the deciding factor is not how big the disappointment, but how one reacts to the problem.

Julius Rosenwald, when he was chairman of the board of Sears, Roebuck and Co., used to say, "When life hands me a lemon, I make lemonade out of it."

"When you get to the end of your rope, tie a knot and hang on," is another way of saying it.

The mother of Dwight D. Eisenhower, who was fond of Solitaire often said, "The Lord deals the cards; you play them."

Henry Ward Beecher ties the whole subject up in a package of twenty-three words: "God asks no man whether he will accept life. This is not the choice. You must take it. The only choice is how."

-Baffler-

How thick is the ice cap in Antarctica and what percent
of the world's fresh water does the ice hold?

Did you know....

You are 1/4 inch taller in the morning than you are at night. The cartilage between the vertebrae of your spine gets squashed while you stand and walk around, but recover while you sleep at night.

23 – Getting to the Top of the Ladder

-Ponder-

"Many a man gets to the top of the ladder and then finds
out it has been leaning against the wrong wall."

—Unknown

-Proverb-

"Only a simpleton believes what he is told! A prudent
man checks to see where he is going."

—Proverbs 14:15, The Living Bible

-Principle-

Two tired donkeys approached a stream on a hot day. One was carrying a load of salt, and the other a huge pack of sponges. The first donkey, carrying the salt, went down into the stream where the salt soon dissolved.

When he came out on the other side, he called back to his fellow donkey, saying what a marvelous experience he had as he lost his burden in the cooling stream.

Whereupon the second donkey plunged into the stream, but the sponges soaked up the water and caused him to drown.

Moral: Don't play "Follow-the-Leader" unless you have a fairly good idea where he's headed!

-Baffler-

How high does a "hill" have to be before it's considered a "mountain"?
500'   1,000'   1,500'   2,000'   3,000'   4,000'   5,000'

Did you know....

A restaurant survey has determined that people who eat
the most in restaurants tend to tip the least.

-Ponder-

"You cannot climb the ladder of success with your hands in your pockets."

—Zig Ziglar

-Proverb-

"Hard work means prosperity, only a fool idles away his time."

—Proverbs 12:11, The Living Bible

-Principle-

Gene Stallings tells of an incident when he was defensive backfield coach of the Dallas Cowboys. Two All-Pro players, Charlie Waters and Cliff Harris, were sitting in front of their lockers after playing a tough game against the Washington Redskins. They were still in their uniforms, and their heads were bowed in exhaustion. Waters said to Harris, "By the way Cliff, what was the final score?"

In our competitive society, we sometimes fail to remember that excellence isn't determined by comparing our score to someone else's. Excellence comes from giving one's best, no matter what the score!

-Baffler-

In 1985 in the city of New York there were 311 people bitten by rats! How many people were bitten by people?

Did you know....

The characteristic tail fins on the cars of the 1950s were inspired by an automotive designer, Harley Earl's fascination with the vertical stabilizers of the F-38 fighter plane.

PONDERS & PRINCIPLES

"We are born princes, and the civilizing process makes us frogs." — Eric Berne

-Ponder-

"Be kind…remember everyone you meet is fighting a hard battle."

—Harvey Thompson

-Proverb-

"Your own soul is nourished when you are kind; it is destroyed when you are cruel."

—Proverbs 11:17, The Living Bible

-Principle-

Jackie Robinson was the first black to play major league baseball. While breaking baseball's racial barrier, he faced jeering crowds in every stadium. While playing one day in his home stadium in Brooklyn, he committed an error. His own fans began to ridicule him. He stood at the second base, humiliated, while the fans jeered.

The shortstop "Pee Wee" Reese came over and stood next to him. He put his arm around Jackie Robinson and faced the crowd. The fans grew quiet. Robinson later said that arm around his shoulder saved his career.

-Baffler-

Why do we cover our mouth when yawning?
(Hint: It's not because of good manners.)

Did you know....

Aside from being a popular food product, peanuts are also used in the production of dynamite.

26 – Money...health, happiness and love

-Ponder-

"Money can't buy health, happiness, love...or even what it did last year."

—Unknown

-Proverb-

"Trust in your money and down you go! Trust in God and flourish as a tree!"

—Proverbs 11:28, The Living Bible

-Principle-

Fortune magazine quotes a comment made by billionaire H. Ross Perot: "Guys, just remember, if you get real lucky, if you make a lot of money, if you go out and buy a lot of stuff—it's gonna break. You got your biggest, fanciest mansion in the world. It has air conditioning. It's got a pool. Just think of all the pumps that are going to go out. Or go to a yacht basin any place in the world. Nobody is smiling, and I'll tell you why. Something broke that morning. The generator's out; the microwave oven doesn't work...Things just don't mean happiness."

-Baffler-

What's the "cottage" in cottage cheese?

Did you know....

In the popular song, "Pop Goes the Weasel," the word "pop" is British slang meaning "to pawn something." The term "weasel" refers to the tools of one's trade. The phrase "Pop goes the Weasel" therefore means you are so broke that you have to pawn the means of your livelihood!

-Ponder-

"Love is measured not in moments of time…but in those timeless moments."

—Reader's Digest

-Proverb-

"Teach a child to choose the right path, and when
he is older he will remain upon it."

—Proverbs 22:6, The Living Bible

-Principle-

In "The Effective Father," Gordan MacDonald wrote: "It is said of Boswell, the famous biographer of Samuel Johnson, that he often referred to a special day in his childhood when his father took him fishing. The day was fixed in his mind, and he often reflected upon many of the things his father had taught him in the course of their fishing experience together.

After having heard of that particular excursion so often, it occurred to someone much later to check the journal that Boswell's father kept and determine what had been said about the fishing trip from the parental perspective. Turning to that date the reader found only one sentence entered: "Gone fishing today with my son; a day wasted." So, you see, we parents need to look at this matter from a new perspective!

-Baffler-

What percentage of the cost of supermarket food goes
to the packages that the goods come in?

Did you know….

In Minnesota, it is illegal to hang men's and women's
undergarments on the same clothesline.

-Ponder-

"Common sense is the knack of seeing things as they
are…and doing things as they ought to be done."

—C. E. Stowe

-Proverb-

"Inexperienced people die because they reject wisdom. Stupid people
are destroyed by their own lack of concern."

—Proverbs 1:32, Good News Bible

-Principle-

It was a 99 degree September day in San Antonio, when a 10-month-old baby girl was accidentally locked inside a parked car by her aunt. Frantically the mother and aunt ran around the auto in near hysteria, while a neighbor attempted to unlock the car with a clothes hanger. Soon the infant was turning purple and had foam on her mouth.

It had become a life-or-death situation when Fred Arriola, a wrecker driver, arrived on the scene. He grabbed a hammer and smashed the back window of the car to set her free.

Was he heralded a hero? He said, "The lady was mad at me because I broke the window. I just thought, what's more important—the baby or the window?"

Sometimes priorities get out of order, and a Fred Arriola reminds us what is important.

-Baffler-

How often does lightning strike the earth's surface in a 24-hour period?

Did you know....

When a male fish begins blowing bubbles in his
aquarium, it means he's ready for breeding.

29 – Marriage and Understanding
...how to have a good fight

-Ponder-

"How many marriages would be better off if the husband and wife
clearly understood that they are on the same side."

—Zig Ziglar

-Proverb-

"The man who finds a good wife finds a good thing;
she is a blessing to him from the Lord."

—Proverbs 18:22, The Living Bible

-Principle-

Even the most committed couple will experience a "stormy" bout every once in a
while. A grandmother, celebrating her golden wedding anniversary, told the secret of
her long and happy marriage. "On my wedding day, I decided to make a list of ten of
my husband's faults which for the sake of our marriage, I would overlook." A guest
asked the woman what some of the faults she had chosen to overlook were. The
grandmother replied, "To tell you the truth, my dear, I never did get around to listing
them. But whenever my husband did something that made me hopping mad, I would
say to myself; 'Lucky for him that's one of the ten.' "

-Baffler-

How did the phrase "Uncle Sam" come to stand for the
U.S. Government Armed Forces?

Did you know....

According to a law in Berea, Ohio...dogs and cats
out after dark were required to wear a tail light!

30 – Friends and Relatives

-Ponder-

"God gives us our relatives; thank God we can choose our friends."

—Ethel Watts Mumford

-Proverb-

"Never abandon a friend—either yours or your father's. Then you won't need to go to a distant relative for help in your time of need."

—Proverbs 27:10, The Living Bible

-Principle-

Not long ago the world watched as three gray whales, ice-bound off Point Barrow, Alaska, floated battered and bloody, gasping for breath at a hole in the ice. Their only hope was somehow to be transported five miles past the ice pack to open sea.

Rescuers began cutting a string of breathing holes about twenty yards apart in the six-inch-thick ice. For eight days they coaxed the whales from one hole to the next, mile after mile. Along the way, one of the trio vanished and was presumed dead. But finally, with the help of Russian icebreakers, the whales, Putu and Siku, swam to freedom.

In a way, friends are like a string of breathing holes. Battered and bruised, in a world frozen over with greed, selfishness, and hatred, we rise for air from friends who love and encourage us until that day when our ice cap is shattered forever.

-Baffler-

Why did Julius Caesar always wear a laurel wreath on his head?

Did you know....

The yo-yo was originally a deadly Filipino weapon until it was adapted and introduced as a toy in 1929!

31 – Advice...How to Profit From it

-Ponder-

"Many receive advice...only the wise profit from it."

—Syrus

-Proverb-

"A rebuke to a man of common sense is more effective
than a hundred lashes on the back of a rebel."

—Proverbs 17:10, The Living Bible

-Principle-

When the great Knute Rockne was coaching at Notre Dame there began to appear in the school newspaper a column signed "Old Bearskin." It would berate the team as a whole and the individual players. The writer seemed to know who the lazy players were, who read their own press clippings, the ones who broke training, and the ladies' men. There wasn't a player on the team who wouldn't have liked to wring his neck.

When a player would come to practice angry over some comment about him, Rockne would sympathize and say that no person should write such things, and he would be mad too. He would tell the team to "get out there and show Old Bearskin that it wasn't true."

Only after the tragic death of Rockne did the real identity of "Old Bearskin" become known. The coach himself wrote the column and used it to motivate those who received too much publicity.

-Baffler-

How many times does the average person swallow during dinner?

65 - 135 - 185 - 215 - 245 - 295

Did you know....

Most people think that sharks live only in the oceans. However, there is one very ferocious species that lives in fresh water. It is found in Lake Nicaragua in Central America.

32 – Grateful Difficulties

-Ponder-

"I am grateful for all my problems. As each of them was overcome, I became stronger and more able to meet those yet to come. I grew in all my difficulties."

—J. C. Penney

-Proverb-

"When the way is rough, your patience has a chance to grow. So let it grow, and don't try to squirm out of your problems. For when your patience is finally in full bloom, then you will be ready for anything, strong in character, full and complete."

—James 1:3-4, The Living Bible

-Principle-

A few years ago in Winter Park, Florida, a hole began to appear in a certain neighborhood. Gradually, trees began to disappear, but before it was over five cars, a three-bedroom home, and a solid block of land were gone. The hole was as long as a football field and eight stories deep.

Beneath that city block were limestone caverns, once filled with water but now dry. When the caverns were filled with water they were solid. But something had siphoned off the water. When the water was gone, houses, cars, businesses and streets sank down and out of sight.

It's rather easy for anybody to be a victim of certain "sinkholes" in life. Sometimes sinkholes are discovered in the process of trouble. Trouble simply exposes the presence of a sinkhole that might have gone undetected for years. If allowed to stay, that sinkhole would rob us of productivity, confidence and hope.

Trouble is really a friend if it enables you to overcome those hidden sinkholes in your character!

-Baffler-

What percent of the books in the world are written in English?

Did you know....

The Graham cracker was invented by Sylvester Graham, a temperance leader and food fanatic who believed (among other things) that meat causes sexual excess and ketchup causes insanity.

-Ponder-

"The human tongue is only inches from the brain but when
you listen to some folks, they seem miles apart."

—P. K. Sideliners

-Proverb-

"An evil man sows strife; gossip separates the best of friends."

—Proverbs 16:28, The Living Bible

-Principle-

Communication is absolutely essential in life. Words are vehicles of communication. By their use we live connected with others. The teacher, the doctor, the parent, do the majority of their work with words. By words we reveal our personalities and character. By words we do immeasurable good, and by words we can do irreparable harm and injury.

The words used by an individual in a lifetime would be impossible to calculate. However, it has been estimated that a person could speak 30,000 words in a day. If those words were published they would amount to a book of more than one hundred pages.

Three simple rules might help us learn to think before speaking. Ask yourself;

1. Is it true?

2. Is it fair?

3. Is it necessary?

Words are powerful—in fact, history is made by great people and the words they use.

-Baffler-

Why do people look up when thinking?

Did you know....

You can find out whether a mosquito is male or female by letting it land on you. If it bites you, it's female. Only female mosquitoes live on blood. The males live on plant juices.

34 – Adversity...builds character

-Ponder-

"Adversity...introduces people to themselves!"

—Epictetus

-Proverb-

"From a wise mind comes careful and persuasive speech."

—Proverbs 16:23, The Living Bible

-Principle-

Kay Yow was the coach of the 1988 Olympic women's basketball team. The USA team won the gold medal. In an interview she shared what has become her life's message. Yow's message is that *"adversity builds character."*

In 1987 she underwent cancer surgery. That same fall, her North Carolina State women's basketball team suffered their first losing season in Yow's thirteen year coaching tenure. In addition, three of the most highly regarded Olympic hopefuls were lost to injuries.

In the midst of this adversity Yow said, "I searched for meaning but I found two things greater. I found purpose and hope. My hope is my faith...and there's been a great purpose in all this."

Your life's message has potential for powerful encouragement...or discouragement. The choice is up to the individual. One thing is definite, however; everyone has a message they are communicating.

-Baffler-

What percent of the people in America clean out their belly buttons daily?

Did you know....

Black-eyed peas aren't peas. They're beans. On the other hand,
coffee beans aren't beans. They are actually fruit pits.

35 – Controlling Desires

-Ponder-

"You will become as small as your controlling desire;
as great as your dominant aspiration."

—James Allen

-Proverb-

"You must eat the bitter fruit of having your own way, and
experience the full terror of the pathway you have chosen."

—Proverbs 1:31, The Living Bible

-Principle-

An old fable from ancient India tells about four brothers who decided to master a special ability. Time went by, and the brothers met to reveal what they had learned.

"I have mastered science," said the first, "by which I can take but a bone of some creature and create the flesh that goes with it."

"I," said the second, "know how to grow that creature's skin and hair if there is flesh on its bones."

The third said, "I am able to create its limbs if I have the flesh, the skin and the hair."

"And I," concluded the fourth, "know how to give life to that creature if its form is complete."

There upon the brothers went into the jungle where one found the bone of a lion. One added the flesh to the bone, the other grew hair and hide, the third gave it matching limbs, and the fourth gave the lion life.

The ferocious beast arose, and jumped on his creators, killed them all, and vanished into the jungle.

We too have the ability to create that which can devour us. Goals and dreams, possessions and property can easily turn and destroy us.

-Baffler-

How did American soldiers get the nickname "G.I." and what does it stand for?

Did you know....

Castor oil is used as the liquid center of many brands of golf balls.

-Ponder-

"Until you have peace with who you are, you'll never be content with what you have."

—Doris Mortman

-Proverb-

"A little gained honestly, is better than great wealth gotten by dishonest means."

—Proverbs 16:8, The Living Bible

-Principle-

Booker T. Washington describes meeting an ex-slave from Virginia in his book *Up From Slavery*: "I found that this man had made a contract with his master, two or three years previous to the *Emancipation Proclamation*, to the effect that the slave was to be permitted to buy himself, by paying so much per year for his body; and while he was paying for himself, he was to be permitted to labor where and for whom he pleased."

Finding that he could secure better wages in Ohio, he went there. When freedom came, he was still in debt to his master for about three hundred dollars. Notwithstanding that the *Emancipation Proclamation* freed him from any obligation to his master, this man walked the greater portion of the distance back to his old master who lived in Virginia, and placed the last dollar, with interest, in his hands.

Washington said. "In talking to me about this, he knew that he didn't have to pay the debt, but that he had given his word to his master and his word had never been broken. He felt that he could not enjoy his freedom until he had fulfilled his promise."

-Baffler-

What is a group of owls called and how many are in a group?

Did you know....

Believe it or not, *Ripley's Believe It or Not* was not written by Robert Ripley—he was an artist. The column was written almost entirely by Norbert Pearlroth and Douglas Storer for over 50 years. Although Ripley has been dead since 1950, the column still bears his name, even though he never wrote it in the first place.

-Ponder-

"If we don't know the direction in which we are
going…we will end up where we're headed."

—Red Skelton

-Proverb-

"Watch your step. Stick to the path and be safe.
Don't sidetrack; pull back your foot from danger."

—Proverbs 4:26-27, The Living Bible

-Principle-

The minister was officiating at the funeral of a war veteran. The dead man's military friends wished to have a part in the service at the funeral home, so they requested that the young minister lead them down to the casket, stand with them for a solemn moment of remembrance, and then lead them out through a side door. This he proceeded to do, but unfortunately the effect was somewhat marred when the minister picked the wrong door. The result was that they marched with military precision into a broom closet, in full view of the mourners, and had to beat a hasty retreat covered with confusion.

There are two cardinal principles illustrated here. First, if you're going to lead, make sure you know where you are going. Second, if you're going to follow, make sure that you are following someone who knows what he is doing.

-Baffler-

Four out of five people eat corn on the cob _____?
-left to right   -right to left   -in a circle

Did you know….

Charles Goodyear, the originator of vulcanized rubber, was in jail for debt when he started his experiments. Although his discoveries earned large sums of money, he died over $200,000 in debt.

-Ponder-

"For every problem there is a solution which is simple…neat…and wrong!"

—H. L. Mencken

-Proverb-

"Before every man lies a wide and pleasant road
that seems right but ends in death."

—Proverbs 14:12, The Living Bible

-Principle-

An old story tells of a desert nomad who awakened hungry in the middle of the night. He lit a candle and began eating dates from a bowl beside his bed. He took a bite from one and saw a worm in it; so he threw it out of the tent. He bit into the second date and found another worm. Reasoning that he wouldn't have any dates left to eat if he continued, he blew out the candle and quickly ate the rest of the dates.

Many there are who prefer darkness and denial to the light of reality.

-Baffler-

What is the most common street name in America?
Main St. — Park Ave. — 2nd St. — 1st St. — Washington St. — Maple St.

Did you know....

A polar bear can smell you 20 miles away.

39 – Bouncing After You Fall

-Ponder-

"The harder you fall, the higher you bounce."

—American Proverb

-Proverb-

"An evil man is stubborn, but a godly man will reconsider."

—Proverbs 21:29, The Living Bible

-Principle-

For years, the opening of *"The Wide World of Sports"* television program showed "the agony of defeat" of a painful ending to an attempted ski jump. The skier appeared in good form as he headed down the jump, but then, for no apparent reason, he tumbled head over heels off the side of the jump, bouncing off the supporting structure.

What viewers didn't know was that he chose to fall rather than finish the jump. Why? As he explained later, the jump surface had become too fast, and midway down, he realized that if he completed the jump, he would land on the level ground beyond the safe landing area, which could have been fatal.

As it was, the skier suffered no more than a headache from the tumble.

To change one's course in life can be a dramatic and sometimes painful undertaking, but change is better than a fatal landing at the end.

-Baffler-

Part A: What % of runners think about sex while running?
Part B: What % of couples think about running while having sex?

Did you know....

Historians believe that one of the main reasons the French lost at Waterloo was that, at the time of the battle, Napoleon was bedridden with a terrible case of hemorrhoids.

40 – Happiness...the conscious choice

-Ponder-

"Happiness is a conscious choice, not an automatic response."

—Mildred Borthel

-Proverb-

"A wise man restrains his anger and overlooks insults. This is to his credit."

—Proverbs 19:11, The Living Bible

-Principle-

In his book, *Lee: The Last Years*, Charles Bracelen Flood reports that after the Civil War, Robert E. Lee visited a Kentucky lady who took him to the remains of a grand old tree in front of her house. There she bitterly cried that its limbs and trunk had been destroyed by Federal artillery fire. She looked to Lee for a word condemning the North, or at least sympathizing with her loss.

After a brief silence, Lee said, "Cut it down, my dear Madam, and forget it."

It is far better to forgive the injustices of the past than to allow them to remain, let the bitterness take root and it will poison the rest of your life.

-Baffler-

Why was the parachute invented? (Note: It was invented in 1783, 100 years before the airplane.)

Did you know....

Ever notice that an elephant's tusks never seem to be of equal length? It's because elephants, like humans, fish, birds and insects, are either "left-handed" or "right-handed". A "left-handed" elephant tends to use his left tusk more, so the tusk wears down faster.

41 – Quality...the intelligent choice

-Ponder-

"Quality is never an accident; it is always the result of intelligent effort."

—John Ruskin

-Proverb-

"It is pleasant to see plans develop, that is why fools refuse
to give them up even when they are wrong."

—Proverbs 13:19, The Living Bible

-Principle-

Film maker Walt Disney was ruthless in cutting anything that got in the way of a story's pacing. Ward Kimball, one of the animators for *Snow White*, recalls working 240 days on a 4 1/2-minute sequence in which the dwarfs made soup for Snow White and almost destroyed the kitchen in the process. Disney thought it was funny, but he decided the scene stopped the flow of the picture, so out it went.

If the film of our lives is shown, will it be as great as it could have been? A lot will depend on the multitude of "good" things we need to eliminate in order to make way for the "best" things.

-Baffler-

What does the "zip" in zip code stand for?

Did you know....

In the 1890's an American doctor published a treatise warning that chewing gum would "exhaust the salivary glands and cause the intestines to stick together."

42 – Character...coming to grips with difficulties

-Ponder-

"The man of character finds special attractiveness in difficulty...since it is only by coming to grips with difficulty that he can realize his potentialities."

—Charles DeGaulle

-Proverb-

"You are a poor specimen if you can't stand the pressure of adversity."

—Proverbs 24:10, The Living Bible

-Principle-

On December 29, 1987, a Soviet cosmonaut returned to earth after 326 days in orbit. He was in good health, which hasn't always been the case in those record-breaking voyages. Five years earlier, touching down after 211 days in space, two cosmonauts suffered from dizziness, high pulse rates, and heart palpitations. They couldn't walk for a week, and after 30 days, they were still undergoing therapy for atrophied muscles and weakened hearts.

At zero gravity, the muscles of the body begin to waste away because there is no resistance. To counteract this, the Soviets prescribed a vigorous exercise program for the cosmonauts. They invented the "penguin suit," a running suit laced with elastic bands. It resists every move the cosmonauts make, forcing them to exert their strength.

We often yearn for days without difficulty but the truth is, the easier our life is, the weaker our spirit is. Strength grows only by exertion!

-Baffler-

What was the original meaning of the phrase "to beat the band?"

Did you know....

When building a bridge, one of the ingredients you need is sugar. Sugar is added to the mortar because tests show that it increases the mortar's strength.

43 – Happiness and Sharing

-Ponder-

"Happiness is not so much in having as sharing. We make a living by
what we get...but we make a life by what we give."

—Norman MacEwan

-Proverb-

"A true friend is always loyal, and a brother is born to help in time of need."

—Proverbs 17:17, The Living Bible

-Principle-

From 1986 to 1990, Frank Reed was held hostage in a Lebanon cell. For months at a
time, Reed was blindfolded, living in a complete darkness, or chained to a wall and kept
in absolute silence. On one occasion, he was moved to another room, and, although
blindfolded, he could sense others in the room. Yet it was three weeks before he dared
peek out to discover he was chained next to Terry Anderson and Tom Sutherland.

Although he was beaten, made ill, and tormented, Reed felt most the lack of anyone
caring. He said in an interview, "Nothing I did mattered to anyone. I began to realize how
withering it is to exist with not a single expression of caring around. I learned one over-
riding fact: caring is a powerful force. If no one cares, you are truly alone."

All of us have the opportunity to impart life-giving strength to someone, simply
by caring.

-Baffler-

What was the original meaning of the word "turnpike"?

Did you know....

The largest single solid gold object in the world is a bathtub, of all things. It's
located at the Funabara Hotel on Japan's Izu Peninsula and weighs 313 1/2 pounds.

44 – Wealth...What Is It Really?

-Ponder-

"Wealth is not measured by just what we have, but rather what
we have for which we would not take money."

—Unknown

-Proverb-

"It is possible to give away and become richer! It is also
possible to hold on too lightly and lose everything. Yes, the liberal
man shall be rich! By watering others, he waters himself."

—Proverbs 11:24-25, The Living Bible

-Principle-

All of us have seen movies in which someone has been shipwrecked and left to
drift aimlessly on the ocean. As the days pass under the scorching sun, their rations
of food and fresh water give out. The men grow deliriously thirsty. One night, while
the others are asleep, one man ignores all previous warnings and gulps down some salt
water. He quickly dies.

Ocean water contains seven times more salt than the human body can safely
ingest. Drinking salt water prompts dehydration because the kidneys demand extra
water to flush the overload of salt. The more salt water someone drinks, the thirstier
he gets. He actually dies of thirst.

Sometimes it is very difficult to distinguish between what we want and what we need.
Needs and wants can look strangely the same, but the difference can mean life or death.

-Baffler-

What is the most despised household task?

Did you know....

Charles Boyer's most famous line was "Come with me to the Casbah." Jimmy
Cagney was famous for "You dirty rat"; Greta Garbo for "I vant to be alone'"; and
Humphrey Bogart for "Play it again, Sam." The ironic thing is that none of these
actors ever spoke the lines that are now so closely identified with them.

45 – Past and Future

-Ponder-

"As important as your past is, as it relates to the present, is not nearly as important as you see your future."

—Dr. Tony Campolo

-Proverb-

"When a man is gloomy, everything seems to go wrong;
when he is cheerful, everything seems right!"

—Proverbs 15:15, The Living Bible

-Principle-

A man from Colorado moved to Texas and built a house with a large picture window from which he could view hundreds of miles of range land. "The only problem is," he said, "there's nothing to see."

About the same time, a man from Texas moved to Colorado and built a house with a large picture window overlooking the Rockies. "The only problem is I can't see anything," he said. "The mountains are in the way."

Which proves that perspective in life is everything! What is seen in life is most often determined by the angle at which it is viewed.

-Baffler-

In the song *Yankee Doodle* why did Yankee Doodle stick a feather in his cap and call it macaroni? (Did this line really refer to pasta?)

Did you know....

Sunglasses first became popular when movie stars began wearing them during the early days of film-making. The general public soon began wearing them too. Actually, early film actors wore sunglasses not because they wanted to look mysterious or romantic, but because their eyes hurt. The early movie lights designed by the Kliegl brothers were so intensely bright that they caused a painful affliction known as "kliegl eyes."

-Ponder-

"You can't have rosy thoughts about the future when
your mind is full of blues about the past."

—Tidbits

-Proverb-

"Storms come, and the wicked are blown away, but honest people are always safe."

—Proverbs 10:25, Good News Bible

-Principle-

Farmers in southern Alabama were accustomed to planting one crop every year—cotton. They would plow as much as they could and plant their crop. Year after year they lived by cotton.

Then one year the dreaded boll weevil devastated the whole area. So the next year the farmers mortgaged their homes and planted cotton again, hoping for a good harvest. But as the cotton began to grow, the insect came back and destroyed the crop, wiping out most of the farms.

The few who survived those two years of the boll weevil decided to experiment the third year so they planted something they had never planted before—peanuts. The peanuts proved so hardy and the market so ravenous for that product that the farmers who survived the first two years reaped profits that third year which enabled them to pay off all their debts. From that point on, they prospered.

Those same farmers created a monument in the town square—to the boll weevil. They learned that even out of a great disaster, there can be a great delight.

-Baffler-

What do Americans fear the most?

Did you know....

According to an extensive study carried out in California in 1966, pigs are the only mammals other than man that are capable of getting sunburned.

47 – Your Conscience...a beeper from God

-Ponder-

"I value people with a conscience—it's like a beeper from God."

—Robert Orben

-Proverb-

"A man's conscience is the Lord's searchlight exposing his hidden motives."

—Proverbs 20:27, The Living Bible

-Principle-

John bought a new car with a voice warning system. At first John was amused to hear the soft female voice gently remind him that his seatbelt wasn't fastened. John affectionately called this voice the "little woman."

He soon discovered his little woman was programmed to warn him about his gasoline. "Your fuel level is low," she said one time in her sweet voice. John nodded his head and thanked her. He figured that he still had gas enough to go another 50 miles, so he kept on going. A few minutes later, she repeated the same message. And so it went over and over. Although he knew it was the same voice, it seemed to John that the voice sounded harsher each time.

Finally, he stopped his car and crawled under the dashboard. After a quick search, he found the appropriate wires and gave them a good yank. So much for the little woman.

He was still smiling to himself a few miles later when his car began sputtering and coughing—out of gas. John was sure that he heard the little woman laughing.

People like John learn before long that the little voice inside, although ignored or even disconnected, often tells them exactly what they need to know.

-Baffler-

Why is a "Swan Song" a farewell?

Did you know....

According to studies by Dr. August Dvorak of the University of Washington, a typist's fingers travel a total of seven miles during a seven-hour workday.

48 – Be Ready When Duty Calls

-Ponder-

"It's not enough to be ready to go where duty calls . . .
a man must stand where he can hear the call."

—Robert Louis Stevenson

-Proverb-

"Sometimes it takes a painful experience to make us change our ways."

—Proverbs 20:30, Good News Bible

-Principle-

In 1985 a celebration was held in New Orleans at a municipal swimming pool. The party was held to celebrate the first summer in memory without a drowning at any New Orleans city pool. In honor of the occasion, two hundred people gathered, including one hundred certified life guards.

As the party was breaking up and the four life guards on duty began to clear the pool, they found a fully dressed body in the deep end. They tried to revive Jerome Moody, thirty-one, but it was too late. He had drowned, surrounded by lifeguards celebrating their successful season.

-Baffler-

Is public kissing a crime anywhere in the United States?

Did you know....

The ceremony of toasting comes from the custom of dropping a piece of toasted spiced bread into a glass of wine to improve its flavor. When we toast a person we are in effect saying that his presence adds flavor to the party.

49 – The Custom Fit

-Ponder-

"The reason for most folk's dissatisfaction in life is that they are looking for a custom fit in an off-the-rack world."

—Gary Gulbranson

-Proverb-

"Have reverence for the Lord and you will live a long life, content and safe from harm."

—Proverbs 19:23, Good News Bible

-Principle-

There is an old story told of a king who was suffering from a painful ailment, whose astrologer told him that the only cure for him was to find a contented man, get his shirt, and wear it night and day. So messengers were sent through the king's realm in search of such a man, with orders to bring back his shirt.

Months passed, and after a thorough search of the country the messengers returned, but without the shirt.

"Did you find a contented man in all my realm?" the king asked.

"Yes, O King, we found one, just one in all your realm," they replied.

"Then why did you not bring back his shirt?" the king demanded.

"Master, the man had no shirt," was the answer.

-Baffler-

Why was the "necktie" introduced in the 1st Century B.C.?

Did you know....

Velcro was invented in 1948 by a Swiss engineer, George deMestral, who came home from a walk in the woods one day and was irritated to find cockleburs stuck all over his clothes as well as his dog's coat. The hook-and-loop fastener was born. Its name was a combination of velvet and crochet, the French word for hook.

PONDERS & PRINCIPLES

"When in deep water, it's good to keep
your mouth shut." — St. Louis Labor Tribune

50 – Breaking Records

-Ponder-

"Adversity causes some people to break…and others to break records."

—William A. Ward

-Proverb-

"An idea well-expressed is like a design of gold, set in silver."

—Proverbs 25:11, Good News Bible

-Principle-

Woolworth conceived the idea of the Five and Ten Cent Store. That was different. His fortune was measured by millions when he passed away. Wanamaker conceived the idea of one price to everybody in his retail stores. That was different, for at the time he put this policy into effect it was directly contrary to accepted practice throughout the country. Ford determined to build a light, cheap car for millions. That was different. His reward came in the greatest automobile output in the world.

Human progress has often depended on the courage of a man who dared to be different.

-Baffler-

What was the first novel ever written on a typewriter?
(Hint: it was typed on a Remington in 1875.)

Did you know....

Lightning strikes somewhere on earth about 6,000 times every minute. Fortunately, it generally strikes mountain tops and skyscrapers rather than homes and people. If It could be harnessed, a powerful lightning bolt could produce enough energy to lift a large ocean liner six feet into the air.

51 – No Chip on the Shoulder

-Ponder-

"A chip on the shoulder indicates there's wood higher up."

—Jack Herbert

-Proverb-

"It is foolish to speak scornfully of others.
If you are smart, you will keep quiet."

—Proverbs 11:12, Good New Bible

-Principle-

A psychiatrist for the Veteran's Administration says that he has made a startling discovery. He studied two groups of people; the first group was made up of thousands of people who were suffering from mental and emotional disturbances; the second group contained people who were relatively free from such tensions.

The study revealed one very clear fact: those who suffered from extreme tension had one trait in common—they were habitual fault-finders, constant critics of people and things around them. Whereas the men and women who were free of all tensions were the least fault-finding.

It would seem that the habit of criticizing is a mark of the nervous, and of the mentally imbalanced.

-Baffler-

What was the first minimum wage in the United States?
(Hint: it was set in 1938)

Did you know....

From the 1300's to the 1500's it was illegal for an Englishman to eat three meals a day. During the reign of Edward III in the 1300's, Parliament passed a law specifying that people were to eat only two meals a day. The law remained on the books for almost 200 years.

-Ponder-

"Once a job has begun, see it through till its done,
be it big or be it small, do it right or not at all."

—Earl Cunha

-Proverb-

"Work and you will earn a living; if you sit around talking you will be poor."

—Proverbs 14:23, Good News Bible

-Principle-

During the refurbishing of the Statue of Liberty a few years ago, most Americans were amazed at the detail which was revealed in "Lady Liberty." Particularly impressive was the detail on the top of the statue's head. The sculptor did a magnificent and painstaking job with the lady's coiffure, and yet he must have been pretty sure that the only eyes that would ever see this detail would be the uncritical eyes of a seagull. The artist could not have dreamt that any man would ever fly over this head. He was artist enough however to finish off this part of the statue with as much care as he devoted to the face and everything else people would see as they sailed by.

When you are creating a work of art, or any other kind of work, finish the job off perfectly. You never know when a helicopter, or some other instrument not at the moment invented, may come along and find you out! That is what integrity is all about.

-Baffler-

What does "O.K." stand for?

Did you know....

When penguins are imported to zoos in the temperate regions, they often catch colds and die. The Antarctic is so cold it's almost antiseptic, so penguins generally have not built up immunities to various germs.

53 – Don't Borrow Trouble

-Ponder-

"Borrow trouble for yourself if that's your nature,
but don't lend it to your neighbors."

—Rudyard Kipling

-Proverb-

"Being cheerful keeps you healthy. It is slow death to be gloomy all the time."

—Proverbs 17:22, Good News Bible

-Principle-

A recent medical survey states that chronic complainers live longer than people who are always sweet and serene. It claims that their cantankerous spirit gives them purpose for living. Each morning they get up with a fresh challenge to see how many things they can find to grumble about, they derive a great satisfaction from making others miserable.

It could be that complainers do not live longer, however. Maybe it just seems that way to those of us who live around them!

-Baffler-

How much water does a person drink in a lifetime?

Did you know....

The great American poet, Hart Crane, who deliberately drowned himself by jumping overboard from a ship in 1933, was the son of the inventor of "Lifesavers" candy.

-Ponder-

"Every crucial experience can be regarded as a setback—or
the start of a new kind of development."

—Mary Roberts Kinehart

-Proverb-

"Do yourself a favor and learn all you can; then
remember what you learn and you will prosper."

—Proverbs 19:8, Good News Bible

-Principle-

On July 15, 1986, Roger Clemens, the sizzling right-hander for the Boston Red Sox, started his first All-Star Game. In the second inning, he came to bat, something he hadn't done in years because of the American League's designated-hitter rule. He took a few uncertain practice swings and then looked out at his forbidding opponent, Dwight Gooden, who the previous year had won the Cy Young Award.

Gooden wound up and threw a white-hot fast ball past Clemens. With an embarrassed smile on his face, Clemens stepped out of the box and asked catcher Gary Carter, "Is that what my pitches look like?" "You bet it is!" replied Carter.

Although Clemens quickly struck out, he went on to pitch three perfect innings and be named the game's most valuable player. From that day on, he later said, with a fresh reminder of how overpowering a good fast ball is, he pitched with far greater boldness.

-Baffler-

What is the percentage of dog owners in the U.S. who throw
birthday parties for their dogs and invite other dogs to attend?

Did you know....

There are over 600,000 words in the English language. A well-educated person is familiar with only about 20,000 words. In the spoken language, however, fewer than 2,000 words account for fully 99 percent of what we say. Even more astonishing is that only 20 words make up 25 percent of what we say. The two most common words in the spoken language are "I" and "you."

55 – Problems, Solutions and Seeds

-Ponder-

"Every problem has in it the seeds of its own solution. If you don't
have any problems...you don't get any seeds!"

—Norman Vincent Peale

-Proverb-

"Intelligent people want to learn, but stupid people are satisfied with ignorance."

—Proverbs 15:14, Good News Bible

-Principle-

Ten Commandments For Leadership (adapted from Mother Teresa)
1. People are illogical, unreasonable and self-centered. *Love them anyway.*
2. If you do good, people will accuse you of selfish ulterior motives.
   Do good anyway.
3. If you are successful, you win false friends and true enemies. *Succeed anyway.*
4. The good you do today will be forgotten tomorrow. *Do good anyway.*
5. Honesty and frankness make you vulnerable. *Be honest and frank anyway.*
6. The biggest people with the biggest ideas can be shot down by the smallest people with the smallest ideas. *Think big anyway.*
7. People favor underdogs, but follow only top dogs.
   Fight for a few underdogs anyway.
8. What you spend years building may be destroyed overnight. *Build anyway.*
9. People really need help but may attack you if you help them.
   Help them anyway.
10. Give the world the best you have and you'll get kicked in the teeth.
    Give the world the best you have anyway.

-Baffler-

What does the "K" in "K" rations stand for?

Did you know....

Everybody knows what the peace symbol looks like, but few people know where
it comes from. The peace symbol, an inverted Y inside a circle, was devised by British
pacifists during the Cold War by combining the semaphore signs for N and D, standing for nuclear disarmament.

-Ponder-

"It's the little things that make the big things possible. Only close attention
to the fine details of any operation makes the operation first class."

—J. Willard Marriott

-Proverb-

"A wise, mature person is known for his understanding.
The more pleasant his words, the more persuasive he is."

—Proverbs 16:21, Good News Bible

-Principle-

The president of a top executive placement firm identified five points at which
most management failures occur. In order, from the greatest to the least, they are:

1. Personality conflicts
2. Lack of interpersonal skills
3. Language-environment problems
4. Communication problems
5. Failure to break up problems into manageable units

Four of the five have to do with getting along with people. The ability to solve
number problems or make mechanical adjustments pales in comparison to personal
relation skills.

-Baffler-

What does 7-Up stand for? (How did 7-Up get its name?)

Did you know....

The word "quiz" is said to have entered the English language as a result of a bet.
About 1780 a Dublin theatre manager laid a wager that he could introduce a new
word into the language within 24 hours. He went around Dublin writing the word on
every blank wall. By the next day, all of Dublin was asking what the word meant. The
theatre manager won the bet and the word "Quiz" became a permanent part of the
English Language.

57 – Motivation...getting started and keeping going

-Ponder-

"Motivation is what gets you started—but habit is what keeps you going."

—Jim Ryun

-Proverb-

"A lazy man will never have money, but an aggressive man will get rich."

—Proverbs 11:16, Good News Bible

-Principle-

Lech Walsea, a simple Polish worker, became the force behind the Solidarity movement and won the Nobel Peace Prize.

Rachel Carson was introduced to nature through woodland walks with her mother and gave birth to the environmental movement with her book, "The Silent Spring."

Dr. Jonas Salk engaged in a dogged but routine research day in and day out before developing the vaccine that spelled the end of polio.

Rosa Parks refused to move to the rear of the bus and sparked a civil rights revolution.

These and all individuals who make a difference prove the truth of an observation made by German martyr, Dietrich Bonhoffer, who defied the Nazis: "Action springs not from thought, but from a readiness for responsibility."

You don't have to move mountains to make a difference. But when you accept responsibility to improve life in your own little world, you change the world by that much.

-Baffler-

Why is hamburger called "hamburger" when it doesn't contain any ham?

Did you know....

One of a horse's gaits is called a "canter." The word comes from "Canterbury," because Pilgrims supposedly used this swift gait when riding to the shrine of St. Thomas a Becket at Canterbury.

-Ponder-

"What we are is God's gift to us—what we become is our gift to God."

—Louis Nizer

-Proverb-

"Your reward depends on what you say
and do; you will get what you deserve."

—Proverbs 12:14, Good News Bible

-Principle-

A rich man went to a rabbi for help. The rabbi led him to a window. "Tell me what you see."

"People," said the rich man.

The rabbi then led him to a mirror and asked, "What do you see now?"

"I see myself," answered the man.

"In the window there is glass," said the rabbi, "but the glass of the mirror is covered with a little silver. No sooner is the silver added than you cease to see others and see only yourself."

-Baffler-

Why is the hot water faucet on the left
and the cold water faucet on the right?

Did you know....

According the extensive study, a man is twice as likely
to fall out of a hospital bed as a woman.

59 – Skydiving...packing your own chute

-Ponder-

"There are certain rules about skydiving you should always keep in mind...like never having an argument with your wife while she's packing your chute."

—Current Comedy

-Proverb-

"Sensible people will see trouble coming and avoid it, but an unthinking person will walk right into it and regret it later."

—Proverbs 27:12, Good News Bible

-Principle-

Ivan McGuire died not long ago at the age of 35. His death at a young age was not due to an automobile accident or a terminal illness. He was not murdered, nor did he commit suicide. The skydiver forgot to put on his parachute before he jumped out of the airplane.

McGuire, who aspired to be the best skydiving photographer, evidently was so excited over filming some other skydivers that he failed to put on his parachute.

Forget those things which are excess baggage, but be careful not to forget the essential. Parachutes are not excess baggage.

-Baffler-

What does it mean to "watch your P's and Q's?"

Did you know....

When the Washington Monument opened in 1888, men took the elevator but women were required to climb the 897 steps of the memorial. It was thought improper for men to accompany women in such an enclosed space for the 12 minutes that the elevator took to rise to the top of the 555-foot-tall monument.

60 – Nothing Without Sweat

-Ponder-

"Nothing of a worthwhile, durable nature in this world
has ever been produced without sweat!"

—Herbert Lockyer

-Proverb-

"No matter how much a lazy person may want something, he will never
get it. A hard worker will get everything he wants."

—Proverbs 13:4, Good News Bible

-Principle-

Once there lived an excellent baseball player named George "Shotgun" Shuba. He was a good hitter but always laughed when people praised his "natural swing." As a 16-year-old boy he had made up his mind he did not want to go into the steel mills of Youngstown, Ohio, where his family had worked for generations. Shuba knew he had good baseball skills, but would have to learn to hit major-league pitching. He knotted a piece of rope so that a row of knots covered the strike zone from top to bottom and then hung the rope from a rafter in his basement. Using a heavily weighted bat, Shuba swung at the strike zone on that rope 600 times every day from age 16 until he made it into the majors.

George Shuba had some natural talent, but it was his hard work that made him a major leaguer. This principle is true in every area of life!

-Baffler-

What is the reason we use the phrase "upset his apple cart" to mean disaster?

Did you know....

The Brookings Institution is a world-famous "think tank" in Washington, D.C. It does research into the most complicated and complex problems that face mankind. Ironically, its founder, multi-millionaire Robert S. Brookings, made his fortune in a somewhat less complicated field, the manufacturing of clothespins.

61 – The Gray Hair of Age

-Ponder-

"You know you're old when you've lost all your marvels!"

—Merry Browne

-Proverb-

"We admire the strength of youth and
respect the gray hair of age."

—Proverbs 20:29, Good News Bible

-Principle-

To celebrate their 50th wedding anniversary, the couple returned to their honeymoon hotel. After retiring the wife said, "Darling, do you remember how you stroked my hair?" and so he stroked her hair. She reminded him of the way they cuddled, and so they did. With a sigh she said, "Won't you nibble my ear again?" With that the husband got out of bed and started to leave the room. The wife sat up in bed, upset, and said, "Where are you going?" He replied, "To get my teeth!"

-Baffler-

Why was the umbrella developed…and how long ago?

Did you know….

Do you know hummingbirds are the
only birds that can fly backwards?

-Ponder-

"We can tell our values by looking at our checkbook stubs."

—Gloria Steinem

-Proverb-

"Truth, wisdom, learning, and good sense—these are worth
paying for, but too valuable to sell."

—Proverb 23:23, Good News Bible

-Principle-

Toward the end of his life, Albert Einstein removed the portraits of two scientists, Newton and Maxwell, from his wall and replaced them with the portraits of Gandhi and Schweitzer. He explained it was time to replace the image of success with the image of service.

By the way, whose portraits hang on your wall?

-Baffler-

When was the last time California went through an entire
day without a traffic fatality? (What year?)

Did you know....

They say that diamonds are a girl's best friend. However, diamonds
were generally worn only by men until the 15th century.

63 – The Cost of Living...It's Going Up
...But It's Still a Bargain

-Ponder-

"The cost of living keeps going up—but it's still a bargain!"

—Unknown

-Proverb-

"The more easily you get your wealth, the sooner you will lose it.
The harder it is to earn, the more you will have."

—Proverbs 13:11, Good News Bible

-Principle-

In early 1989, 600 adults in 6 of our largest cities whose household incomes exceeded $100,000 were polled by the Roper Organization about what they considered "the most important life-style necessities."

The answers display the torrid American love affair with gadgetry: Seventy-nine percent of those polled said they couldn't live without a microwave oven. Forty-nine percent said they couldn't survive without a telephone answering machine. Thirty-six percent wouldn't make it without a V.C.R.

These were not answers to poorly worded questions. The study asked the affluent to distinguish between luxuries—"things they may enjoy owning, but could live without" and necessities—"things or services that have become so important they are thought to be necessities."

Among the same affluent citizens who could not contemplate life without the microwave, only thirty percent rated quality of education for their children a necessity.

-Baffler-

Why is blue associated with baby boys and pink with baby girls?

Did you know....

During your lifetime, you eat about 60,000 pounds of food,
the equivalent in weight of six elephants.

64 – Live a Day at a Time

-Ponder-

"Live one day at a time and make it a masterpiece."

—Dale West

-Proverb-

"An intelligent person aims at wise action,
but a fool starts off in many directions."

—Proverbs 17:24, Good News Bible

-Principle-

Linda Ellerbee, television journalist, claims she actually got this letter from a little girl. It read:

Dear Miss Ellerbee,
When I grow up, I want to do exactly what you do.
Please do it better!

For the sake of those who come after us, we need to do what is right. Then we need to do it better!

-Baffler-

What percentage of men and what percentage of women
pull apart their "Oreo" cookies before they bite?

Did you know....

The first recorded labor strike took place in 1160 B.C. when laborers on Pharaoh Rameses III tomb went on strike to demand a cost of living increase.

65 – Trouble and Motives

-Ponder-

"Maybe the Lord lets some people get into trouble because
...it is the only time they ever think of him."

—Nuggets

-Proverb-

"You may think everything you do is right, but the Lord judges your motives."

—Proverbs 16:2, Good News Bible

-Principle-

In New York three of the great magicians of the world gathered for a dinner meeting:

Harry Houdini, the great escape artist who could free himself from handcuffs and sealed chests wound round with chains and rope; Blackstone, who could make people appear and disappear; and Dunninger, the mind reader who could tell you the numbers on the dollar bills in your pocket. Dunninger had brought the other two in his car.

When they came out of the restaurant, Dunninger, mental genius that he was, found that he had mislaid his keys and could not open the car door. Blackstone tried, but for once his magic failed him. He just couldn't do anything with that door. And Houdini, who claimed he could get any lock open, under any circumstances, could not conquer this one. They just stood and stared at the locked door—and then sent for a man from the automobile agency.

We try to solve all sorts of riddles in human life; we do all kinds of tricks with human personality. But there comes a time when human experts fail and we are help-less. That's when we go to the manufacturer.

-Baffler-

38% of the people in America clean out their belly buttons daily! Now—how is that percentage broken down between men and women?

_____% Men   _____% Women

Did you know....

Peter Mark Roget, the author of the famous "Roget's Thesaurus,"
was a medical doctor by profession. Working in his spare time,
it took him fifty years to finish the book.

66 – Truth...it shall make you free

-Ponder-

"The truth shall make you free—but first it shall make you miserable."

—Barry Stevens

-Proverb-

"People who listen when they are corrected will live, but those
who will not admit that they are wrong are in danger."

—Proverbs 10:17, Good News Bible

-Principle-

Dorchester County, Maryland, recently purchased new modular units to be used as a temporary jail until a permanent facility under construction could be completed. Like all new buildings, these units had some embarrassing flaws in workmanship. Less than two weeks after the prisoners were transferred, two of them escaped. Their method was ingenious. They used the cover of a Bible to pry open the malfunctioning lock on a back door and made good their escape. Fortunately, the two men were captured a short time later. However, their use of the Bible gives new meaning to Jesus' words, "you will know the truth and the truth will make you free."

-Baffler-

What percentage of people in America save their leftover food?

Did you know....

Up until 1987, unmarried couples who lived together in Massachusetts could be punished by being taken to the gallows and made to stand there with a rope around their necks, receiving 39 lashes. The town of Sharon, Massachusetts, threatened to cite the 1784 law against two of its employees, and it took an act of the State Legislature to get the law off the books.

67 – Staying on the Right Track

-Ponder-

"Even if you're on the right track, you'll get
run over if you just sit there."

—Will Rogers

-Proverb-

"Always remember what you have learned.
Your education is your life—guard it well."

—Proverbs 4:13, Good News Bible

-Principle-

H. G. Wells told the story of a young Sultan whose beautiful wife died. In her memory he built a memorial stone, and then over the years added an altar, then a grotto. Over the grotto he built a temple, and finally around it a lovely city. In the midst of all this beauty the original stone had become quite out of place and insignificant, and eventually had to be removed.

Our lives can be like that. We establish the right priorities, but as the years pass we can lose that sense of importance in the midst of all the good things we add. The original stone is forgotten.

-Baffler-

In the *Wizard of Oz*, what is Dorothy's last name?

Did you know....

Contrary to what you would expect, blond
beards grow faster than dark beards.

-Ponder-

"Sometimes a majority simply means that all the fools are on the same side."

—Claude McDonald

-Proverb-

"People who do not get along with others are interested only in themselves; they will disagree with what everyone knows is right."

—Proverbs 18:1, Good News Bible

-Principle-

Althea Simmons is the chief congressional lobbyist of the N.A.A.C.P. and the director of the Civil Rights organization's Washington Bureau. She recalls that the most dehumanizing incident of her life took place in the late 1950's.

Simmons, her sister, and a white male law student were trying to desegregate a lunch counter in Dallas, Texas. The trio walked up to the lunch counter in a downtown bus station and sat down. No one shouted at them or said anything. No one wiped the counter where they were sitting. Instead, the three were ignored totally. Everyone in the lunchroom acted as if they didn't exist. For five to six hours they sat at the counter.

She said, "Nobody made any kind of gesture that could be perceived as hostile. We just didn't exist. Even now it's painful because I am a person and for all practical purposes, I did not exist."

-Baffler-

Averagers say the typical citizen eats __% of their daily food intake after 6:00 P.M.?
_____25% _____40% _____60% _____80%

Did you know....

Many anthropologists think that prehistoric man sang long before he developed the ability to communicate by speech.

69 – Bridge Builders and Toll Takers

-Ponder-

"There are two kinds of people in this world—bridge builders and toll takers."

—Kingsley Morse

-Proverb-

"Wise people walk the road that leads upward to life,
not the road that leads downward to death."

—Proverbs 15:24, Good News Bible

-Principle-

The Roman Catholic Archdiocese of Boston had found itself in some rather dire circumstances. One year it ordained only 5 new priests—45 fewer than were needed to maintain current staffing levels.

Then someone hit on an idea—a 30-second commercial spot to be released over several Boston-area television stations. The commercial begins with a blur of affluent images—a gold watch, a diamond bracelet, champagne, cocktails, pearls, and caviar. Then the scene goes black followed by a tag line: "A world that doesn't deny itself anything could use a few men who do." The closing depicts a priest's hands holding up a communion wafer.

Whether or not advertising for clergy is appropriate, the question asked is very relevant. With all the glitter and glitz in our world today, there is a desperate need for people who are willing to forsake all for a higher calling.

-Baffler-

Did "007" have any significance for James Bond
beyond representing his "license to kill"?

Did you know....

According to criminologists, the odds of finding two sets of fingerprints exactly alike are about one in a *billion trillion*. A duplicate set has never been found.

70 – Going Farther Than You Can See

-Ponder-

"If a man will go as far as he can see, he will be
able to see farther when he gets there."

—Bits and Pieces

-Proverb-

"An intelligent person learns more from one rebuke than
a fool learns from being beaten a hundred times."

—Proverbs 17:10, Good News Bible

-Principle-

Everyone makes mistakes!

Imagine if you had been the president of the Michigan bank who advised Henry
Ford's lawyer not to invest in the new motor company, assuring him, "The horse is
here to stay, but the automobile is only a novelty."

Or there was Gary Cooper's comment about Clark Gable accepting the role of
Rhett Butler, which he had turned down: "'Gone With The Wind' is going to be the
biggest flop in Hollywood history. I'm just glad it will be Clark Gable who's falling flat
on his face and not Gary Cooper."

Or the Boston sports writer who summed up young Ted Williams by saying, "I
don't believe this kid will ever hit half a singer midget's weight in a bathing suit."
Whatever that meant, he was most certainly wrong!

Everyone makes mistakes, including the experts. The key is not to live in the mistakes of the past but to move forward, learning from those mistakes.

-Baffler-

What seven colors make up a rainbow?

Did you know....

You can tell what time it is merely by looking at a flower. Many flowers open at
different times of the day. Morning glories open between 5 and 6 A.M.; daisies
between 8 and 9, and tulips between 10 and 11.

71 – Making Mistakes

-Ponder-

"If you must make mistakes, it will be more to your
credit if you make a new one each time."

—Construction Digest

-Proverb-

"What you think is the right road may lead to death."

—Proverbs 16:25, Good News Bible

-Principle-

A tough store manager was walking through the packing room one day when he saw a young man lounging on a shipping crate, whistling and relaxing. He asked how much he was paid.

"$120 a week," the young man answered. At that, the manager said, "Here's a week's pay. Get out!"

The manager immediately found the department head and demanded to know who had hired the young man.

"We didn't hire him," came the reply. "He was just here to pick up a package."

Assumptions can be costly. We'd better find out what's going on before we jump into the fray.

-Baffler-

What is the most common time of the day to have a fatal heart attack?

Did you know....

Prisoners in Paris' infamous fortress, the Bastille, were each given three bottles of wine to drink every day. This kept them in such a state of mellow inebriation that they were virtually incapable of escaping.

-Ponder-

"Today's accent may be on youth—but the stress is still on the parents."

—Earl Wilson

-Proverb-

"Children just naturally do silly and careless things, but
a good spanking will teach them how to behave."

—Proverbs 22:15, Good News Bible

-Principle-

Sometimes we need to learn to adapt to situations, like the teenage boy who came in about an hour after his curfew. As he got home he killed the car lights, cut the ignition, took his shoes off, and did everything possible to slip in quietly. It was 2:00 A.M., and as he walked down the hall a light came on and his mother called out, "John, what time is it?"

"It's midnight, momma," he replied. But just at that moment the cuckoo clock let out two cuckoos. So John stood there and cuckooed ten more times!

-Baffler-

What is the least common time of the day for a fatal heart attack?

Did you know....

According to the ancient code of Hammurabi, the early Babylonian legal code, it was proper to put your wife up as collateral for a loan. If you didn't repay the loan, the creditor could seize your wife. The code stipulated, however, that the creditor could only keep her for three years and that he was required to return her in as good condition as she was when she came.

73 – Genius in Working Clothes

-Ponder-

"Common sense is genius dressed up in work clothes."

—Ralph Waldo Emerson

-Proverb-

"Sensible people always think before they act, but
stupid people advertise their ignorance."

—Proverbs 13:16, Good News Bible

-Principle-

A man came into a bank and wanted to borrow $5. He was told that the bank did not lend such small sums.

"But," he went on, "lending money is your business isn't it?"

The banker admitted it was.

"Well, I've got good security," said the stranger, "and I want to borrow $5."

Finally the banker agreed to make the loan. When the note was drawn and the interest of 30 cents paid, the stranger drew from his pocket $10,000 worth of government bonds and handed them over as security. Before the banker could recover from his astonishment the stranger said, "Over at the other bank they wanted to charge me $10 just for a safety deposit box to keep these things in."

-Baffler-

Why are Piggy Banks called "Piggy Banks"?

Did you know....

In the famous 1944 movie *To Have and Have Not* actress Lauren Bacall's singing voice was dubbed in by a 14-year-old boy who grew up to become the famous singing star, Andy Williams.

-Ponder-

"You may be disappointed if you fail, but you are doomed if you don't try."

—Beverly Sills

-Proverb-

"Do not lose your courage, then, because it brings with it a great reward."

—Hebrews 10:35, Good News Bible

-Principle-

Charles Kettering, the noted scientist and inventor, believed the easiest way to overcome defeat was to ignore completely the possibility of failure.

He used to tell the story of how he had once given a tough assignment to a young research worker at the General Motors laboratory just to see how he would react to a difficult problem. Mr. Kettering forbade him to examine notes on the subject that were filed in the library. These notes were written by expert research men and contained statistics to prove that the assignment was impossible. The young research worker did not know this, of course, so he went to work with confidence that he would succeed.

He did succeed too. He didn't know it couldn't be done—so he did it!

-Baffler-

What is the average age at which people first start smoking?

Did you know....

The catch phrase "right-on," appears in Shakespeare's
Julius Caesar (Act 3, Scene 2).

PONDERS & PRINCIPLES

© 2004 Tania von Allmen for Ponders & Principles LLC

"You cannot climb the ladder of success with your hands in your pockets." — Zig Ziglar

75 – Aim in Life...make it high

-Ponder-

"Before you decide about your aim in life—check your ammunition."
—Executive Speechwriter Newsletter

-Proverb-

"To the man with insight, it is all clear; to the well-informed, it is all plain."
—Proverbs 8:9, Good News Book

-Principle-

Success has always been associated with the ability to focus goals and purposes and develop one-track minds.

A widow was playing bridge with three other ladies in the retirement home where they lived. A man walked in—a new resident.

One of the ladies waved at him and spoke: "Hello! You're new here aren't you?"

He replied, "Yes I am. As a matter of fact I just moved in, and I was taking a little stroll around to look the place over."

Another lady asked, "Where did you move from?"

He replied, "Oh, I was just released after twenty years in San Quentin.

Surprised, one of the ladies asked, "San Quentin? What were you in for?"

"Well, I murdered my wife," he answered.

Immediately this little widow lady perked up and said, "Oh, then you're single...?"

Now that's a one-track mind!

-Baffler-

22% of women like the way that they look in the nude. So now—what percentage of men are pleased with their own appearance in the nude?

Did you know....

The bloodhound is the only animal whose evidence
is admissible in American courts.

76 – Caring...the risk of feeling

-Ponder-

"Caring about others...running the risk of feeling
...and leaving an impact on people brings happiness."

—Rabbi Harold Kushner

-Proverb-

"Whenever you possibly can, do good to those who need it."

—Proverbs 3:27, Good News Bible

-Principle-

Ten Commandments Of Human Relations
1. Speak to people. There is nothing as nice as a cheerful word of greeting.
2. Smile at people. It takes 72 muscles to frown; 14 to smile.
3. Call people by name. The sweetest music is the sound of one's own name.
4. Be friendly and helpful.
5. Be cordial. Speak and act as if everything you do is a genuine pleasure.
6. Be genuinely interested in people. You can like everybody if you try.
7. Be generous with praise—cautious with criticism.
8. Be considerate of the feelings of others. It will be appreciated.
9. Be thoughtful of the opinion of others.
10. Be alert to give service. What counts most in life is what we do for others.

-Baffler-

How much older is the average groom than the average bride?

Did you know....

Studies have shown that raindrops are not raindrop-shaped. They are generally round or spheroid and some studies say they are sometimes doughnut-shaped.

-Ponder-

"There are only two ways of getting on in the world:
by one's own industry—or by the stupidity of others."

—Jean Dela Bruyere

-Proverb-

"You are the one who will profit if you have wisdom,
and if you reject it, you are the one who will suffer."

—Proverbs 9:12, Good News Bible

-Principle-

Thomas A. Edison, the great inventor, was talking one day with the governor of North Carolina, and the governor complimented him on his inventive genius.

"I am not a great inventor," said Edison.

"But you have over a thousand patents to your credit, haven't you?" queried the governor.

"Yes, but about the only invention I can really claim as absolutely original is the phonograph," was the reply.

"Why, I'm afraid I don't understand what you mean," said the governor.

"Well, explained Edison, "I guess I'm an awfully good sponge. I absorb ideas from every source I can, and put them to practical use. Then I improve them until they become of some value. The ideas which I use are mostly the ideas of other people who don't develop them themselves."

-Baffler-

Of the recorded 82,230 nose jobs performed in 1986,
how many were performed on men?

Did you know....

The bee is the only insect that produces food that is eaten by man.

78 – Doing Your Duty

-Ponder-

"He who does his duty is a hero whether
anyone rewards him for it or not."

—George Failing

-Proverb-

"Stupid people are happy with their foolishness,
but the wise will do what is right."

—Proverbs 15:21, Good News Bible

-Principle-

A certain Eskimo man was taken on one of the expeditions to the North Pole a number of years ago. Later, as a reward for his faithful service, he was brought to New York City for a short visit. He was amazed at what he saw. When he returned to his native village, he told stories of buildings that rose into the very face of the sky; of streetcars, which he described as houses that moved along the trail, with people living in them as they moved; of mammoth bridges; artificial lights, and all the other dazzling sights to be seen in the Big Apple of that day.

His people looked at him coldly and walked away. They began to call him Sagdluk, meaning "The Liar," and this is the name he carried in shame to his grave. Long before his death his original name was forgotten.

History is replete with misunderstood geniuses, tortured artists and unappreciated prophets. Greatness has its price. The pioneer, the pathfinder, the innovator risks ridicule every time. Maybe that is why there are so few of them around.

-Baffler-

What does the word "tips" stand for when it comes to service?

Did you know....

According to the medical definition of the word, an imbecile is
more intelligent than an idiot but less intelligent than a moron.

-Ponder-

"If the government commission had worked on the horse, you would have had the first horse that could operate its knee joint in both directions. The only trouble is…it couldn't have stood up."

—Peter Drucker

-Proverb-

"A fool does not care whether he understands a thing or not; all he wants to do is show how smart he is."

—Proverbs 18:2, Good News Bible

-Principle-

Events in Washington D.C., concerning the confirmation of a Supreme Court Justice have caused much concern. These events remind us of the surgeon, the architect, and the politician who were arguing as to whose profession was the oldest.

"Eve was made from Adam's rib," said the surgeon, "and that surely was a surgical procedure."

"Maybe," said the architect, "But prior to that, order was created out of chaos, and that was an architectural job."

"But," interrupted the politician, "somebody had to create the chaos first."

-Baffler-

Where and how did the counting rhyme
"Eeny, Meeny, Miny, Mo" originate?

Did you know....

Henri Charpentier, the famous chef of one of the Princes of Wales, accidentally invented Crepes Suzettes when the dessert he was making caught on fire. It was named for a young girl who witnessed the conflagration.

-Ponder-

"Don't worry about your mistakes—some of the dullest people don't make any."

—Robert D. Hahn

-Proverb-

"Enthusiasm without knowledge is not good;
impatience will get you into trouble."

—Proverbs 19:2, Good News Bible

-Principle-

Two Kentucky farmers who owned racing stables had developed a keen rivalry. One spring, each of them entered a horse in a local steeplechase. Thinking that a professional rider might help him outdo his friend, one of the farmers engaged a crack jockey. The two horses were neck and neck with a large lead over the rest of the pack at the last fence, but suddenly both fell, unseating their riders.

The professional jockey remounted quickly and rode on to win the race.

Returning triumphantly to the paddock, the jockey found the farmer who had hired him fuming with rage. "What's the matter?" the jockey asked. "I won, didn't I?"

"Oh, yea," roared the farmer. "You won all right, but you crossed the finish line on the wrong horse."

In his hurry to remount after the fall, the jockey had jumped on his competitor's horse. Success is meaningless unless we are in the right.

-Baffler-

How does a catfish "taste" its prey?

Did you know....

The huddle used in American football was invented at Gaulladet College, a university for the deaf in Washington, D.C., to prevent the opposing team from seeing their hand signals.

81 – Worry and Trouble...how to avoid it

-Ponder-

"Worry is interest paid on trouble before it falls due."

—William Inge

-Proverb-

"Worry can rob you of happiness, but kind words will cheer you up."

—Proverbs 12:25, Good News Bible

-Principle-

No problem was ever solved by worrying. It is much too heavy a consumer of energy to be productive. The following are three ways to minimize worries:

1. When confronted with a problem that worries you, do not keep going over it. Come to a decision once and for all. Most worry is caused by indecision.

2. Having made a decision, stick to it. Any positive action is usually better than no action. Don't make the mistake of never expecting to make a mistake.

3. Decide where thought ends and worry begins. Worrying is not the same as thinking. Clear thinking is constructive. Worry is destructive.

-Baffler-

What state in the United States is the world's largest producer of toothpicks?

Did you know....

According to a hospital study, the average new-born
baby spends 113 minutes a day crying!

-Ponder-

"Adults set behavior patterns—children copy them."

—Unknown

-Proverb-

"Pay close attention, son, and let my life be your example."

—Proverbs 23:26, Good News Bible

-Principle-

"The ten behaviors kids want most from their parents were identified in an interview with 100,000 children, ages 8 to 14, from 24 countries and social backgrounds. Children reported that they:

1. Didn't want parents to argue in front of them.
2. Wanted to be treated with the same affection as other children in the family.
3. Didn't want to be lied to.
4. Wanted mutual tolerance from both parents.
5. Wanted friends welcomed in the home.
6. Wanted comradeship with parents.
7. Wanted parents to answer questions.
8. Didn't want to be punished in front of neighborhood kids.
9. Wanted parents to concentrate on their good points, not weaknesses.
10. Wanted parents to be constant in their affections and moods.

-Baffler-

How can you identify the sex of a glowworm?

Did you know....

Thomas Jefferson is credited with inventing the coat hanger.

83 – Lay a Firm Foundation

-Ponder-

"A successful man is one who can lay a firm foundation
with the bricks others throw at him."

—David Brinkley

-Proverb-

"If you are lazy, you will never get what you are after;
but if you work hard, you will get a fortune."

—Proverbs 12:27, Good News Bible

-Principle-

It was the spring of 1947. A new young baseball player had shown up in Yankee Stadium. He was a catcher. No one ever looked less like an athlete than this guy. People wondered if the Yankee organization had lost its mind, and this was before George Steinbrenner. This new catcher was strange looking. He was short, squat, rotund and clumsy. He looked more like something out of a circus, than a professional ball player. They made fun of the way he walked, and the way he looked with a catcher's mask on. He swung at bad pitches, had problems behind the plate, his throwing was wild. He was criticized and laughed at, but he would not quit.

He spent extra hours in the batting cage; he studied rival hitters; he threw thousands of times to second base to improve his accuracy. Eventually he turned public opinion. He would become one of America's most loveable personalities.

This determined ball player was Yogi Berra.

-Baffler-

In what country are Japanese people considered Caucasian?

Did you know....

In an attempt to escape the U.S. Cavalry, Geronimo, the famous Apache Indian chief, jumped from a high cliff into a river, supposedly shouting his name, "Geronimo!" The incident was featured in a 1940 movie and inspired paratroopers during World War II to shout "Geronimo!" as they jumped.

84 – Holding the Torch

-Ponder-

"We cannot hold a torch to light another's
path without brightening our own."

—Ben Sweetland

-Proverb-

"A good man's words are like pure silver;
a wicked man's ideas are worthless."

—Proverbs 10:20, Good News Bible

-Principle-

In 1947, a professor at the University of Chicago, Dr. Chandraseklar, was scheduled to teach an advanced seminar in astrophysics. At the time, he was living in Wisconsin, doing research at the Yerkes Astronomical Observatory. He planned to commute twice a week for the class, even though it would be held during the harsh winter months.

Registration for the seminar, however, fell far below expectations. Only two students signed up for the class. People expected Dr. Chandrasekhar to cancel, lest he waste his time. But for the sake of two students, he taught the class, commuting 100 miles round trip through back country roads in the dead of winter.

His students did their homework. Ten years later, in 1957, they both won the Nobel prize for physics. So did Dr. Chandraseklar in 1983.

-Baffler-

What is the largest animal living today? What is the
largest animal that ever lived on the earth?

Did you know....

The husband of the woman depicted in the *Mona Lisa* is said to have
disliked the painting so much that he refused to pay for it.
It once hung in the bathroom of Francis I, the King of France.

85 – Choosing a Friend

-Ponder-

"Be slow in choosing a friend, slower in changing."

—Benjamin Franklin

-Proverb-

"Some friendships do not last, but some friends are more loyal than brothers."

—Proverbs 18:24, Good News Bible

-Principle-

An English publication offered a prize for the best definition of a friend, and among the thousands of answers received were the following:

"One who multiplies joys, divides grief."
"One who understands our silence."
"A volume of sympathy bound in cloth."
"A watch which beats true for all time and never runs down."

But here is the definition that won the prize:
"A friend...the one who comes in when the whole world has gone out."

-Baffler-

What is the most common <u>first</u> name in the world?

Did you know....

When ants travel in a straight line, expect rain.
When they scatter, expect fair weather.

86 – The Right Condition

-Ponder-

"It is doubtful if anyone ever made a success of anything who waited until all the conditions were 'just right' before starting."

—Unknown

-Proverb-

"If you listen to advice and are willing to learn, one day you will be wise."

—Proverbs 19:20, Good News Bible

-Principle-

Winner Versus Loser

1. A winner says, "Let's find out"; a loser says, "Nobody knows."

2. When a winner makes a mistake, he says, "I was wrong." When a loser makes a mistake, he says, "It wasn't my fault."

3. A winner goes through a problem; a loser goes around it, and never gets past it.

4. A winner makes commitments; a loser makes promises.

5. A winner says, "I'm good, but not as good as I ought to be." A loser says, I'm not as bad as a lot of other people are."

6. A winner tries to learn from those who are superior to him. A loser tries to tear down those who are superior to him.

7. A winner says, "there ought to be a better way to do it." A loser says, "That's the way it's always been done here."

-Baffler-

What is the most common <u>last</u> name in the world?

Did you know....

Generally speaking, if your cat nudges your feet in the morning, it wants to stay inside. If it nudges your face, it wants to go out.

87 – Always Doing Right

-Ponder-

"Always do right—that will gratify some people and astonish the rest."

—Mark Twain

-Proverb-

"Conceited people can never become wise,
but intelligent people learn easily."

—Proverbs 14:6, Good News Bible

-Principle-

The Roman philosopher and statesman, Cicero, said this 2,000 years ago, and it is still true.

THE FIVE MISTAKES OF MAN

1. The delusion that personal gain is made by crushing others.

2. The tendency to worry about things that cannot be changed or corrected.

3. Insisting that a thing is impossible because we cannot accomplish it.

4. Refusing to set aside trivial preference.

5. Neglecting development and refinement of the mind, and not acquiring the habit of reading and studying.

-Baffler-

What is the largest organ in the human body?

Did you know....

It will save you money if you buy the right size refrigerator-freezer for your family. You need a total of eight cubic feet of space for two people, plus one foot for each additional family member.

-Ponder-

"A few kind words take only seconds to say
...but their echoes can go on for years!"

—Executive Speechwriter Newsletter

-Proverb-

"Good people will be rewarded for what they say, but those
who are deceitful are hungry for violence."

—Proverbs 13:3, Good News Bible

-Principle-

Wilfred Funk, a noted lexicographer and dictionary publisher suggests the ten most impressive words in the English language.

"Alone"	- the most bitter word
"Mother"	- the most revered word
"Death"	- the most tragic word
"Faith"	- brings greatest comfort
"Forgotten"	- the saddest word
"Love"	- the most beautiful word
"Revenge"	- the most cruel word
"Friendship"	- the warmest word
"No"	- the coldest word
"Tranquillity"	- the most peaceful word

-Baffler-

What is the smallest tree in the world?

Did you know....

You should have a least four people for any caving expedition. If someone is injured, two people can go for help while one stays with the injured spelunker. That way, no one is in the cave alone.

-Ponder-

"Half the world is composed of people who have something to say and can't
. . . and the other half, who have nothing to say and keep on saying it."

—Robert Frost

-Proverb-

"Thoughtless words can wound as deeply as any
sword, but wisely spoken words can heal."

—Proverbs 12:18, Good News Bible

-Principle-

The following are some of the "The Most Important Words" in the English language:

THE SIX MOST IMPORTANT WORDS: "I admit I made a mistake."
THE FIVE MOST IMPORTANT WORDS: "You did a good job."
THE FOUR MOST IMPORTANT WORDS: "What is your opinion?"
THE THREE MOST IMPORTANT WORDS: "If you please."
THE TWO MOST IMPORTANT WORDS: "Thank you."
THE MOST IMPORTANT WORD: "We"
THE LEAST IMPORTANT WORD: "I"

-Baffler-

In which three sports is left-handed play illegal?

Did you know....

To estimate the surface area of your body, multiply the
surface area of the palm of your hand by 100.

-Ponder-

"The world is moved not only by the mighty shoves of heroes,
but also the aggregate of the tiny pushes of each honest worker."

—Helen Keller

-Proverb-

"Arrogance will bring your downfall, but if you are humble,
you will be respected."

—Proverbs 29:23, Good News Bible

-Principle-

A sea captain and his chief engineer were arguing over who was most important to the ship. To prove their point to each other, they decided to swap places. The chief engineer ascended to the bridge, and the captain went to the engine room.

Several hours later, the captain suddenly appeared on deck covered with oil and dirt. "Chief!" he yelled, waving aloft a monkey wrench. "You have to get down there. I can't make her go!"

"Of course you can't," replied the chief. "She's aground!"

On a team we don't excel each other; we depend on each other.

-Baffler-

What do Noel Coward, Thomas Edison, Sean O'Casey,
Charles Dickens and Mark Twain have in common?

Did you know....

People are more likely to remember you if you always wear the same outfit.

-Ponder-

"A man's reputation is the opinion people have of him,
but his character is what he really is."

—Jack Miner

-Proverb-

"Wise men will gain an honorable reputation,
but stupid men will only add to their disgrace."

—Proverbs 3:25, Good News Bible

-Principle-

A young English boy was called "Carrot Top" by others and given "little chance of success" by some teachers. He ranked third lowest in class: grade average for English was 95%, history 85%, mathematics 50%, and Latin 30%.

His teacher's report read: "The boy is certainly no scholar and has repeated his grade twice. He also has a stubborn streak and is sometimes rebellious in nature. He seems to have little or no understanding of his schoolwork, except in the most mechanical way. At times, he seems almost perverse in his ability to learn. He has not made the most of his opportunities."

Later, the boy settled down to serious study and soon the world began to hear about Winston Churchill.

-Baffler-

How can you tell whether someone is right or
left-handed by looking at their hands?

Did you know....

Try to buy a car made on a Wednesday. Assembly-line workers are off-rhythm on Mondays and Tuesdays because of the weekend. They're tired and bored on Thursdays and Fridays because of the week. This makes cars built on Wednesdays the best.

-Ponder-

"The only people with whom you should try to
get even...are those who have helped you."

—Mae Maloo

-Proverb-

"A good man's words are a fountain of life, but a
wicked man's words hide a violent nature."

—Proverbs 10:11, Good News Bible

-Principle-

Henry Ford once said that the ability to encourage others is one of life's finest assets. The auto inventor and manufacturer knew the power of encouragement. He had learned of it as a young man.

Memorable to him was the time, at the beginning of his career, when he made drawings of his newly built engine for Thomas Edison. Young Ford had endured criticism and ridicule. Most mechanical experts of the day were convinced that electric carriages would be the popular passenger cars of the future.

But attending a dinner one evening at which Edison was present, Ford began explaining his engine to the men nearest him at the table. He noticed Edison, seated several chairs away, was listening. Finally the great man moved closer and asked Ford to make a drawing.

When the crude sketch was completed, Edison studied it intently, then suddenly banged his fist on the table. "Young man," he said, "that's the thing! You have it!"

Years later, Ford recalled "The thump of that fist on the table was worth worlds to me."

-Baffler-

The modern 7-inch-long lead pencil can draw a line how long in length?

Did you know....

The best time to have a garage sale is the first weekend of the month,
because people who get paid monthly have more money to spend then.

-Ponder-

"It's not just who you know, but 'when'
you know them that really counts."

—Rodney R. Weckworth

-Proverb-

"Never tell your neighbor to wait until
tomorrow if you can help him now."

—Proverbs 3:28, Good News Bible

-Principle-

The ice cream cone is a case of necessity being the mother of invention.

Charles E. Menches was one of 50 vendors selling saucers of ice cream at the 1904 Louisiana Purchase Exposition in St. Louis, MO. Business was booming on a hot August day when he ran out of clean saucers.

Menches turned to the stand next to his, operated by a Syrian named Hamwi who had come to the fair from Damascus to sell zalabia—a wafer-like pastry baked on a waffle iron. Hamwi is supposed to have rolled his still soft zalabia into a cornucopia, which Menches filled with ice cream and handed to a customer. Success was instantaneous.

-Baffler-

On an average day, 814 Americans enlist in the armed forces.
How many of those are women?

Did you know....

A resting human gives off as much heat as a 150-watt light bulb. You can use this fact to keep the temperature in a greenhouse constant, even as you come and go. Just turn the light out whenever you go in.

-Ponder-

"The average man, who does not know what to do with his life,
wants another one which will last forever."

—Anatole France

-Proverb-

"Wisdom offers you a long life, as well as wealth and honor."

—Proverbs 3:16, Good News Bible

-Principle-

A recent survey found that the average adult spends about one-third of his waking time bored!

Famed economist Stuart Chase once sat down to figure his own personal calendar. There is, he said, an ascending scale of human values and somewhere on it there is a line between living and mere existing. In how many hours of the week, he asked himself, had he truly and intensively lived? In how many had he just existed? Out of the 168 hours of the week, he found that he had been "alive" only 40 hours, or about 25% of the total time!

-Baffler-

Which muscle in your body gets the greatest day-to-day workout?

Did you know....

If stacked one atop the other, the red blood cells of the
body would create a tower 31,000 miles high.

-Ponder-

"We are not at our best perched at the summit—we are
climbers and at our best when the way is steep."

—John W. Gardner

-Proverb-

"It is better to be an ordinary man working for a living
than to play the part of a great man and go hungry."

—Proverbs 12:9, Good News Bible

-Principle-

Talking with John Dewey several months before his nineteenth birthday, a young doctor blurted out his low opinion of philosophy. "What's the good of such claptrap?" he asked. "Where does it lead you?"

The great philosopher answered quietly, "The good of it is that you climb mountains."

"Climb mountains?" retorted the youth, unimpressed. "And what's the use of doing that?"

"You see other mountains to climb," was the reply. "You come down, climb the next mountain, and see still others to climb." Then, putting his had gently on the young man's knee, Dewey said, "When you are no longer interested in climbing mountains to see other mountains to climb, life is over."

-Baffler-

What are the five most universal things that people dream about?

Did you know....

At age 43 you can still see how a man looked as an adolescent,
yet—for the first time—you can see how he'll look as an old man.

-Ponder-

"Millions long for immortality who do not know what
to do with themselves on a rainy Sunday afternoon."

—Susan Ertz

-Proverb-

"Keep God's laws and you will live longer;
if you ignore them, you will die."

—Proverbs 19:16, Good News Bible

-Principle-

A research scientist in Switzerland has proven that a night's rest does not balance the day's work. A workman for example, breathes 30 ounces of oxygen during Monday's work, but used 31 ounces. At the close of the day he is 1 ounce short. He goes to sleep and breathes more oxygen than he uses, so that in the morning he has gotten back five-sixths. The night's rest does not balance the day's work.

On Sunday morning he is six-sixths of an ounce in debt to nature, a whole ounce, a whole day behind so that he must rest a whole day to get in balance with nature. So, week by week a worker is restored.

But if he neglects to take a weekly rest, he "runs down" and dies before his time.

Another scientist from Clark University confirms the conclusions and has proven that the nerve cells are not fully recovered from a day's wear by a night's rest; and that they must be recovered every few days, or nervous exhaustion is invited.

-Baffler-

Who has the keener senses, men or women?

Did you know....

You can estimate the weight of your skin by dividing your weight by 16.

-Ponder-

"Wisdom consists not so much in knowing what to do
in the ultimate as in knowing what to do next."

—Herbert Hoover

-Proverb-

"It is the Lord who gives wisdom; and from him
comes knowledge and understanding."

—Proverbs 2:6, Good News Bible

-Principle-

An Arab Proverb

He that knows not and knows not that he knows not;
He is a fool—shun him

He that knows not and knows that he knows not;
He is simple—teach him!

He that knows and knows not that he knows;
He is asleep—wake him!

He that knows and knows that he knows;
He is a wise man—follow him!

-Baffler-

Julius Caesar, Hannibal and Napoleon had something
unusual in common. What was it?

Did you know....

When choosing the color of your new car, choose a color that matches the ads for
your particular model—that color will most likely grab a used-car buyer's eye as well.

-Ponder-

"Blessed is the man who is too busy to worry in the
daytime and too sleepy to worry at night."

—Phil Marquart

-Proverb-

"Go ahead and be lazy; sleep on, but you will go hungry."

—Proverbs 19:15, Good News Bible

-Principle-

The people who dismissed deep thinkers like Albert Einstein as "dreamers" were right, a Boston sleep researcher says.

Dr. Ernest Hartmann said his studies show those who need more than nine hours of sleep every night are worriers who apparently mull over their problems while they dream.

Those who sleep fewer than six hours a night, like Thomas Edison and Napoleon, tend to be efficient people who push problems aside and get on with the job, he said.

"Tortured geniuses might be more likely to be long sleepers," said Hartman. "Great men in the sense of practicality, effectiveness—administrators, applied scientists, political leaders—may tend to be short sleepers."

-Baffler-

If laid end-to-end, the body's blood vessels would be how long?

Did you know....

If there's dew on the spider webs in the grass in the morning, it won't rain

-Ponder-

"The secret of success is to be like a duck—smooth and
unruffled on top, but paddling furiously underneath."

—Unknown

-Proverb-

"Plan carefully and you will have plenty; if you act
too quickly, you will never have enough."

—Proverbs 21:5, Good News Bible

-Principle-

At the close of the first day of the battle of Shiloh, a day of severe Union reverses, General Grant was met by his much discouraged Chief of Staff, McPherson, who said,

"Things are bad, General. We have lost half our artillery and a third of the infantry. Our line is broken, and we are pushed back nearly to the river." Grant made no reply, and McPherson asked impatiently what he intended to do. "Do? Why, reform the lines and attack at daybreak. Won't they be surprised?"

Surprised they were, and routed before nine o'clock. Every person that succeeds meets such a crises, and must avert disaster with a prompt reforming of lines and early attack.

-Baffler-

At what age does your nose stop growing?

Did you know....

The occurrence of a heart attack is very rare when one's cholesterol level is less than 150. (National Heart, Lung and Blood Institute study, 1984)

PONDERS & PRINCIPLES

"The secret of success is to be like a duck — smooth and unruffled on top, but peddling furiously underneath." — Unknown

-Ponder-

"Men are wise in proportion not to their experience
but to their capacity for experience."

—George Bernard Shaw

-Proverb-

"Bad people will get what they deserve. Good
people will be rewarded for their deeds."

—Proverbs 14:14, Good News Bible

-Principle-

An old Indian legend tells about a vicious snake who terrorized everyone in the neighborhood until the day he met a wandering holy man. Naturally, the snake couldn't hurt a holy man, and the meeting wound up with the snake listening to a stiff lecture on being nice to people. The holy man left after the snake promised not to bite anybody.

He kept his promise, though his patience was sorely tried. His neighbors thought he was being good because he'd grown too old to fight, and they threw rocks at him. By the time the holy man visited him again, the snake was looking pretty seedy. "You and your ideas!" he said.

"My friend," said the holy man, "I told you not to bite anybody, but I didn't forbid you to kiss!"

-Baffler-

How many UFO sightings will be reported today?

Did you know....

Any time a mechanic starts a conversation by telling you how lucky you are that you brought your car in when you did, plan on spending at least $100!

101 – Hard work and Trust

-Ponder-

"Don't bother about genius, don't worry about being clever, but place
your trust in hard work, perseverance, and determination."

—Sir Frederick Treves

-Proverb-

"A lazy man who refuses to work is only killing himself."

—Proverbs 21:25, Good News Bible

-Principle-

Hotelier Cesar Ritz was a perfectionist. A few hours before the gala opening of the
Ritz Hotel in Paris, Ritz came into the dining room. By six o'clock the last prepara-
tions had been made. Ritz sat down at a table. He noticed at once that it was about
two centimeters too high. So were a second and third table. Ritz gave a few orders.
By eight o'clock the legs of all the tables in the dining room had been shortened by
two centimeters.

Ritz's son, Charles, now chairman of the board, remembers that his father tried
out every new mattress he ordered by sleeping one night on it. If he didn't sleep well,
the mattress was returned.

-Baffler-

Why is it most economical to fill a gas tank early in the morning?

Did you know....

Every hour you spend in a smoky bar is equal
to smoking one or two cigarettes.

-Ponder-

"Those who refuse to learn from history are condemned to repeat it."

—George Santayana

-Proverb-

"When you stop learning, you will soon neglect what you already know."

—Proverbs 19:27, Good News Bible

-Principle-

In "The Decline and Fall of the Roman Empire," completed in 1787, Edward Gibbon lists the following reasons for that fall:

1. *The rapid increase of divorce*; the undermining of dignity and sanctity of the home, which is the basis of human society.
2. *Higher and higher taxes*, and the spending of public money for free bread and entertainment for the populace.
3. *The mad craze for pleasure*; sports becoming every year more exciting and more brutal.
4. *The building of gigantic armaments* when the real enemy was within; the decadence of the people.
5. *The decay of religion*—faith fading into mere form—losing touch with life and becoming impotent to guide the people.

Maybe these five tell us something about our present national situation.

-Baffler-

The National Institute on Aging found that persons in one particular profession outlive the rest of the population by as much as 20 years. What profession is it?

Did you know....

In 1750 America, the typical life span was 40 years.

103 – Women!

-Ponder-

"If you think women aren't explosive…drop one!"

—Gerald F. Lieberman

-Proverb-

"Be faithful to your own wife, and give your love to her alone."

—Proverbs 5:15, Good News Bible

-Principle-

In 1978, in San Bernadino, California, a classified advertisement came out listing a 1973 Porsche automobile for the remarkable price of just $5.00. Of course, everyone thought it was a mistake, but the advertisement came out exactly the same way a second time.

When the advertisement ran a third time, a young man found it impossible to resist, so he made the call to the number listed. To his surprise, he discovered that the price was not a mistake. The man rushed over to see this $5.00 Porsche and discovered that it was absolutely immaculate. It was obvious that the auto had been someone's pride and joy.

Finally he asked the woman why she was selling an auto worth thousands for a mere $5.00. The lady answered, "This is my husband's car. He ran off with his secretary to Canada. I just received a letter from him requesting that I sell the car and send him half." Then with a note of glee she said, "I sure would like to see the look on his face when he gets his $2.50!"

-Baffler-

There is one sport in which neither the spectators nor the participants
know the score or the leader until the contest ends. What is it?

Did you know....

Gardenias and orange blossoms both have lovely fragrances, but combine the two flowers in a bouquet and the smells neutralize each other. The bouquet will have no aroma at all.

-Ponder-

"A leader cannot invent motivation, he can only unlock it."

—Unknown

-Proverb-

"Kind words bring life, but cruel words crush your spirit."

—Proverbs 15:4, Good News Bible

-Principle-

A famous millionaire took pride in never giving a tip for good service or expressing thanks to any employees for a job well done. One New Year's Day, he experienced an unforgettable tragedy. His chief accountant committed suicide. The books were found to be in perfect order, the affairs of the dead man—a modest bachelor—were prosperous and in perfect order. The only letter left by the accountant was a brief note to his wealthy employer. It read: "In 30 years, I have never had one word of encouragement. I'm fed up."

-Baffler-

Do you know where the most heavily used pay
phone in the United States is located?

Did you know....

When United Artists was casting the 1964 film *The Best Man*, about a U.S. President, someone suggested Ronald Reagan be offered the starring role. The UA executive dismissed the idea, explaining, "Reagan doesn't have the presidential look."

-Ponder-

"The hardest arithmetic to master is that which
enables us to count our blessings."

—Reflection

-Proverb-

"Patient persuasion can break down the strongest
resistance and can even convince rulers."

—Proverbs 25:15, Good News Bible

-Principle-

Thanksgiving might not be celebrated in the United States today, were it not for a patient, persistent woman named Sarah Hale.

The first Thanksgiving Day was celebrated by the Pilgrim fathers in 1621. In 1789, President George Washington issued a Thanksgiving Day Proclamation to commemorate the first Pilgrim celebration. But Thomas Jefferson, the third president of the United States discontinued it, calling Thanksgiving "a kingly practice."

Then in 1828, Mrs. Hale began campaigning for the restoration of Thanksgiving as a national holiday. She wrote letters and sought appointment with national leaders from the president down. Time after time she was rebuffed and told this was none of her business.

Finally, in 1863 President Lincoln listened seriously to her plea. He proclaimed the fourth Thursday of November to be the official "National Thanksgiving Day."

By the way, this day was not finally ratified by Congress until 1941!

-Baffler-

Who authored the poem *Mary Had a Little Lamb?*

Did you know....

The Alexander Column in Leningrad (St. Petersburg) was built in 1834 during a bitterly cold winter. Workers mixed mortar for the bricks with vodka instead of water to keep it from freezing.

-Ponder-

"It is better to say 'thank you' and not mean it,
than to mean it and not say it."

—Unknown

-Proverb-

"Have reverence for the Lord, be humble, and you will
get riches, honor, and a long life."

—Proverbs 22:4, Good News Bible

-Principle-

There was once a good king in Spain called Alfonso XII. It came to the king's attention that the pages of his court forgot to ask God's blessing on their daily meals, so he determined to teach them a lesson. He invited all the pages to a lavish banquet. The table was spread with all kinds of good things and the guests ate with evident relish; but none remembered to ask God's blessing on the food.

During the feast a dirty, ill-clad beggar entered, seated himself at the royal table and ate and drank to his heart's content. The pages were amazed and expected the king to send the beggar away, but not a word was said. When the beggar finished he left without saying a word. Finally the pages could keep their silence no longer and they began to criticize the beggar for his ingratitude and presumption.

The king silenced them by saying, "Bolder and more audacious than this beggar have you all been. Every day you sit down to a table supplied by the bounty of your Heavenly Father, yet you ask not His blessing, nor express to Him your gratitude."

-Baffler-

Where does the dust in your house come from?

Did you know....

During World War II, it was discovered that the liquid inside young coconuts can be used as a substitute for blood plasma in an emergency.

-Ponder-

"A thankful heart is not only the greatest virtue,
but the parent of all other virtues."

—Unknown

-Proverb-

"Smiling faces make you happy, and good news makes you feel better."

—Proverbs 15:30, Good News Bible

-Principle-

An elderly lady was ushered into Abraham Lincoln's private office. Mr. Lincoln asked, "What can I do for you Madam?" Placing a covered basket on the table she said, "Mr. President, I have come here today not to ask any favor for myself or for anyone. I heard that you were very fond of cookies and I came here to bring you this basket of cookies!"

Tears trickled down the gaunt face of the great President. He stood speechless for a moment; then he said, "My good woman, your thoughtful and unselfish deed greatly moves me. Thousands have come into this office since I became President, but you are the first one to come asking no favor for yourself or somebody else!"

Remember: Nothing is more honorable than a grateful heart!

-Baffler-

Which is heavier a cup of skim milk, a cup of whole milk, or a cup of cream?

Did you know....

In nearly every language around the world, the word for
"mother" begins with an "m" sound.

-Ponder-

"We are born princes, and the civilizing process makes us frogs."

—Eric Berne

-Proverb-

"Evil people look for ways to harm others;
even their words burn with evil."

—Proverbs 16:27, Good News Bible

-Principle-

Three monkeys were discussing the theory of evolution. Sitting in a tree, one says to the others, "Listen you two. There's a rumor going around that can't be true—that man descended from our noble race. Why, the very idea is a dire disgrace!"

"You'll never see a monkey build a fence around a coconut tree and then let all the coconuts go to waste, forbidding all others a taste. Here's another thing a monkey won't do; go out at night and get drunk, or use a gun or knife to take another monkey's life. Man may have descended, but he didn't descend from us!"

-Baffler-

In 1919 a hydrofoil boat set a world's water speed record of over seventy miles per hour. Who was the boat's creator and pilot?

Did you know....

Dancing to *The Star-Spangled Banner*
is against the law in several states.

-Ponder-

"The really tough thing about true humility
…is that you can't brag about it."

—Anonymous

-Proverb-

"A fool's pride makes him talk too much;
a wise man's words protect him."

—Proverbs 14:3, Good News Bible

-Principle-

In a certain pond on a certain farm were two ducks and a frog. These three were the best of friends. All day long they used to play together. But as the hot summer days came, the pond began to dry up and soon there was such a little bit of water, they all realized they would have to move. Now the ducks could easily fly to another place, but what about their friend the frog?

Finally it was decided that they would put a stick in the bill of each duck, and then the frog would hang onto the stick with his mouth and they would fly him to another pond. And so they did.

As they were flying, a farmer out in his field looked up and saw them and said, "Well, isn't that a clever idea! I wonder who thought of it?"

The frog said, "I did…"

Pride is a deadly, dangerous trap!

-Baffler-

What is the safest time in a person's life?

Did you know....

Lighting a cigar with a $100 bill, that grand gesture of the tycoon, can be performed legally and at no cost if you blow out your light in time. So long as you save more than half of any damaged bill in recognizable form, you can exchange it for a new one at any Federal Reserve bank.

-Ponder-

"Discouragement is like a rash…if it is scratched, it spreads rapidly."

—Dan Hill

-Proverb-

"When people are happy, they smile, but when
they are sad, they look depressed."

—Proverbs 15:13, Good News Bible

-Principle-

According to legend, the devil once advertised his tools for sale at a public auction. When the prospective buyers assembled, there was an oddly shaped tool which was labeled "not for sale." Asked to explain why this was, the devil answered, "I can spare my other tools, but I cannot spare this one. It is the most useful implement I have. It is called DISCOURAGEMENT, and with it I can work my way into lives otherwise inaccessible. When I get this tool into a person's life, the way is open to plant anything there I want."

The moral of the legend is obvious: never leave the door open for discouragement! When discouragement moves in, he is never satisfied to occupy a single room, he must occupy your whole house!

-Baffler-

Do you know who the first person was who is known
to have died of radiation poisoning?

Did you know....

Tidal waves on the open ocean sometimes reach speeds of more
than five hundred nautical miles per hour.

-Ponder-

"When in deep water, it's a good idea to keep your mouth shut."

—St. Louis Labor Tribune

-Proverb-

"The Lord hates evil thoughts, but he is
pleased with friendly words."

—Proverbs 15:26, Good News Bible

-Principle-

If you have ever thought "there ought a be a law" against negative people spreading their poisonous influence, there is good news!

A man was once court-martialed and sentenced to a year's imprisonment for being a discourager. It happened during the Boer War at the siege of Lady Smith. The fortunes of the town and garrison were hanging in the balance. A certain civilian would go along the battle lines and speak discouraging words to the men on duty. He struck no blow for the enemy, not one. He was just a discourager at the critical time. The court-martial judged it a crime to speak disheartening words in an hour like that.

Discouragement can grow like a malignant cancer, spreading its poison and strangling life wherever it goes. If not rooted out, transformed, or re-directed, disaster will surely result.

-Baffler-

All dogs have a pink tongue, except for one type that's
tongue is jet black? What kind of dog is that?

Did you know....

You can cut a starfish into several chunks and each piece
will grow back into a complete starfish.

-Ponder-

"Before marriage a man yearns for a woman—afterward the "Y" is silent."

—W. A. Clark

-Proverb-

"Look after your sheep and cattle as carefully as you can, because wealth is not permanent. Not even nations last forever."

—Proverbs 27:23-24, Good News Bible

-Principle-

Andrew Carnegie was a generous supporter of the New York Philharmonic. One year the society's secretary came as usual to Carnegie's mansion, this time requesting a donation of $60,000.00. Carnegie was just about to sign a check when he paused and said, "No, I've changed my mind. Surely there are other people who like music enough to help with their own money." He then told the secretary to go out and raise half the necessary amount, promising to match it with the other half when this was done.

The following day the secretary was back, announcing that he had raised the required amount. Carnegie commended the man's enterprise and wrote out his check for $30,000.00. As he handed it over he said, "Would you mind telling me who gave you the other half?"

"Not at all," replied the secretary. "It was Mrs. Carnegie."

-Baffler-

Which two states in the U.S. have NOT adopted Daylight Savings Time?

Did you know....

Thomas Edison averaged one new patent every two weeks of his adult life.

-Ponder-

"Reputations are made by searching for things
that can't be done and doing them."

—Unknown

-Proverb-

"If you have to choose between a good reputation
and great wealth, choose a good reputation."

—Proverbs 22:1, Good News Bible

-Principle-

In 1872, George Westinghouse took out his first patent for an automatic air brake that would function far more quickly and safely than the clumsy hand brakes then in use. The railroad companies, however, were deeply suspicious of the invention. When Westinghouse wrote Cornelius Vanderbilt, president of the New York Central Railroad, pointing out the advantages of the air brake, Vanderbilt returned the letter with the words "I have no time to waste on fools," scrawled on the bottom.

The president of the Pennsylvania Railroad saw the possibilities of the new brake and gave Westinghouse money to develop his invention. The tests were successful and news of them reached Vanderbilt. A letter was written from Vanderbilt to Westinghouse requesting that Westinghouse come to see him. Back came the letter, endorsed "I have no time to waste on fools!"

—George Westinghouse

-Baffler-

What is a simple way to test if you have hard or soft water in your home?

Did you know....

Natural gas has no smell. The unpleasant odor is added artificially as
a safety precaution so that people can detect gas leaks.

114 – Angel's Wings

-Ponder-

"In the night of death, hope sees a star, and listening love
can hear the rustle of an angel's wings."

—Robert Ingersoll

-Proverb-

"Anyone who is alive in the world of the living has some hope;
a live dog is better off than a dead lion."

—Ecclesiastes 9:4, Good News Bible

-Principle-

Years ago the S-4 submarine was rammed by another ship and quickly sank. The entire crew was trapped in its prison house of death. Ships rushed to the scene of the disaster off the coast of Massachusetts. Inside the sunken submarine, men clung bravely to life, as the oxygen slowly gave out.

As rescuers arrived, a diver was sent down to the submarine. The diver placed his ear to the side of the vessel and listened. He heard a tapping noise. Someone, he learned, was tapping out a question in the dots and dashes of the Morse Code. The question came slowly: "Is...there...any...hope?"

Someone has said that if you could convince a person there was no hope, he would curse the day he was born. Hope is an indispensable quality of life.

-Baffler-

General Motors introduced its compact Chevy Nova to the Latin American market with an expensive promotion, but the car didn't sell. Why?

Did you know....

A rat can go without water longer than a camel can.

115 – Remember to Practice

-Ponder-

"When you are not practicing—remember: Someone...somewhere
...is practicing...and when you meet him—he will win!"

—Senator Bill Bradley

-Proverb-

"He who tills his land will have plenty of bread,
but he who pursues vain things lacks sense."

—Ecclesiastes 3:22, Good News Bible

-Principle-

Raymond Berry was a great pass receiver for the Baltimore Colts in the late '50s and '60s. What is unusual is that Berry did not have the physical attributes of the other top players. He wasn't very strong; he wasn't very fast. In fact, he had a bad back and wore contact lenses. But he became one of the most productive pass receivers in the history of the National Football League.

The secret of this unusual athlete can be summed up in one word—PRACTICE. He practiced more than any other receiver before or since, catching the ball from every conceivable angle, running patterns until they were perfect, working with his quarterback Johnny Unitas, until they knew each other's minds. All this practice is what made him a super-star, because as Berry put it, "In a game there is little time to think. Good practice habits keep you toned so you can do right things automatically."

-Baffler-

Why can't you make a good cup of tea on the top of Mt. Everest?

Did you know....

In any group, usually the person doing the least
talking is the one with the most power.

-Ponder-

"Adversity introduces people to themselves."

—Epictetus

-Proverb-

"The Lord makes you go through hard times, but he himself will be there to teach you, and you will not have to search for him any more."

—Isaiah 30:20, Good News Bible

-Principle-

John Todd was a product engineer, and he traveled frequently. As most travelers do, he would often forget his shampoo and be forced to use bath soap. Then came his solution—to sell hotels on providing free toiletries to their guests with the brand names on one side and the hotel's name on the other.

Because John Todd forgot his shampoo, he created the opportunity. The customized hotel amenities industry was born. By the way, John Todd's company recently reported revenues of $11.7 million!

-Baffler-

Which is taller—the Eiffel Tower or the Washington Monument?

Did you know....

Any time your lips feel dry, you need water.

-Ponder-

"When one door of opportunity closes, another opens; but often we look so long at the closed door…we don't see the one which has been opened for us."

—Helen Keller

-Proverb-

"Always remember what you have learned.
Your education is your life—guard it well."

—Proverbs 14:13, Good News Bible

-Principle-

A Brooklyn-based adventurer was on a fur-trapping expedition in Labrador. He noticed that the Eskimo froze Caribou meat in the dry arctic air, and when it was thawed and cooked months later, it was still flavorsome and tender. He reasoned that the secret of their food freezing success was in the quickness with which they froze their food. Returning home, the adventurer developed the equipment and procedures which became the basis for today's frozen food industry.

His name—Charles Birdseye, the founder of General Foods. All because of a hunting trip to Labrador. Profitable ideas can be discovered all around us if we are alert!

-Baffler-

The largest McDonald's in the world opened in January, 1990,
with 700 seats and 27 cash registers. Where is it?

Did you know....

Ten people will raise the temperature of a
medium-size room one degree per hour.

118 – Talent and Genius

-Ponder-

"Talent is a flame…Genius is a fire!"

—Ben Williams

-Proverb-

"People with no regard for others can throw whole cities into turmoil.
Those who are wise keep things calm."

—Proverbs 29:8, Good News Bible

-Principle-

The story is told of a heavy bronze bell that had sunk into a river in China. The efforts of various engineers to raise it had been to no avail. At last a clever native priest asked permission to make the attempt, on the condition that the bell should be given to his temple. He then had his assistants gather an immense number of bamboo rods. These are hollow, light and practically unsinkable. They were taken down by divers, one by one, and fastened to the bell. After many thousands of them had thus been fastened, it was noticed that the bell began to move, and when the last one had been added, the buoyancy of the accumulated rods was so great that they actually lifted that enormous mass of bronze to the surface.

Sometimes we may be tempted to believe that our bamboo rod is too small and light to make any difference. The key is to remember that our contribution can and should lend strength to the whole.

-Baffler-

The increase in the cost of a first-class postage stamp (to 29 cents) which happened in early 1991 was not unusual. How many times did the U.S. Post Office raise the cost of a first-class stamp between 1960 and 1990?

Did you know....

One out of five items costing under $75 that you buy at a garage sale will end up in your garage sale within the next 1.5 years.

-Ponder-

"Drive carefully—your car is not the only thing that can be recalled by its maker!"

—Soundings

-Proverb-

"It is foolish to follow your own opinions. Be safe and
follow the teachings of wiser people."

—Proverbs 28:26, Good News Bible

-Principle-

The patrolman had stopped a driver late at night. The man knew he had not been speeding; so he asked the officer, "What did I do wrong?"

"You are driving without a rear light," the officer replied. The man got out of his car to look and suddenly began to go to pieces. "Oh, oh, oh," he cried. "This is terrible. I don't know what I'm going to do. How in the world did this happen without me knowing it?"

"Calm down," the officer said. "It isn't all that bad. Not having a rear light isn't that serious."

"Rear light?" the man screamed. "I don't care about the light. What about my boat and trailer?"

-Baffler-

What is pictured on the back of a $10 bill?

Did you know....

Each winter, squirrels lose about half their nuts
because they forget where they stored them.

-Ponder-

"Ears are openings to the mind."

—Malcolm Forbes

-Proverb-

"A warning, given by an experienced person to someone willing to listen, is more valuable than gold rings or jewelry made of the finest gold."

—Proverbs 25:12, Good News Bible

-Principle-

It was the most important football game of the season, and the defense was being torn apart by the opponent's aggressive lineman. So the coach called his toughest player over and said, "Jones, we've go to do something. I want you to get in there and get belligerent and get vindictive. Do you understand?" "Sure thing, Coach," said Jones, and he ran out into the field...but nothing happened. Jones didn't block, he didn't charge; Instead he seemed to be just roaming about the field looking one way and then the other. Finally, the coach sent in a replacement and when Jones trotted back to the bench, the coach was furious. "What's the matter with you?" he screams. "I thought I told you to get belligerent and get vindictive?" "I tried," Jones complained. "I really did, honest, Coach. I looked real hard, but I couldn't find those names on any jersey out there?"....That's called a communication gap!

-Baffler-

In fiction, where can Gillikin Country, Munchkin Country, Quadling Country, and Winkie Country all be found?

Did you know....

The island of Alcatraz gets its name from the Spanish word for *Pelican*.

-Ponder-

"Next to a happy family and a few good friends, the best human
gift that God can give us is a worthy adversary."

—The Cresset

-Proverb-

"To like sin is like making trouble. If you brag all the time,
you are asking for trouble."

—Proverbs 17:19, Good News Bible

-Principle-

A lion was king of the jungle. One day as he paraded through the jungle he met a rabbit. He said, "Who is the king of the jungle?" The rabbit said, "You are." Next the lion came to a deer and asked the elegant creature, "Who is king of the jungle?" The deer said, "You are, Mr. Lion." So he walked on and met a tall giraffe, towering higher than all of the creatures in the jungle. The lion looked up to the giraffe and roared, "Who is king of the jungle?" The giraffe bowed his head, bent his neck, until his eyes were even with the lion, and said, "You are, Mr. Lion."

Proudly, the beast went on his way until he ran into a huge bull elephant with tusks six feet long. He looked up at the monstrous creature and roared, "Who is the king of the jungle?" The elephant, without saying a word, swung his trunk back and forth, wrapped it around the lion's body, lifted him up, whirled him around, then slapped him against the side of a mountain. The lion, dazed, struggled to his feet, staggered over to the elephant, and said, "Just because you didn't know the answer, you don't have to get so mad."

Competition demands that you know for sure, who you are and who "they" are!

-Baffler-

How much does the *Plymouth Rock* weigh?

Did you know....

Mothballs in your tool chest will keep tools from rusting.

-Ponder-

"Keep your fears to yourself, but share your courage with others."

—Robert Louis Stevenson

-Proverb-

"The wicked run when no one is chasing them, but an honest person is brave as a lion."

—Proverbs 28:1, Good News Bible

-Principle-

A very wealthy man bought a huge ranch in Arizona, and he invited some of his closest associates in to see it. After touring some of the 1500 acres of mountains, rivers, and grasslands, he took everyone to the house. The house was as spectacular as the scenery, and out back was the largest swimming pool imaginable. However, this giant swimming pool was filled with alligators. The owner explained it this way: "I value courage more than anything else. Courage is what made me a billionaire. In fact, I think that courage is such a powerful virtue that if anybody is courageous enough to jump in the pool, swim through those alligators and make it to the other side, I'll give them anything they want, anything—my house, my land, my money." Of course, everybody laughed at the absurd challenge and preceded to follow the owner into the house for lunch...when they suddenly heard a splash. Turning around they saw this guy swimming for his life across the pool, thrashing at the water, as the alligators swarmed after him. After several death defying seconds, the man made it, unharmed to the other side. The rich host was amazed, but he stuck to his promise. He said, "You are indeed a man of courage—just tell me what you want, and it's yours." The swimmer, breathing heavily, looked up at the host and said, "I just want to know one thing—who pushed me in that pool?"

The line between courage and fear is often a very narrow line.

-Baffler-

A "Spermologer" doesn't study sperm. What does he do?

Did you know....

Less than five percent of the paperwork filed in the average
office is ever seen again by anyone for any reason!

-Ponder-

"I think God is going to come down and pull civilization over for speeding."

—Steven Wright

-Proverb-

"Any enterprise is built by wise planning, becomes strong through common sense, and profits wonderfully by keeping abreast of the facts."

—Proverbs 24:3-4, Living Bible

-Principle-

There is a sports metaphor for the times we are living in that is particularly appropriate to the changing and volatile environment. There is a game called Chinese baseball. The game is played exactly like the American baseball with one major exception, and that is: the minute the ball leaves the pitcher's hand—the fielders can do anything they want! They can actually mass all the bases together and run away with them. They can separate second and third bases by another thirty yards if they like. For a weak hitter, all the players might line up in the infield. For a slow runner, after he hits the ball, the first baseman could actually carry the base into left field, all the way to the wall! Naturally, it's total chaos!

The point is nations, people and companies would be just as chaotic without planning, specific direction, and clear goals.

-Baffler-

He is called "the Father of Our Country." But how many children did George Washington actually have?

Did you know....

The is no evidence whatsoever that cedar chests or closets act as moth repellents.

-Ponder-

"As we grow older it seems that life is sometimes unfair—
however, 'fair' is not a grown-up concept."

—Dale Frye

-Proverb-

"Long life is the reward of the righteous; gray hair is a glorious crown."

—Proverbs 16:31, Good News Bible

-Principle-

The song says, "Fairy tales can come true, it can happen to you, if you're young at heart."

But what if you're old and gray?

If so, you're probably depicted in most fairy tales as a villainous witch, blind soul, poor beggar or village idiot, says Allen Chinen in *Modern Maturity* magazine.

In a report to the American Psychiatric Association, Chinen said that out of 2,500 fairy tales, only two percent featured older people as wise or productive. When they were presented positively, their characters were supernatural and unrealistic (i.e., a fairy god-mother or a wise magician).

The result, concluded Chinen, is that yet another generation of young people will grow up with very few positive or well-drawn images of older people and old age.

-Baffler-

How long did Sleeping Beauty sleep before the
handsome prince came to awaken her?

Did you know....

Although their name means "100-legged," most centipedes have fewer than 50 legs. There are some centipedes, though, that have as many as 200 legs.

PONDERS & PRINCIPLES

© 2004 Tania von Allmen for Ponders & Principles LLC

"The harder you fall, the higher you bounce."
— American Proverb

125 – Daring to Fail

-Ponder-

"Those who dare to fail miserably can achieve greatly!"

—Robert Kennedy

-Proverb-

"So let us not become tired of doing good; for if we do not give up,
the time will come when we will reap a harvest."

—Galatians 6:9, Good News Bible

-Principle-

In the 1820's there was a young journalist who became famous for coining the phrase, "Remember the Alamo." But Gail Borden's real ambition was to invent a way to condense food so that it would stay edible for a long time. Said Borden: "I mean to put a potato into a pillbox, a pumpkin into a tablespoon, and a watermelon into a saucer." At every opportunity he would experiment on guests serving concentrated soups and foods. For the 1850 California Gold Rush, Borden invented the dehydrated meat biscuit; however, it was a boat trip home from England that sparked "the idea," an idea born out of a tragedy. On board ship, Borden saw children die as a result of drinking contaminated milk. He vowed to dedicate his life to finding a way to make milk safe for human consumption.

Through his experiments with meat biscuits, Borden knew food could be kept fresh over long periods of time if moisture was reduced. He put a gallon of milk in a kettle and boiled off the water. The experiment failed. It had an unpleasant, burnt taste. While visiting a Shaker colony in New York, Borden found the answer—he saw maple sugar condensed in a vacuum-sealed pan. Because of the vacuum-sealed pan, less heat was needed to evaporate, reducing the burnt taste.

It worked and the U. S. Army placed the first big order for 500 pounds of condensed milk. Borden did more than invent a process and created what is now a multi-billion dollar company; he founded the modern dairy industry. On his tombstone was inscribed his life's motto: "I tried and failed. I tried again and succeeded."

-Baffler-

Which of the following vegetables are not used to make V-8 juice?
beet   cabbage   carrot   spinach

Did you know....

The brain continues sending out electrical wave
signals as long as 37 hours after death.

-Ponder-

"Sound travels slowly—sometimes the things you say when your kids
are teenagers, don't reach them 'til they're in their 40's."

—Orben's Current Comedy

-Proverb-

"Respected people do not tell lies, and fools have nothing worthwhile to say."

—Proverbs 17:7, Good News Bible

-Principle-

An alumnus returned to visit his old dorm and his old dorm room. As luck would
have it, there was someone in and so he knocked and was admitted. He asked the
young man if he could look around and was given permission. "Good heavens" said
the former student, "that chair is the same old chair I had when I was a student here
ten years ago. And that desk is the same old desk—see, here are my initials!" And he
went on saying. "same old bed, same old furniture, same old windows." Then he went
to the closet and opened it, whereupon he found a coed. "Oh that, sir, is my sister,"
said the young student. "Yes," said the alumnus, "and that is the same old story."

-Baffler-

To a stamp collector, what does "E.F.O.'s" mean?

Did you know....

The stock market usually goes up in years in which the NFL team
wins the Super Bowl, and down when the AFL team wins.

-Ponder-

"Adversity has the effect of eliciting talents which in prosperous circumstances would have lain dormant."

—Homer

-Proverb-

"Only a wise man knows what things really mean.
Wisdom makes him smile and makes his frowns disappear."

—Ecclesiastes 8:1, Good News Bible

-Principle-

A certain chicken farmer had a real problem. Every spring his land was almost totally flooded. Even though the floods caused him horrendous problems, he refused to move. When the waters would back up onto his land and flood his chicken coops, he would race to move his chickens to higher ground. Some years, hundreds of them drowned because he couldn't move them out in time.

One year after suffering heavy losses from a particularly bad flood, he came into the farm house and in a voice filled with despair, told his wife, "I've had it. I can't afford to buy another place. I can't sell this one. I don't know what to do!"

His wife calmly replied, "Buy ducks."

-Baffler-

What do you call the dot over the letter "i"?

Did you know....

In an average lifetime, the human body produces
more than 25,000 quarts of saliva.

-Ponder-

"Keep away from people who try to belittle your ambitions. Small people always do that, but the really great ones make you feel that you, too, can become great."

—Mark Twain

-Proverb-

"What you say can preserve life or destroy it; so you must accept the consequences of your words."

—Proverbs 18:21, Good News Bible

-Principle-

At age 16, Andor Foldes was already a skilled pianist, but he was experiencing a troubled year. In the midst of the young Hungarian's personal struggles, one of the most renowned pianists of the day came to Budapest. Emil von Sauer was famous not only for his abilities; he was also the last surviving pupil of the great Franz Liszt. Von Sauer requested that Foldes play for him. Foldes obliged with some of the most difficult works of Bach, Beethoven, and Schumann. When he finished, von Sauer walked over to him and kissed him on the forehead. "My son," he said, "when I was your age I became a student of Liszt. He kissed me on the forehead after my first lesson, saying, 'Take good care of this kiss—it comes from Beethoven, who gave it to me after hearing me play.' I have waited for years to pass on this sacred heritage, but now I feel you deserve it."

-Baffler-

Where did the idea of signing an "X" for a kiss come from?

Did you know....

The annual output of a single coffee tree amounts to about one pound of ground coffee.

-Ponder-

"A good man dies when a boy goes wrong."

—Unknown

-Proverb-

"Discipline your son, and you can always be proud of him.
He will never give you reason to be ashamed."

—Proverbs 29:17, Good News Bible

-Principle-

A young successful attorney said: "The greatest gift I ever received was a gift I got one Christmas when my Dad gave me a small box. Inside was a note saying, "Son, this year I will give you 365 hours, an hour every day after dinner. It's yours. We'll talk about what you want to talk about, we'll go where you want to go, play what you want to play. It will be your hour!"

"My dad not only kept his promise," he said, "But every year he renewed it—and it's the greatest gift I ever had in my life. I am the result of his time."

-Baffler-

What is the purpose of the ball on top of a flagpole?

Did you know....

It wasn't until 20 years after he wrote *Take Me Out to the Ball Game* that Albert von Tilzer actually saw his first one.

130 – Diplomacy

-Ponder-

"Diplomacy is the art of letting the other fellow have your way."

—Herman Van Roijen

-Proverb-

"The most stupid fool is better off than someone
who thinks he is wise, when he is not."

—Proverbs 26:12, Good News Bible

-Principle-

The foreign diplomat was unable to speak English. When the lunch bell rang at the United Nations Assembly, he stood behind a man at the food counter and heard him order apple pie and coffee. So he ordered apple pie and coffee too. For the next two weeks he kept ordering apple pie and coffee. Finally, he decided he wanted to try something else so he listened attentively while another man ordered a sandwich. "Ham sandwich," he said to the counter man.

"White or rye?" the counter man asked.

"Ham sandwich," the diplomat repeated.

"White or rye?" the counter man asked again.

"Ham sandwich," the diplomat replied.

The counter man grew very angry. "Look Mac," he roared, shaking his fist under the diplomat's nose, "do you want it on white or rye?"

"Apple pie and coffee," answered the diplomat.

-Baffler-

When *The Tonight Show* debuted (as *Tonight*) in 1954, who was its host?

Did you know....

A fly's taste buds are in its feet.

-Ponder-

"The way to make a fortune is to come up with something that is:
Low Priced—Habit forming—Tax Deductible."

—Unknown

-Proverb-

"What good people want always results in good; when the
wicked get what they want, everyone is angry."

—Proverbs 11:23, Good News Bible

-Principle-

Early in his amazing career, Thomas Edison invented a machine that recorded votes. With a flick of a switch, a legislator could vote for or against a proposal without leaving his desk. The tedious business of marking ballots and counting them was no longer necessary. Edison eagerly headed for Washington to demonstrate his new machine. He was praised for his inventiveness, but his machine was rejected. The chairman of the Committee explained why: "Filibustering and delay in tabulating votes are often the only way we can defeat bad or improper legislation." he told Edison.

Edison was stunned. The invention was good; it worked. But it wasn't needed. Edison said later, "There and then I made a vow that I would never invent anything which was not wanted."

No rule for success is more fundamental than that. Give the people what they want.

-Baffler-

What is the most popular name for a dog in the U.S.?

Did you know....

It's the fat in beef and pork that gives them their characteristic tastes. If all the fat were removed from these meats, the Dept. of Agriculture says, you wouldn't be able to taste any difference between them.

-Ponder-

"No dream comes true until you wake up and go to work."

—Banking

-Proverb-

"Being lazy will make you poor, but hard work will make you rich."

—Proverbs 10:4, Good News Bible

-Principle-

There is a very thin line between the top five percent of real achievers and the rest of the pack. This fine line of demarcation is "the winner's edge."

On the professional golf tour in the United States, only a few shots separate the top money winners from the rest of the tour. In baseball, the American and National League batting champions every year actually only hit safely about 20 to 30 more times in an entire season than those who didn't make the top 10 in the batting average finals. Just a few strokes of the bat in a different way separates the true champion from the average professional. In the Olympic Games, the difference between the gold medal winner and the fourth place non-metal winner is often only two-tenths of a second. And so, the winning edge is only a degree here and a few strokes there, or a few swings here and a couple of tenths of a second there. The talent in professional football is so nearly equal that the score at the end of the game is a matter of inches and split second timing.

What is true on the athletic field is true in every other walk of life. The real leaders in business, in the professional community, in education, in government, and in the home draw upon a special winning edge that separates them from the rest of society.

-Baffler-

According to polls, which of these presidents had the highest
overall approval rating after one year in office?
A. George H. W. Bush   B. Jimmy Carter   C. Richard Nixon   D. Ronald Reagan

Did you know....

Most newborn babies cry without tears until they are three to six weeks old.

-Ponder-

"Don't let the little things get you down—there's no need
to pole-vault over mice manure."

—Dan Hill

-Proverb-

"The hopes of good men lead to joy, but wicked
people can look forward to nothing."

—Proverbs 10:28, Good News Bible

-Principle-

Those inventive people, the Italians, have a custom. As midnight on New Year's
Eve approaches, the streets are clear. There is no traffic; there are no pedestrians;
even the policemen take cover. Then at the stroke of midnight, the windows of the
houses fly open. To the sound of laughter, music, and fireworks, each member of the
family pitches out old crockery, detested ornaments, hated furniture and a whole cat-
alogue of personal possessions which remind them of something in the past year they
are determined to wipe out of their minds.

-Baffler-

On July 22, 1962, the Mariner I space probe was launched from Cape Canaveral,
Florida, programmed to provide the first close-up view of the planet Venus. It fell into
the Atlantic four minutes after lift-off, an $18.5 million loss for the U.S. space pro-
gram. What was later determined to be the cause this failure?

Did you know....

The U. S. Postal Service has assured diet-conscious customers that there is no
more than one tenth of a calorie in the glue on the back of each postage stamp.

-Ponder-

"No matter what a man's past may have been, his future is spotless."

—John R. Rice

-Proverb-

"Some people ruin themselves by their own actions and then blame the Lord."

—Proverbs 19:3, Good News Bible

-Principle-

The Koreans have a curious New Year's custom. Desiring to forget unpleasant things and make a fresh start, each person determines what bad habits he would like to eliminate and what past deeds he wants forgiven. Then he writes the names of those evils on a kite and flies it high into the air. When it is almost out of sight, he cuts the string. As the kite takes a nosedive and disappears from sight, he thinks that all his faults and all previous transgressions are forever removed.

-Baffler-

Long Beach, Miami Beach, Palm Beach—there are dozens of coastal resort cities with "Beach" in their names. However, there is only one town in the United States name simply "Beach." Where is it?

Did you know....

During World War II the U. S. Navy used world-champion chess player Reuben Fine to calculate probabilities of where enemy subs might surface.

135 – No Excuse!

-Ponder-

"Ninety-nine percent of failures come from people who
have the habit of making excuses."

—George Washington Carver

-Proverb-

"Let other people praise you—even strangers; never do it yourself."

—Proverbs 27:2, Good News Bible

-Principle-

Managing performance means giving feedback and reinforcement. The ultimate form of feedback is a scoreboard.

A scoreboard is created not so much different from the ones in sports: a graph is used to chart employees' performance and production. It works! Not just in keeping score, but improving the score. People actually improve the score simply because someone pays attention—often for the first time—to what they are doing.

Intel Corporation used a scoreboard for their facilities maintenance group. The maintenance group had been mediocre for years despite all kinds of methods, programs, pressure, and inducement. Then the company started a program in which each building was "scored." The score was then compared with those given other buildings. The condition of the facilities improved immediately. No money or any other rewards was given, but the arena of competition made all the difference in performance.

-Baffler-

Why is it more difficult to find a specific address in
Tokyo than any other city in the world?

Did you know....

Our taste buds begin to atrophy after the age of 45,
and flavor perception drops significantly.

-Ponder-

"The average person puts only 25% of his energy and ability into his work. The world takes off its hat to those who put in more than 50% of their capacity and stands on its head for those few and far between souls who devote 100%."

—Andrew Carnegie

-Proverb-

"A hard-working farmer has plenty to eat.
People who waste time will always be poor."

—Proverbs 28:19, Good News Bible

-Principle-

Lee Iacocca says, "When I leave, I guess my only legacy will be to leave on the wall my commandments of management—my distillation of 44 years in the business world:"

1. Hire the best—smart, dedicated people.
2. Get your priorities straight and keep a hot list of what you're trying to do.
3. Say it in English and keep it short—no bureaucratic double-talk.
4. Never forget it is the line organization—not the staff—that makes money.
5. Delegate, but set limits on the size of their playing field.
6. Keep some mavericks around who disagree.
7. Remember the fundamentals.

-Baffler-

The *Guinness Book of World Records* was first published in 1955.
Nineteen years later, in 1974, it got into itself: Why?

Did you know....

In one survey of first-graders, a large percentage chose
Diarrhea as the most poetic-sounding female name!

137 – The Bum Steers

-Ponder-

"It's not the bulls and bears you need to avoid...it's the bum steers."

—Chuck Hillis

-Proverb-

"Stupid people always think they are right. Wise people listen to advice."

—Proverbs 12:15, Good News Bible

-Principle-

A young teller aspired to be a success in the banking business. Upon hearing that the president of the bank was retiring, the young teller made an appointment with the wise old banker. He did not want to miss out on the opportunity to learn from the retiree the secret of his success.

Walking into the president's impressive office he wasted no time by saying, "Sir, you have done a great job and made a tremendous success of yourself. I too want to succeed in this business. To what do you owe your success?"

The old gentleman replied, "Two words—good decisions."

The teller said, "Okay, I understand that, but how do I make good decisions?"

The president said, "One word—experience."

"Yes sir, that makes sense," replied the teller, "but how do I get that experience?"

"Two words," answered the wise president, "bad decisions!"

-Baffler-

Do toilet-seat covers really protect us against anything?

Did you know....

Women smile more than men. One can find immediate proof
of this by thumbing through any high-school yearbook.

-Ponder-

"If a fellow isn't thankful for what he's got, he isn't likely
to be thankful for what he's going to get."

—Frank H. Clark

-Proverb-

"Be thankful in all circumstances. This is what God wants
from you in your life in union with Christ Jesus."

—I Thessalonians 5:18, Good News Bible

-Principle-

Pete had become lost in the desert and had been chasing mirages. He thought to himself, I'll follow this last one. It was a deserted town with a well in the very center. As he pumped the handle in a futile attempt for water he saw a note nailed to a post. It said, "Look behind the rock where a five-gallon bucket of water will be found." Then the note warned against drinking or using the water for anything besides priming the pump. The note went on to say that "every drop of water was needed, but when it is primed all the water you desire will come forth." One last instruction read, "Please fill the bucket of water and place it behind the rock for the next weary soul who might happen to come along."

How hard it is to give up a "sure thing" for something we cannot see at the moment. The temptation is for immediate gratification which results in selling out too quickly.

It may just be that now is a good time to start priming the pump, rather than indulging our immediate desires!

-Baffler-

Where did the term "fall guy" originate?

Did you know....

According to one survey, two-thirds of the men in
America believe in love at first sight.

-Ponder-

"Nothing in the world can take the place of persistence. The slogan 'PRESS ON' has solved and always will solve the problems of the human race!"

—Calvin Coolidge

-Proverb-

"Look straight ahead with honest confidence; don't hang your head in shame."

—Proverbs 4:24, Good News Bible

-Principle-

There's a belief that certain people do everything right—that they never make mistakes, and their plans never fail. There is the presumption that only if you're perfect, all the time, only then do you have the "right stuff" to succeed. In reality however, nothing could be further from the truth.

Consider the following facts:

The greatest quarterbacks complete only six out of ten passes.

The best basketball players only make about half of their shots.

Major league baseball players make it to first base only 25% of the time—and that includes walks.

Top oil companies, even with the consultation of expert geologists, find only one well in ten.

A successful T.V. actor is turned down twenty-nine out of thirty times after auditioning for roles in commercials.

Winners in the stock markets make money on only two out of five investments.

Persistence is the gold mine for success!

-Baffler-

What is the most popular perfume in the world?

Did you know....

Brazil nuts are seeds, not nuts (but they do come from Brazil).

140 – Be a Smiler

-Ponder-

"The fellow who can smile when things go wrong has probably
just thought of somebody he can blame it on."

—Grit

-Proverb-

"Sensible people accept good advice.
People who talk foolishly will come to ruin."

—Proverbs 10:8, Good News Bible

-Principle-

With the recession affecting more and more Americans, there is renewed comparison of American business with Japanese business. The announcement by gigantic General Motors of cuts in their North American operations inevitably revives talk of slowing the steady stream of imported cars which are filling the highways.

Unfortunately, someone who talks like that is often the person who drinks Brazilian coffee out of an English cup while devouring French pastry while sitting on his Danish furniture after coming home in his German car from seeing an Italian movie, then blows his top because his business is bad, picks up his Japanese-made ball-point and writes to his congressman to demand that the government stop the flood of foreign imports.

-Baffler-

Why did pirates wear an earring in a pierced ear?

Did you know....

Tarantula spiders have been known to live for over two years without eating.

-Ponder-

"Just because nobody disagrees with you does not necessarily
mean you are brilliant...maybe you're the boss!"

—Construction Digest

-Proverb-

"If your goals are good, you will be respected, but if you are
looking for trouble, that is what you will get."

—Proverbs 11:27, Good News Bible

-Principle-

One of the largest department stores in the world is in London, England.
Selfridge's owes a great deal of its success to H. Gordon Selfridge who considered
himself more than a mere boss. He saw himself as a leader of people. When analyzing
the difference between being a boss and being a leader, here is what he believed:

1. The boss drives his people; the leader coaches them.
2. The boss depends on authority; the leader on good will.
3. The boss inspires fear; the leader inspires enthusiasm.
4. The boss says "I"; the leader says "We."
5. The boss fixes the blame for the breakdown; the leader fixes the breakdown.
6. The boss says "go"; the leader says "let's go!"

-Baffler-

Do you know your elephant trivia? How much liquid
can an elephant hold in its trunk?

Did you know....

The first stewardesses were on United Airlines, in 1930,
and they had to be registered nurses.

-Ponder-

"Trust your hunches—they're usually based on facts
filed away just below the conscious level."

—Dr. Joyce Brothers

-Proverb-

"If you refuse good advice, you are asking for trouble;
follow it, and you are safe."

—Proverbs 13:13, Good News Bible

-Principle-

Andrew Carnegie was once asked about the secret to his remarkable success. Carnegie replied, "I owe it all to my flashes."

When pressed to explain, Carnegie said, "All my life, I woke up early in the morning, and always there came to my mind with the waking, a flash telling me what to do that day, and if I followed those flashes, I always succeeded."

An interviewer inquired if Carnegie likened the flashes to heavenly visions like those in the Bible?

"Call it that if you like," Carnegie answered, "or call it flashes; but it was the following of those silent admonitions and directions which brought me the success you say I have achieved."

-Baffler-

Where is the "warmest" part of your body?

Did you know....

The flu was first described by Hippocrates, in 412 B.C.

143 – Dying of Thirst

-Ponder-

"When you're dying of thirst, it's too late to think of digging the well."

—Unknown

-Proverb-

"Wisdom is in every thought of an intelligent man;
fools know nothing about wisdom."

—Proverbs 14:33, Good News Bible

-Principle-

Lewis Waterman was an insurance agent. After working on a client for several weeks, he persuaded the man to take out a large policy. Waterman called on him with the contract ready for signature. He placed it on the desk and took a fountain pen from his pocket. As he opened it, it began to leak, and ink ran over the contract. Waterman hurried back to his office for another policy form. By the time he returned, however, the man had changed his mind.

Waterman was so disgusted that he gave up the insurance business and, in turn, devoted his time to the development of a reliable fountain pen, founding the prestigious company that now carries his name. The Waterman fountain pen, one of the highest quality fountain pens in the world—an opportunity created, all because Lewis Waterman had a problem signing a contract.

-Baffler-

What are American's two most favorite foods?

Did you know....

Charles Bronson got his first part in a movie, *You're In the Navy Now* (1951) because "he could belch on cue."

-Ponder-

"Awareness of the reality of life means squeezing
the most you can out of each day."

—O. A. Battista

-Proverb-

"Pay attention to what you are taught, and you will be
successful; trust in the Lord, and you will be happy."

—Proverbs 16:20, Good News Bible

-Principle-

The allotment of time into months and years is a human contrivance and, therefore, artificial; but there is still something symbolic about taking down an old calendar and hanging a new one. Entering a new year gives one the feeling of leaving one country and reaching the port of entry to a new one. Ahead of us is the challenge and the opportunity to make a fresh start at all sorts of things.

Looking back over the past twelve months, we give thanks that, despite the hazards of modern civilization and despite overstrenuous living, we still have our health in body and mind. We can be grateful that we have not been asked to pay the consequences of our stupidest mistakes.

-Baffler-

What percentage of American women think their feet are too big?

Did you know....

The first known contraceptive was crocodile dung,
used by the Egyptians in 2000 B.C.

145 – The Optimist

-Ponder-

"The optimist proclaims that we live in the best of all possible worlds;
and the pessimist fears this is true."

—James Branch Cabell

-Proverb-

"Someone who is sure of himself does not talk all the time.
People who stay calm have real insight."

—Proverbs 17:27, Good News Bible

-Principle-

Every great society in history—from the Greek city state to American democracy was founded on recognition and respect for the individual. These societies grew and prospered as the dynamic contribution of the individual was encouraged to flower. These same societies decayed as individuals were restricted and oppressed. How often we forget this lesson in history.

Some in our midst have studied their history well. They know that when others are saying "I can't," the time is ripe to say "I can." These people are to be commended because this is in the best tradition of American free enterprise. One complaint, however—the wrong people are saying "I can."

-Baffler-

On the average, how much time does a working woman spend a day cooking?
How much time does a working man spend a day cooking?

Did you know....

About 1 million Americans say they drink Coca Cola for breakfast.

-Ponder-

"Fear brings on mediocrity; it dulls creativity
and sets one up to be a loser in life."

—Fran Tarkenton

-Proverb-

"A person's thoughts are like water in a deep well, but
someone with insight can draw them out."

—Proverbs 20:5, Good News Bible

-Principle-

One advertising genius, when asked what the secret was to his thirty years of success, replied, "My experience has convinced me that imagination is not a gift; it is a habitual way of using your mind."

Creativity is restricted by *perceptual blocks*. The mind falls into a habit of viewing things in a certain way. It is restrained by *emotional blocks*. The mind falls into the habit of thinking about things in the established way. It is repressed by emotional blocks. The mind falls into the habit of feeling about things in an accepted way.

The creative mind, however, is not bound by these filters, but has adopted the habit of challenging the accepted, of questioning the established.

-Baffler-

Where did the name for the "Baby Ruth" candy bar originate?

Did you know....

It's the Law: In Washington, D.C. no building
can be taller than the Capitol.

-Ponder-

"The will to win is not nearly as important as the will to prepare to win."

—Bobby Knight

-Proverb-

"After all, you must make careful plans before you fight a battle,
and the more good advice you get, the more likely you are to win."

—Proverbs 21:6, Good News Bible

-Principle-

When Bobby Dodd was football coach for Georgia Tech, he confided that one of the secrets to his teams' success was that he paid the officials—to come to practice! One day a week he paid a regular officiating crew, the same people who would officiate at college games each weekend, to work Georgia Tech's scrimmages, so that the team would become used to practicing under game conditions.

The result was that, under Dodd's leadership, Georgia Tech teams had the fewest penalties of any major college team.

Dodd's view was that it's not practice that makes perfect—it's perfect practice that makes perfect. It doesn't help to practice mistakes!

-Baffler-

Every year, the average human being has how many dreams?

Did you know....

N.Y. Yankee Babe Ruth once tried marketing his own brand of candy, "Babe Ruth's Home Run Candy," but the Curtiss Candy Co. (who made the "Baby Ruth") took him to court and enjoined him from using his own name!

-Ponder-

"It is a fine thing to have ability, but the ability to
discover ability in others is the true test."

—Elbert Kipling

-Proverb-

"They (proverbs) can make an inexperienced person clever
and teach young men how to be resourceful."

—Proverbs 1:4, Good News Bible

-Principle-

A wealthy Ohio farmer was approached by a young man named Jamie, asking for a job. The farmer hired Jamie and allowed him to sleep in the barn.

Over the ensuing weeks and months, Jamie proved to be a hard worker and a valuable employee—so much that he was given responsibility over some of the other workers.

One day, Jamie went to the farmer and announced that he and the farmer's daughter had fallen in love. The young worker asked for the daughter's hand in marriage. The farmer was incensed; he exclaimed, "I've treated you well and this is how you repay me! You do not deserve such good treatment. Get your things and go!" Jamie left and the farmer never heard from him again.

Years later, the farmer was cleaning in the barn and came to an area where Jamie used to sleep. When the straw was swept away, he was startled to find the place where Jamie carved his full name in the wood. It read: James A. Garfield.

The farmer was astounded to find that his undeserving farm hand had gone on to become a general, then President of the United States. He could have been father-in-law to the President, but he never recognized Garfield for what he was.

-Baffler-

Where is the coldest place in the world?

Did you know....

It takes up to two million flowers to make one pound of honey.

-Ponder-

"You know you are old if all your baby pictures are in black and white."

—Dean Sheridan

-Proverb-

"Have reverence for the Lord, and you will live longer.
The wicked die before their time."

—Proverbs 10:27, Good New Bible

-Principle-

You're getting old if...

...you remember how to get undressed in a Pullman car.

...when you pick a hobby, the first consideration is to pick one where you can sit down.

...your friends don't ask how you feel, but ask you where you hurt.

...the little old lady that you help across the street is your wife.

...you feel like the morning after, and there wasn't a night before.

...you remember when Queen Elizabeth was a princess.

-Baffler-

Where did the saying "raining cats and dogs" come from?

Did you know....

You have about 10 gallons of water inside you,
making up about 60% of your weight.

PONDERS & PRINCIPLES

"A chip on the shoulder indicates there's wood higher up." — Jack Herbert

-Ponder-

"No one can make you feel inferior without your consent."

—Eleanor Roosevelt

-Proverb-

"Your joy is your own; your bitterness is your own.
No one can share them with you."

—Proverbs 14:10, Good News Bible

-Principle-

One man had built his grocery business into a rather substantial chain of small grocery stores. But this man's son who had just completed graduate school with a degree in economics, was appalled at the ancient accounting system his father used.

"Dad," he said, "why don't you let me organize a modern system for you so you'll know if you're making any profit."

"Son," he said, "I want you to know that when I started this business after the war, all I had was the shirt on my back. I have worked all these years and have managed to put you and your two sisters through college. Our home is paid for. We vacation in the Bahamas twice a year. We own two cars and we still manage to pay our taxes. The way I figure it is that we don't need any new-fangled modern system when the old one is working so well."

"And how do you know it's working so well?" the son asked.

"Because when I add it all together and take away the cost of the shirt on my back, it comes out that everything else is profit."

-Baffler-

Do you know which state has had the most Miss Americas
since the pageant began in 1921?

Did you know....

M&M's were introduced in 1940 for U.S. soldiers,
so their hands wouldn't be sticky.

151 – Building a Home

-Ponder-

"A house is built of logs and stone, of piles and posts and piers;
a home is built of loving deeds that stand a thousand years."

—Victor Hugo

-Proverb-

"The Lord puts a curse on the homes of wicked men,
but blesses the homes of the righteous."

—Proverbs 3:33, Good News Bible

-Principle-

Professor Nick Stinnett, Chairman of the Department of Human Development and the Family at the University of Nebraska, headed a research project to discover "what makes families strong." Their team observed and interviewed 3,000 strong families in South America, Switzerland, Austria, Germany, South Africa, and the United States. From all this research they concluded that strong families have six main qualities:
1. Commitment to the family.
2. Spend time together.
3. Have good family communication.
4. Express appreciation to each other.
5. Have a spiritual commitment.
6. Able to solve problems in a crises.
Strong families don't just happen—they take work!

-Baffler-

What is the animal with the largest eyes on earth?

Did you know....

The *Beatles* sold over 125 million singles and
85 million LPs in less than a decade.

-Ponder-

"Some folks pay a compliment like they went down in their pocket for it."

—Kin Hubbard

-Proverb-

"Insincere talk that hides what you are really thinking
is like a fine glaze on a cheap clay pot."

—Proverbs 26:23, Good News Bible

-Principle-

Two duck hunters were known for their contrasting outlooks on life. One was an eternal optimist, while the other lived out the role of the ever negative pessimist. The optimist set out to get a positive response from his negative friend by training his dog to retrieve ducks by walking on the water.

When opening day arrived, the optimist couldn't wait to show off his dog. Soon enough the first ducks flew over, and he shot the first duck of the season. Confident that his dog would generate a positive remark from his pessimistic friend, he sent his dog after the duck. Just like he had been trained, the dog walked out on the water and retrieved the duck. The proud hunter beamed with pride only to hear his pessimistic friend say, "Got a dog who can't swim, huh."

-Baffler-

What percentage of the American population never read books?

Did you know....

You are more likely to get stung by a bee on a
windy day than in any other weather.

153 – Nature's Ends

-Ponder-

"Nature gave man two ends…one to sit on and one to think with. Ever since then, man's success or failure has been dependent on the one he used most."

—George R. Kirkpatrick

-Proverb-

"Not even the world of the dead can keep the Lord from knowing what is there; how then can a man hide his thoughts from God."

—Proverbs 15:11, Good News Bible

-Principle-

Do you think vertically, traditionally, or laterally? Professor Edward De Bono of Oxford suggests we can know by problem solving.

For instance; A company moved into a new high rise and discovered that there were not enough elevators. Employees were disgruntled because there were overlong waits for the elevators. After careful consideration, four options were suggested;

1. Speed up the elevators or arrange for them to stop at certain floors during rush hours.

2. Stagger working hours to reduce elevator demand at either end of the day.

3. Install mirrors around entrances of all elevators.

4. Install new elevator shafts and increase the number of elevators.

If you chose the first, second, or fourth option, then you are a vertical or traditional thinker. If you chose the third possibility, then you are a lateral thinker. When the third possibility was employed, it worked. The workers no longer noticed the wait when they were preoccupied with looking at themselves! The problem was not so much the lack of elevators as the impatience of the employees.

-Baffler-

He was a clergyman living in Trinidad. He sent several species of tropical fish to the British Museum, including a tiny specimen which now bears his name. Who was this man, and what was the name of the fish (the same name, of course).

Did you know....

"Gilligan's Island" was man-made, located in the middle of an artificial lake at CBS's Studio Center in Hollywood, and surrounded by painted landscapes, artificial palm trees, and wind machines, and cost $75,000 to build.

-Ponder-

"Riches are mental, not material."

—B. C. Forbes

-Proverb-

"Better to be poor and fear the Lord than to be rich and in trouble."

—Proverbs 15:16, Good News Bible

-Principle-

The money or place or fame which our endeavors may bring when crowned with so-called success will not give all the joy we anticipated; such things may charm, may tickle our vanity, may effervesce a hectic sort of happiness for a little while; but soon we find our teeth grating at the core. The consciousness of the worthwhileness of the achievement itself can alone produce in us a state of happiness. Riches are mental, not material!

-Baffler-

Eleven-year-old Frank Epperson accidentally left a mixture of powdered soda mix and water on his back porch one winter night in 1905. The next morning, he found the stuff frozen, with the stirring stick standing straight up in the jar. What had Frank accidentally created?

Did you know....

Per capita, Finns drink the most coffee in the world.

-Ponder-

"The greatest natural resource that any country can have is its children."

—Danny Kaye

-Proverb-

"Son, don't forget what I teach you. Always remember what I tell you to do.
My teaching will give you a long and prosperous life."

—Proverbs 3:1-2, Good News Bible

-Principle-

Erma Bombeck once wrote, "Someday when my children are old enough to understand the logic that motivates a parent, I will tell them:

I loved you enough to ask where you were going, with whom, and what time you would be home.

I loved you enough to insist that you save your money and buy a bike for yourself even though we could afford to buy one for you.

I loved you enough to be silent and let you discover that your new best friend was a creep.

I loved you enough to let you see anger, disappointment, and tears in my eyes. Children must learn their parents are not perfect.

I loved you enough to let you assume the responsibility for your actions, even when the penalties were so harsh they almost broke my heart.

But most of all, I loved you enough to say 'no' when I knew you would hate me. Those were the most difficult battles of all. I am glad I won them, because in the end you won something too."

-Baffler-

"A box without hinges, key, or lid.
Yet golden treasure inside is hid."
This is a riddle by J. R. Tolkien. Do you know what the answer is?

Did you know....

The U. S. waived any claim to the moon by signing the Treaty on Exploration and Use of Outer Space in 1967. This established the lunar surface as the property of all mankind.

-Ponder-

"A good listener is not only popular everywhere, but
after awhile he even knows something."

—Unknown

-Proverb-

"The Lord has given us eyes to see with and ears to listen with."

—Proverbs 20:12, Good News Bible

-Principle-

A recent survey revealed that three out of every four bosses have traits that bother employees. The three most frequently mentioned problems were:

(1) Not listening well
(2) Being ambiguous
(3) Communicating poorly. Only two percent of the workers said that low pay or other compensation issues bothered them.

The issue is communication, and the implications are obvious. Successful bosses must focus on four priorities:

(1) Work on becoming a "people person." Treat employees the way you want them to treat the customer
(2) Be clear on deadlines and expectations
(3) Provide feedback regularly
(4) Realize that employees like to get information about the company from their immediate supervisor.

-Baffler-

Where did the term "Peeping Tom" originate?

Did you know....

A few '60s fast-food flops you never ate at: Johnny Carson's
"Here's Johnny's!" restaurants; Mahalia Jackson's Glori-Fried Chicken;
Mickey Mantle's Southern Cooking; Tony Bennett's Spaghetti House.

-Ponder-

"The results of life are your intentions."

—Denise Monsoor

-Proverb-

"Human wisdom, brilliance, insight—they are of no help if the Lord is against you."

—Proverbs 21:30, Good News Bible

-Principle-

It's not easy . . . . .
> To apologize.
> To begin over.
> To take advice.
> To be unselfish.
> To admit error.
> To be charitable.
> To be considerate.
> To avoid mistakes.
> To be broad-minded.
> To forgive and forget.
> To think and then act.
> To keep out of a rut.
> To make the best of little.
> To shoulder deserved blame.
> To maintain a high standard.
> To recognize the silver lining.

But it always pays to keep on trying!

-Baffler-

In the course of a decade, a man is likely to shave off how much, in weight, of whiskers?

Did you know....

Dragnet was once the most popular cop show in TV history. It began as the top show on radio, and in December, 1951, began its official run on TV, remaining popular for 11 years.

-Ponder-

"The man who removes a mountain begins by carrying away small stones."

—Chinese Proverb

-Proverb-

"Help your brother, and he will protect you like a strong city wall,
but if you quarrel with him, he will close his doors to you."

—Proverbs 18:19, Good News Bible

-Principle-

According to the Birmingham News, Herman Ostery of Bruno, Nebraska, needed to relocate his barn. His only apparent option was to tear it down and rebuild at the new site. Not wanting to do that, he came up with an idea that was original and exciting. He contacted all his neighbors and after some discussion they collectively agreed to literally pick up the barn and move it.

Using hydraulic jacks to get the barn off the ground, 328 of Herman's friends and neighbors picked up the barn and carried it 110 feet to the new location. Impossible? Herman estimated that each person only lifted and carried about 50 pounds.

Many tasks are impossible for one person to accomplish. But if we all work together and carry our fair share of the load, just think of what can be accomplished!

-Baffler-

A hard rain falls at the rate of about _____ m.p.h.

Did you know....

There are 132 Hawaiian Islands, spread over 1,500 square miles.

-Ponder-

"Accountability: No individual raindrop ever
considers itself responsible for the flood."

—Anonymous

-Proverb-

"You will never succeed in life if you try to hide your sins. Confess them
and give them up; then God will show mercy to you."

—Proverbs 28:13, Good News Bible

-Principle-

Accountability is a word that some people have trouble recognizing and most
have trouble applying in their lives. In our modern society, we have done away with
the idea of being accountable or responsible for our actions, beliefs, ideas, circumstances, and successes or failures. When something goes wrong, we point our finger
at everyone and everything instead of ourselves. It does not matter whether we are
wrong; no way will we take blame for anything. Not only is everyone else blamed for
mistakes, but everything gets blamed for the things that happen to us.

Failure to instill some sense of accountability will produce, and is producing, a
lack of motivation. There is no accountability towards anything or anyone. If
America is to move beyond mediocrity we must have men, women, and young people who stand responsible for their actions; and if they make a mistake—admit it and
accept what comes with the mistake.

-Baffler-

How many times a day to you think the average person laughs?

Did you know....

From 1840 to 1980, every president elected in a year that ended in zero
died while in office. Only Ronald Reagan managed to escape the
presidential curse—and he barely survived an assassination attempt.

-Ponder-

"The glory of great men should always be measured
by the means they have used to acquire it."

—Duc de la Rochefoucauld

-Proverb-

"Get all the advice you can, and you will succeed; without it, you will fail."

—Proverbs 15:22, Good News Bible

-Principle-

Napoleon's genius has been attributed to many things, but, above all, he was a superb natural leader of men. He was acutely aware that his own success depended on his men being willing and even eager to follow him. He devised a unique technique to inspire men individually. Before visiting a regiment he would ask the officer in charge for the name of a soldier who had served well in previous campaigns, but who had not been given the credit he deserved.

Napoleon would then learn everything about him, where he was born, the names of his family, his exploits in battle, etc.

Later, upon passing this man while reviewing the troops, and at a signal from the officer, Napoleon would stop, single out the man, greet him warmly, ask about his family, compliment him on his bravery, then pin a medal on the grateful soldier.

The gesture worked. After the review, the other soldiers would remark, "You see, he knows us—he remembers."

-Baffler-

At noon and midnight, the hour and minute hands of a clock are exactly coincident with each other. How many other times between noon and midnight do the hour and minute hands cross?

Did you know....

In his 48 years with the FBI, Hoover never made an arrest or conducted an investigation. According to a top aide, Hoover didn't even know how to use a gun.

-Ponder-

"The only real voyage of discovery consists not in
seeking new landscapes, but in having new eyes."

—Marcel Proust

-Proverb-

"Fire tests gold and silver; a person's reputation can also be tested."

—Proverbs 27:21, Good News Bible

-Principle-

The American painter, John Sargent, once painted a panel of roses that was highly praised by critics. It was a small picture, but it approached perfection.

Although offered a high price for it on many occasions, Sargent refused to sell it.
He considered it his best work and was very proud of it.

Whenever he was deeply discouraged and doubted his abilities as an artist, he
would look at it and remind himself, "I painted that." Then his confidence and ability would come back to him.

There are times when everyone doubts themselves. The harder our work is, the
more creatively demanding it is, the more vulnerable we are to such doubts.

We can't live on past achievements, but we can use them for inspiration.
Everyone should have a "high water mark" to look back on—something we can be
proud of and say, "I did that once and I can do it again."

-Baffler-

Are you more likely to catch a person's cold from shaking
hands with them, or from their sneezes?

Did you know....

The Hula Hoop originated in Australia, where it was a bamboo exercise
ring used in gym classes. It was introduced in America in 1958.

-Ponder-

"You can't depend on your judgment when your imagination is out of focus."

—John F. Kennedy

-Proverb-

"It is better to meet a mother bear robbed of her cubs than to
meet some fool busy with a stupid project."

—Proverbs 17:12, Good News Bible

-Principle-

A man was hired to paint lines on a newly resurfaced portion of an interstate highway. The first day he painted 109 miles, and his supervisor, impressed by such an effort, told him he would recommend a promotion and a raise in pay if he kept up that pace. But the next day he was only able to paint five miles. On the third day he did only one mile and when he reported in at quitting time, he was fired. "It isn't my fault," he muttered as he walked away shaking his head. "I kept getting farther away from the can."

Sometimes it is necessary to go all the way back to the beginning to accomplish things. But sometimes we need only take the can with us.

-Baffler-

Your eyes and nose are the warmest parts of your body.
What are the coldest parts of your body?

Did you know....

Only two percent of American homes don't have a Bible in them.

-Ponder-

"Do not be disturbed at being misunderstood; be
disturbed rather at not being understanding."

—Chinese Proverb

-Proverb-

"It is dangerous to be concerned with what others think of you,
but if you trust the Lord, you are safe."

—Proverbs 29:25, Good News Bible

-Principle-

The story was told of General Robert E. Lee: Hearing General Lee speak in the highest terms to President Davis about a certain officer, another officer, greatly astonished, said to him, "General, do you know that the man of whom you speak so highly to the President is one of your most bitter enemies, and misses no opportunity to malign you?"

"Yes," replied General Lee, "but the President asked my opinion of him; he did not ask for his opinion of me."

-Baffler-

Why are "Three Musketeers" candy bars called "Three Musketeers?"

Did you know....

According to Flexner's "I Hear America Talking," there are an estimated 600,000 words in our English language—but the average American only understands around 2-3% of them…and actually uses only half that amount.

-Ponder-

"Don't worry if a rival imitates you—because while
he follows in your tracks he can't pass you."

—Uplift Magazine

-Proverb-

"People learn from one another, just as iron sharpens iron."

—Proverbs 27:17, Good News Bible

-Principle-

Someone said, "Sometimes I think my competitors do more for me than my friends do; my friends are too polite to point out my weaknesses, but my competitors go to great expense to advertise them.

My competitors are efficient, diligent, and attentive; they make me search for ways to improve my product and my service.

If I had no competitors, I might be lazy, incompetent, inattentive; I need the discipline they enforce on me.

I salute my competitors; they have been good to me. God bless them all."

-Baffler-

Where would you have to be to see the sun
rise on the Pacific and set on the Atlantic?

Did you know....

Fairy tales are seldom about fairies.

-Ponder-

"A good thing to remember is that you can't save face if you lose your head."

—Unknown

-Proverb-

"People with a hot temper do foolish things; wiser people remain calm."

—Proverbs 14:17, Good News Bible

-Principle-

Anger puts a person at a disadvantage in every undertaking in life. The story is told that when Sinbad and his sailors landed on one of the tropical islands, they saw high up in the trees coconuts which could quench their thirst and satisfy their hunger. The coconuts were too high for Sinbad and his sailors to reach them, but in the branches were many chattering apes. The men began to throw sticks and stones at the apes. The monkeys became so enraged they began to seize the coconuts and hurl them down at the men on the ground. This was just what Sinbad and his men wanted. They got the apes angry so that the apes would gather their food for them.

When we indulge in anger, we usually play right into the hands of our enemies!

-Baffler-

Lassie was the most successful animal actor ever, starring in seven feature films and a TV series that ran for 19 years. But there wasn't just one Lassie. How many were there, and how many of them were female?   (Lassie was portrayed as a she-dog.)

Did you know....

Four out of five adults in the U.S. drink coffee, putting away an average of two cups a day. That adds up to about a third of the world's supply.

-Ponder-

"Never be so busy bringing home the bacon that you forget the applesauce."

—Unknown

-Proverb-

"Selfish people are in such a hurry to get rich that they do
not know when poverty is about to strike."

—Proverbs 28:22, Good News Bible

-Principle-

For all those who feel that life is too busy, full of too many activities and obligations, you can relate to the young woman who detested housework and saw absolutely no need for it. When the young man to whom she was engaged showed her a house he planned to buy, she commented:

"A home, why do I need a home? I was born in a hospital, educated in a college, courted in an automobile, and expect to be married in a church. We can live out of the delicatessen and paper bags. I spend my mornings on the golf course, my afternoons at my clubs, and then my evenings at the movies. When I die I am going to be buried at the undertaker's. All I really need is a garage!"

To this we say, "Good luck, You will need it!"

-Baffler-

Can you name the shortest-lived primetime series in TV history?
(Hint: It was premiered on ABC on February 5, 1969.)

Did you know....

Queen termites can live for up to 100 years.

-Ponder-

"An archaeologist is the best husband any woman can have
...the older she gets, the more interested he is in her."

—Agatha Christie

-Proverb-

"A nagging wife is like water going drip-drip-drip on a rainy day."

—Proverbs 27:15, Good News Bible

-Principle-

Ten henpecked husbands formed themselves into a sworn society for resisting poisonous oppression of their wives. At the first meeting they were sitting and talking, when suddenly the ten wives, who had gotten wind of the movement, appeared on the scene. There was a general stampede and nine of the husbands bolted like rats through a side door, only one remained unmoved to face the music. The ladies merely smiled contemptuously at the success of their raid and went home. The nine husbands then agreed that the bold tenth man who had not run away should be appointed their president; but on coming to offer him the post, they found he had died of fright!

-Baffler-

Donald Duck comics were banned from libraries in Finland. Why?

Did you know....

Levi's were invented for the California gold miners in 1873.

-Ponder-

"Whatever has our attention…determines our direction in life."

—Mitch Harrison (Youth Pastor)

-Proverb-

"Happy is the man who becomes wise—who comes to have understanding."

—Proverbs 3:13, Good News Bible

-Principle-

One of the most popular aquarium fish is the shark. It is interesting to note that if you catch a small shark and confine it, it will stay a size proportionate to the aquarium. Sharks can be six inches long and yet fully mature. But if you turn them loose in the ocean, they grow to their normal length of eight feet.

The exact same thing can happen to people. It is not unusual to see a six-inch person swimming around in their safe, comfortable little puddle. However, it is only when we are thrust into the larger arena of life—only then can we become great.

-Baffler-

What well-known actor played the title role of
I Was a Teenage Werewolf in 1957?

Did you know....

Robert O. Welch, the inventor of the Sugar Daddy,
is also the founder of the John Birch Society.

169 – Pride...the pain of stupidity

-Ponder-

"Pride is the anesthetic that dulls the pain of stupidity."

—Unknown

-Proverb-

"People who are proud will soon be disgraced. It is wiser to be modest."

—Proverbs 11:2, Good News Bible

-Principle-

Greek mythology tells of two wrestlers who participated in the Olympic games. One was older and greatly experienced in his craft, while the other was young and inexperienced. Often these two would wrestle before the crowds, and always the older man would win. Through the years the young wrestler built up a great hatred in his heart toward his older foe because of the many humiliating defeats at his hands. Time and again his pride was offended. Finally, the older wrestler died and a bronze statue of him was erected in the arena in memory of his many victories.

One night the young man, whose heart was filled with hatred, went to the statue. Climbing up, he grabbed it around the waist and shouted, "Now, my great foe, I'll show you who is the greatest. Beat me now if you can!" As he struggled trying to topple it, he fell to the ground and the statue fell on top of him, crushing him to death. His pride had destroyed his very life.

-Baffler-

Texas is the most expensive place in the U.S. to get a divorce.
Which state is the cheapest?

Did you know....

You can feed 24 people with one ostrich egg.

-Ponder-

"If one advances confidently in the direction of his dreams,
and endeavors to live the life which he has imagined, he will meet
with a success unexpected in common hours."

—Henry D. Thoreau

-Proverb-

"Being wise is better than being strong; yes,
knowledge is more important than strength."

—Proverbs 24:5, Good News Bible

-Principle-

THINKING
If you think you are beaten, you are;
If you think you dare not, you don't.
If you want to win but don't think you can,
It's almost a cinch you won't.

If you think you'll lose, you're lost;
For out in the world we find
Success begins with a person's will:
It's all in the state of mind.

If you think you're outclassed, you are;
You've got to think high to rise;
You've got to be sure of yourself before
You can ever win a prize.

Life's battles don't always go
To the stronger and faster man;
But sooner or later the man who wins
Is the man who thinks he can.

—Walter D. Wintle

-Baffler-

The most-watched film in history is _____?

Did you know....

Porcupines have more than 30,000 quills.

-Ponder-

"There are a lot of people who mistake their imagination for their memory."

—Josh Billings

-Proverb-

"Be kind and honest, and you will live a long life;
others will respect you and treat you fairly."

—Proverbs 21:21, Good News Bible

-Principle-

Two monks were traveling a muddy road during a downpour. Around a bend in the road, they met a lovely girl unable to cross the intersection. One monk immediately took the girl in his arms and carried her through the mud and onto more secure ground.

The monks continued their hike, not speaking a word to each other, until they reached their temple lodging that night. Finally, the monk who had not helped the girl could restrain himself no longer: "We monks never go near females," he challenged, "most particularly not young and pretty ones. It is dangerous, it is tempting fate. Why did you do it?"

In a quiet spirit, the other monk replied, "I left the girl there. Are you still carrying her?"

-Baffler-

What percentage of dog and cat owners talk to their pets?

Did you know....

The real James Bond was an ornithologist, not a spy.

-Ponder-

"An age is called dark, not because the light fails to shine,
but because people refuse to see it."

—James A. Michener

-Proverb-

"Arrogance causes nothing but trouble. It is wiser to ask for advice."

—Proverbs 13:10, Good News Bible

-Principle-

Once a little town in the British Isles built a new jail which supposedly had an escape-proof cell. The great escape artist, Harry Houdini, was invited to come and see if he could escape from it.

The Great Houdini accepted the invitation. He had previously boasted that the jail had not been made that could hold him. On the appointed day, Houdini entered the cell and the jailer shut the door behind him. The great escape artist heard the noise of steel against steel as the jailer slipped the key into the lock. Once the jailer had gone, Houdini took out his tools and began to work on the cell door. An hour passed, then two. What had worked to open the locks on so many doors did not seem to work on these. Houdini couldn't understand it; it had seemed so simple. Finally, after admitting defeat, Houdini leaned against the door in his fatigue—and the door opened! You see, the jailer had never locked it. The only place the door was locked was in the Great Houdini's mind!

And so it is with most of us. If we would just unlock our minds, the impossible would become possible!

-Baffler-

What is the #1 thing U.S. families fight about more than anything else?

Did you know....

The most extras ever used in a movie was 300,000,
for the film *Gandhi* in 1981.

-Ponder-

"The past should be a springboard, not a hammock."

—Ivern Bell

-Proverb-

"If you want people to like you, forgive them when they wrong you.
Remembering wrongs can break up a friendship."

—Proverbs 17:9, Good News Bible

-Principle-

In 1880, James Garfield was elected President of the United States, but after only six months in office, he was shot in the back with a revolver. He never lost consciousness. At the hospital, the doctor probed the wound with his little finger to seek the bullet. He couldn't find it, so he tried a silver-tipped probe. Still he couldn't locate the bullet.

They took Garfield back to Washington D. C. Despite the summer heat, they tried to keep him comfortable. He was growing very weak. Teams of doctors tried to locate the bullet, probing the wound over and over.

The President hung on through July, through August, but in September he finally died—not from the wound, but from infection. The repeated probing, which the physicians thought would help the man, eventually killed him.

So it is with people who dwell too long on their shortcomings and failures.

-Baffler-

How many Americans believe in UFO's (percentage)?

Did you know....

Opposite sides of a dice cube always add up to 7.

-Ponder-

"No man is worthy to succeed until he's willing to fail."

—A. W. Tozer

-Proverb-

"It is better to be patient than powerful. It is better to
win control over yourself than over whole cities."

—Proverbs 16:32, Good News Bible

-Principle-

Thomas A. Edison's plant was on fire. As he hopelessly watched it burn, taking his costly experiments up in flames, he called his son Charles, "Come!" he said. "You'll never see anything like this again!" Then he called his wife. As the three stood gazing, Edison said, "There go all our mistakes. Now we can start over afresh." In two weeks he started rebuilding the plant, and it was not long before he invented the phonograph.

That's the power of perspective!

-Baffler-

The saying "pay through the nose" comes from ninth-century Ireland, meaning to pay a high price. Do you know what "paying through the nose" was referring to?

Did you know....

The bronze razor archaeologists took out of King Tut's
tomb was still sharp enough to use.

PONDERS & PRINCIPLES

"Every problem has in it the seeds of its own solution. If you don't have problems... you don't get any seeds!" — Norman Vincent Peale

-Ponder-

"If you're going to be able to look back on something and
laugh about it—you might as well laugh about it now."

—Marie Osmond

-Proverb-

"A cheerful heart does good like medicine, but a broken spirit makes one sick."

—Proverbs 17:22, The Living Bible

-Principle-

Scientists have been studying the effect of laughter on human beings and have found, among other things, that laughter has a profound and instantaneous effect on virtually every important organ in the body. Laughter reduces health-sapping tensions and relaxes the tissues as well as exercising the most vital organs. It is said that laughter, even when forced, results in beneficial effect on us, both mentally and physically. Next time you feel nervous and jittery, indulge in a good laugh. It's nature's best remedy for trouble.

-Baffler-

Do you have any "phobias?" How about "pantophobia?"
It is the fear of _____?"

Did you know....

The dog on the Cracker Jack package is named Bingo, after the folk
song that generations of kids were forced to learn in grade school.

-Ponder-

"The fellow who never steps on anybody's toes is probably standing still."

—Franklin P. Jones

-Proverb-

"Nothing will stand in your way if you walk wisely,
and you will not stumble when you run."

—Proverbs 4:12, Good News Bible

-Principle-

Here's how the Chicago Times in 1865 evaluated Lincoln's Gettysburg Address the day after its delivery: "The cheek of every American must tingle with shame as he reads the silly, flat, and dish-watery utterances of a man who has to be pointed out to intelligent foreigners as the President of the United States."

In a public speech, the great Daniel Webster expressed his doubts concerning the ultimate success of American railroads. He argued that frost on the rails would prevent a train from moving; or, if it did move, it could not be brought to a stop.

And most people who loaned money to Robert Fulton for the development of his proposed steamboat did so with the stipulation that their names be kept secret, for fear they might be ridiculed for backing such an absurd idea.

-Baffler-

What percentage of Americans think that the
best way to get rich is to win a lottery?

Did you know....

In high school, Robin Williams was voted "Least Likely to Succeed."

-Ponder-

"When you are educated, you'll believe only half of what you hear
...when you're intelligent, you'll know which half!"

—Jerome Perryman

-Proverb-

"Son, pay attention and listen to my wisdom and insight. Then you will know how
to behave properly, and your words will show that you have knowledge."

—Proverbs 5:1-2, Good News Bible

-Principle-

When Sir Walter Raleigh was imprisoned in the Tower of London, he decided to spend the time writing a history of the world. He had covered about two hundred pages when, one morning, he was interrupted by a great noise in the prison courtyard. Two prisoners working there had become involved in a violent argument. Blows were struck. Inmates clung to the barred windows of their cells and yelled encouragement until the guards tore the men apart just in time to avoid mayhem.

Raleigh went to his desk and threw away his history, noting that he couldn't even decide who was right in what was happening right under his eyes!

-Baffler-

More Hollywood films have been made about one particular sport
than any other. Which sport do you think that is?

Did you know....

From the bottom of a well, you can actually see the stars during the daytime.

-Ponder-

"Did you ever stop to think that paying alimony is like
keeping up the payments on a car with four flats?"

—Laugh In

-Proverb-

"Be happy with your wife and find your joy with the girl you married."

—Proverbs 5:18, Good News Bible

-Principle-

Banks have long printed checks in a wide spectrum of colors; some have offered checks with floral or scenic backgrounds. A modest-sized bank in San Francisco has gone one step further. Its customers can bring in their own photograph or drawing and have them printed onto a standard check form.

Undeterred by the higher cost, more than 500 customers signed up for the illustrated checks. But perhaps the most imaginative—and vindictive—customer is the one who ordered special checks to be used solely for making his alimony payments. They show him beautifully kissing his new wife.

-Baffler-

How many days each year is there no sun at the North Pole?

Did you know....

J. Paul Getty, at one time the richest man in the world,
had a pay phone in his mansion.

-Ponder-

"Character is like a tree and reputation like its shadow—the shadow
is what we think of it...the tree is the real thing."

—Abraham Lincoln

-Proverb-

"Be honest, and you will be safe. If you
are dishonest, you will suddenly fall."

—Proverbs 28:18, Good News Bible

-Principle-

I went to see my psychiatrist to be psychoanalyzed.
To find out why I killed my cat and blackened my wife's eyes.
He put me on a downy couch to see what he could find,
And this is what he dredged up from my subconscious mind.
When I was one, my mommy hid my dolly in the trunk.
And so it follows naturally that I am always drunk.
When I was two, I saw my father kiss the maid one day,
And that's why I suffer now from kleptomania.
When I was three, I suffered ambivalence from my brothers,
And so it follows naturally that I poisoned all my lovers.
I'm so glad I have learned the lesson it has taught;
That everything I do is someone else's fault.

—Anna Russell

-Baffler-

In what country do people live the longest?

Did you know....

The first baseball team to put numbers on their
uniforms were the N. Y. Yankees, in 1929.

-Ponder-

"A diamond is just a hunk of coal that made good under pressure."

—Rodney R. Weckworth

-Proverb-

"Work hard at whatever you do, because there will be no action, no thought, no knowledge, no wisdom in the world of the dead—and that is where you are going."

—Ecclesiastes 9:10, Good News Bible

-Principle-

On a Friday morning, an eager young student from Stanford University stood before Louis Janin seeking part-time employment. "All I need right now," said Janin, "is a stenographer." "I'll take the job," said the eager applicant, "but I can't come back until next Tuesday."

On Tuesday he reported for duty. "Why couldn't you come back before Tuesday?" Janin wanted to know. "Because I had to rent a typewriter and learn to use it," was the unexpected answer! The zealous typist was Herbert Hoover.

Never underestimate the power of personal motivation!

-Baffler-

If you could find an autograph by Julius Caesar, how much would it be worth?

Did you know....

Before 1859, baseball umpires didn't crouch behind the catcher—they sat in rocking chairs.

-Ponder-

"The best gift to your enemy is forgiveness; an opponent—tolerance;
a friend—your heart; your child—a good example; to all men—charity."

—Unknown

-Proverb-

"A friend means well, even when he hurts you. But when an
enemy puts his arm around your shoulder—watch out!"

—Proverbs 27:6, Good News Bible

-Principle-

A Chinese emperor was informed that some of his enemies had caused an insurrection in one of the areas of his domain. He said to his officers: "Follow me, and we shall soon conquer them!" As soon as the mutineers saw the emperor approaching, they gave in and surrendered.

His officers expected to receive his orders to kill these mutineers, but he never issued such an order.

The first thing that this emperor said to his enemies was that he loved them and he was not going to harm them.

One of his officers asked him, "Your Majesty, is this the way you fulfill your promise of conquering your enemies? You had told us that you were going to conquer your enemies, but you forgave them and you are treating them as if they were friends."

"Yes," answered the emperor. "I promised to destroy my enemies. I kept my word. They are no more my enemies, I made them my friends."

The easiest way to destroy your enemies is to make them your friends. And who of us does not need more friends?

-Baffler-

An ice cream sundae will warm you more than hot chocolate. Why?

Did you know....

More than 20,000,000 Americans read their horoscope every day.

-Ponder-

"The world is moving so fast these days that the man who says it can't be done is generally interrupted by someone doing it."

—Elbert Hubbard

-Proverb-

"There is more hope for a stupid fool than for someone who speaks without thinking."

—Proverbs 29:20, Good News Bible

-Principle-

After satisfying himself that there must be some absolute limits to human strength, speed, agility and endurance, Brutus Hamilton, coach of the U. S. Olympic team about 20 years ago compiled a list of what he considered to be the "ultimate" in track and field performances. No one, said Hamilton out of confidence based on long experience, would ever run the 100 yard dash in less than 9.2 seconds or the mile in less than 3 minutes, 57.8 seconds. No one would ever put the shot more than 62 feet, throw the discus more than 200 feet, do better than 7 feet, 1 inch in high jump, 27 feet in the long jump, or 16 feet in the pole vault.

Since then, in every case, someone has. Which goes to prove there are no absolute limits on what a person can or cannot do!

-Baffler-

How many females have appeared on U.S. currency?

Did you know....

Eskimos have over 100 words for ice.

-Ponder-

"Character is much easier kept than recovered."

—Thomas Paine

-Proverb-

"Rich people always think they are wise, but a poor person
who has insight into character knows better."

—Proverbs 28:11, Good News Bible

-Principle-

At a U. S. arsenal a few years ago, a large gun was, marked "Condemned." The attendant pointed out some indentations about the size of a pinhead which dotted the gun in several places. They did not appear to go deeper than a thirty-second of an inch; and yet the gun was condemned. There might be a weakness extending through the entire gun so that in war the mighty engine capable of hurling half a ton of metal a dozen miles and hitting a target with fine accuracy might, under the heat of battle and strain of powder, burst into a thousand fragments.

Wise is the person who realizes that a tiny flaw may destroy our character and hurt others also—no matter how perfect we may think we are on other points!

-Baffler-

Only one of the Seven Wonders of the Ancient World still exists.
Which one is it?

Did you know....

In 1989, Americans bought over 7,000 Harlequin romance books every hour.

-Ponder-

"The dictionary is the only place where
success comes before work."

—Arthur Brisbane

-Proverb-

"Some people are too lazy to put
food in their own mouths."

—Proverbs 26:15, Good News Bible

-Principle-

The sooner a person is convinced that there are no shortcuts in life, the better. Some people never learn it. To the end of their lives they have an idea that there is a shortcut to wealth, a shortcut to reputation, a shortcut to health, a shortcut to happiness—if only they could find it They walk along the high road with a continual sense of grievance. Every now and then they deviate to the right or left to step in the fields of desire, but it always ends in their coming back to the main road again, a little behind where they left it.

-Baffler-

The American slogan, "In God We Trust"
was adopted in what year?

Did you know....

A housefly can carry germs as far as
15 miles from the original source.

-Ponder-

"Happiness is not having what you want, but wanting what you have."

—Rabbi Hyman Judah Schachtel

-Proverb-

"The customer always complains that the price is too high,
but then he goes off and brags about the bargain he got."

—Proverbs 20:14, Good News Bible

-Principle-

When Benjamin Franklin was seven years old, a visitor gave him some small change. Later, seeing another boy playing with a whistle, young Benjamin gave the boy all his money for it. He played the whistle all over the house, enjoying it, until he discovered that he had given four times as much as the whistle was worth. Instantly, the whistle lost its charm. As he grew older, Franklin generalized this principle. When he saw a man neglecting his family for political popularity, or a miser giving up friendship for the sake of accumulating wealth, he would say, "He pays too much for his whistle."

Too often we pay much too great a price for something that looks and sounds so good and promises so much. Fish are hooked because they are attracted to something that looks like food. Don't be fooled, there are many whistles that are not worth the price!

-Baffler-

No one likes to lick postage stamps because of the taste (bad).
Do you know what the glue on postage stamps is made from?

Did you know....

The heads of a two-headed snake will fight over
food—even though they share one stomach.

-Ponder-

"One of the most annoying things about weather forecasts
is that they're not wrong all the time either."

—Farm Journal

-Proverb-

People who promise things that they never give
are like clouds and wind that bring no rain."

—Proverbs 25:14, Good News Bible

-Principle-

Weathermen have failed so often in forecasting the weather that they now hide behind such statements as, "There is a 10% or a 20% chance of rain." So, if it rains or not, they are safe in their prediction.

The only "fool-proof" weather prediction is the "rope weather gauge." It seems a tourist stopped at a combination service station and general store. Sitting out in front was an elderly gentleman, holding a short piece of rope.

"What's the rope for, sir?" the visitor asked.

"It's a weather gauge," replied the old man.

Puzzled, the tourist asked, "How can a rope tell the weather?"

"Simple, sonny," said the old man. "When it swings back and forth the wind is blowing. When it gets wet, it's raining."

-Baffler-

Michael Jackson's *Beat It* is said to have been inspired by a
1961 award-winning film. Do you know which film?
(Hint: The first two words spoken in the film are "Beat it!")

Did you know....

The Charleston Chew candy bar was introduced during the roaring
twenties when the Charleston dance craze was in full swing.

187 – Song of Life

-Ponder-

"The triumph song of life would lose its melody without its minor keys."

—Sunshine

-Proverb-

"Be glad about this, even though it may now be necessary for you
to be sad for a while because of the many kinds of trials you suffer.
Their purpose is to prove that your faith is genuine."

—1 Peter 1:6-7, Good News Bible

-Principle-

A maker of violins searched all his life for wood that would serve for making violins with a certain beautiful and haunting resonance. At last he succeeded when he came into possession of wood gathered from the timberline, the last stand of the trees of the Rockies, 12,000 feet above sea level. Up there, where the wind blows so fiercely and steadily that the bark to windward has no chance to grow, where the branches all point one way, and where a tree to live must be very strong. That is where the world's most resonant wood for violins is born and lives and dies.

So it is with us human creatures. The sweetest music in life comes from those whose existence has been tested by ill winds and blustery circumstances, but in the face of it all, they stand firm!

-Baffler-

There is one particular vegetable that Americans grow at home more often than any other vegetable or fruit. Do you grow _____ ?

Did you know....

60% of all new cars sold in the '80s were recalled for some defect!

-Ponder-

"If you want a place in the sun, you have to put up with a few blisters."

—Abigail Van Buren

-Proverb-

"A lazy person is as bad as someone who is destructive."

—Proverbs 18:9, Good News Bible

-Principle-

A team of Russian scientists have been conducting experiments aimed at discovering whether a life of ease shortens or lengthens life. A report on the outcome claims:

"A series of experiments were staged on animal life spans. Some animals were provided with ideal conditions of life—quiet, fresh air, plenty of food, and no cares whatever. Sleep if you like, play if you want. The fur of the animals began to gloss."

"Another group of animals was placed in conditions that involved cares and joys, setbacks and surprises of all kinds."

Researchers found "the first to fall sick and break down were animals existing in ideal conditions." Now the researchers are trying to establish "whether the same holds good for human beings."

-Baffler-

Here's a new word for your vocabulary, or
do you already know what a *Ranarium* is?

Did you know....

Vivien Leigh made only $15,000 for playing
Scarlett O'Hara in *Gone With the Wind*.

-Ponder-

"Why does a slight tax increase cost you two hundred dollars
and a substantial tax cut save you thirty cents?"

—Peg Bracken

-Proverb-

"When the king is concerned with justice, the nation will be strong,
but when he is only concerned with money, he will ruin his country."

—Proverbs 29:4, Good News Bible

-Principle-

In this day of government waste, we would do well to learn the lesson of the city of Paris, France. It all started with the mayor examining the huge Paris City Hall in search of space. He found a door with a sign on it reading "Bureau of Claims Payments for the Flood of 1910." Upon entering, two white-bearded octogenarians looked like startled Rip Van Winkles. A little questioning produced the fact that the claims were all paid. In fact, the last claim was paid in 1913.

But no one ever came and told them to stop work, so they had spent the years drawing their pay and "tidying things up before submitting their final report to the city elders."

-Baffler-

How much water does the average American use each day?

Did you know....

There are about a million earthquakes every year.
Most are so small they don't even register.

-Ponder-

"What we obtain too cheap...we esteem too lightly."

—Thomas Paine

-Proverb-

"The more easily you get your wealth, the less good it will do you."

—Proverbs 20:21, Good News Bible

-Principle-

A young man was applying for a factory job. Asking for the owner, he found himself in the presence of a nervous, fidgety man who looked hopelessly emaciated. "The only vacancy here," he told the applicant, "is a vice-presidency. The man that takes that job must shoulder all my worries."

"That's a tough job," said the young man. "What's the salary?"

"I'll pay you one hundred thousand a year if you will really take over all my worries."

"Where is the one hundred thousand coming from?" asked the applicant, cautiously.

"That is your first worry," replied the owner!

-Baffler-

When did the last Dodo Bird die?

Did you know....

According to a book called *The Want Makers*, "Pepsi's 'Come Alive with the Pepsi Generation' was reportedly translated on billboards in Taiwan as 'Pepsi brings your ancestors back from the dead.'"

-Ponder-

"Your mind is like a parachute…it only works when it's open."

—Unknown

-Proverb-

"Give a silly answer to a silly question, and the one who asked it
will realize that he is not as smart as he thinks."

—Proverbs 26:5, Good News Bible

-Principle-

Talking with John Dewey several months before his ninetieth birthday, a young doctor blurted out his low opinion of philosophy. "What's the good of such claptrap?" he asked. "Where does it lead?"

The great philosopher answered quietly, "The good of it is that you climb mountains."

"Climb mountains!" retorted the doctor, unimpressed. "And what's the use of doing that?"

"You see other mountains to climb," was the reply. "You come down, climb the next mountain, and see still others to climb."

Then Dewey said, "When you are no longer interested in climbing mountains to see other mountains to climb, life is over."

-Baffler-

What was Vice-President Dan Quayle's favorite film?

Did you know....

It is illegal to own pets in China.

192 – Effortless Failures

-Ponder-

"The only thing that happens without effort is failure."

—Dave Huusko

-Proverb-

"A laborer's appetite makes him work harder,
because he wants to satisfy his hunger."

—Proverbs 16:26, Good News Bible

-Principle-

When you feel that being persistent is a difficult task, think of the bee. A red clover blossom contains less than one-eighth of a grain of sugar; 7,000 grains are required to make a pound of honey. A bee, flitting here and there for sweetness, must visit 56,000 clover heads for a pound of honey; and there are about sixty flower tubes to each clover head. When a bee performs that operation 60 times 56,000, or 3,360,000 times, it secures enough sweetness for only one pound of honey!

-Baffler-

John Wayne appeared in 153 movies.
How many of them was he NOT the star?

Did you know....

The first coin bearing the name of the United States of America was the "Fugio cent" of 1787. It bore the motto, "Mind your business."

-Ponder-

"To stand upon the ramparts and die for our principles is heroic, but to sally forth to battle and win for our principles is something more than heroic."

—Franklin D. Roosevelt

-Proverb-

"Reverence for the Lord is an education in itself. You must be humble before you can ever receive honors."

—Proverbs 15:33, Good News Bible

-Principle-

The true test of whether a person is educated, regardless of how many years were spent in school, is the ability to choose wisely and courageously under any circumstance. Every minute and every hour of the day, we are confronted with choices. Most of us will make intelligent decisions when it's easy. The question is: Will we have the courage to do the intelligent thing when it is unpopular, inconvenient, or possibly embarrassing?

Many times decisions are not easy. For some, they have meant life itself.

David Livingston dying in a grass hut in Africa for his ideals; Mark Twain at sixty years of age bankrupt, shouldering his debts and starting out on a heart-breaking lecture tour to earn enough money to be out of debt in four years so he could start life all over again. These men could testify to the price paid for courageous decisions. Small minds, lazy minds, weak minds, always take the easiest way. In life, the line of least resistance is always the busiest boulevard.

-Baffler-

Who is pictured on the $100 bill?

Did you know....

By law, no living person can be portrayed on a money bill of the United States.

-Ponder-

"We must produce a great age or see the collapse
of the upward striving of our race!"

—Alfred North Whitehead

-Proverb-

"It is better to listen to the quiet words of a wise man
than to the shouts of a ruler at a council of fools."

—Ecclesiastes 9:17, Good News Bible

-Principle-

Those of us who are privileged to live in this day and time are living in the most sophisticated culture ever to have developed on planet Earth. The twentieth-century was the age of the atom, of space travel, of the computer, and other remarkable scientific achievements. The twentieth-century man celebrates his mentality but not his humanity. He strives to shove out his mental horizons, but neglects to cultivate the humane side of his nature.

The real question of the future is whether man can learn to educate his heart as well as his head—whether he can learn to combine mentality with morality.

Loren Eiseley, an American anthropologist, said, "A future worth contemplating will not be achieved solely by flights into space. It will be achieved, if it is achieved at all, only in individual hearts."

-Baffler-

Who was the first to win two consecutive Academy Awards for best actor?

Did you know....

It's not polite to stare, but a butterfly probably can't help it—it has 12,000 eyes!

-Ponder-

"Excellence can be obtained only by the labor of a lifetime.
It is not purchased at a lesser price."

—Samuel Johnson

-Proverb-

"Someone who will not learn will be poor and disgraced.
Anyone who listens to correction is respected."

—Proverbs 13:18, Good News Bible

-Principle-

A number of years ago, the great Paderewski had just completed a concert tour of the United States. Just before going back to Europe, he made this statement:

"There have been moments when I have known completed satisfaction, but only a few. I have rarely been free from the disturbing realization that my playing might have been better."

The secret of Paderewski's greatness lay in his dissatisfaction with his own efforts. As long as he remained unhappy about his playing, he was constantly striving to improve himself. Although the world held him to be perfect, he himself knew his own weaknesses, and he kept constantly at the job of improving his technique.

-Baffler-

Who was "Mother Goose?"

Did you know....

The first silver coins minted were based upon the value of sheep.

-Ponder-

"Until you make peace with who you are, you'll
never be content with what you have."

—Doris Mortman

-Proverb-

"Peace of mind makes the body healthy, but jealousy is like a cancer."

—Proverbs 14:30, Good News Bible

-Principle-

In a small town there was a farmer who had a dog who spent part of his time sitting by the side of a well-traveled highway waiting for big trucks. When the dog saw a large truck come around the corner, he would get ready and as it passed him, he would take out after it down the road, barking and doing his best to overtake it.

One day the farmer's neighbor said, "Sam, do you think that dog of yours is ever going to catch a truck?"

"Well, Bill," Sam replied, "that isn't what worries me. What worries me is what he would do if he caught one!"

Many people are just like that dog. They give their lives pursuing goals that have little value even if they were reached. Sometimes it pays to stop and ask whether we have objectives worth pursuing.

-Baffler-

A poll was taken to see how many dog and cat owners carry pictures
of the pets in their wallets. What do you think the results were?

Did you know....

Philanthropist John D. Rockefeller gave away half of his fortune. He made his first charitable contribution at the age of 16 and by the time he died at 82, he had given away $531,326,842.

-Ponder-

"Success is measured not so much by the position that one has reached in life as by the obstacles which he has overcome while trying to succeed."

—Booker T. Washington

-Proverb-

"…Tears may flow in the night, but joy comes in the morning."

—Psalm 30:5, Good News Bible

-Principle-

The French artist, Renoir, suffered a great deal from an old malady, rheumatism. It was particularly painful for him to continue painting, which he did seated in a chair.

One day a friend passed by while he was forcing himself to work. Noting Renoir's obvious pain, the friend exclaimed, "You have done enough already, Renoir. Why do you continue to torture yourself?"

The great artist looked at him for a long moment and replied, "The pain passes, but the beauty remains."

We all have our moments of pain and our memories of beauty. And it is the beauty in life that sustains us through whatever moments of pain may come.

-Baffler-

If a scientist was to examine one strand of your hair,
what could he learn about you?

Did you know....

Each time your toilet is flushed, it uses 5 to 7 gallons of water—40% of the pure water you use in your house is flushed down the toilet.

-Ponder-

"A problem is something with a solution. If there is no solution
...there is no problem."

—Moshe Dayan

-Proverb-

"If you pay attention when you are corrected, you are wise."

—Proverbs 15:31, Good News Bible

-Principle-

There is a story about Russia in the days of the Czars. In the park of St. Petersburg's Winter Palace there was a beautiful lawn, on that lawn a bench, and next to that bench two guards. Every three hours, the guards were changed. No one knew why. One day an ambitious young lieutenant was put in charge of the Palace Guard. He started wondering, and asking questions. In the end, he found a cobwebby little old man, the Palace historian.

"Yes," the old man said, "I remember. During the reign of Peter the Great, 200 years ago, the bench got a fresh coat of paint. The Czar was afraid the ladies in waiting might get paint on their dresses, so he ordered a guard to watch over the bench. The order was never rescinded. Then in 1908, all the guards of the Palace were doubled for fear of a revolution. So the bench has had two guards ever since.

-Baffler-

What percentage of the cost of food is for transporting it?

Did you know....

The youngest person to earn a million dollars was child film star Shirley Temple. She accumulated wealth estimated at a million dollars before she was ten years old.

-Ponder-

"What life does to you will depend on what life finds in you."

—Dan Hill

-Proverb-

"Men cast lots to learn God's will, but God himself determines the answer."

—Proverbs 16:33, Good News Bible

-Principle-

After a round of golf, former British statesman David Lloyd George and a friend walked through a field in which cows were grazing. They were so absorbed in conversation that they forgot to close the gate when they left the fenced area. Lloyd George happened to notice the open gate, however, and went back to close it.

George told his friend that this little incident reminded him of a doctor who, when dying, was asked by a minister whether there was anything he wanted to say before he slipped away. "No," the doctor replied, "except that through life I think I have always closed the gates behind me." The dying man meant by this that he had learned the secret of putting past failures and disappointments behind him so they wouldn't rob him of his joy and peace.

-Baffler-

The first gold record ever awarded went to Glenn Miller for what song?

Did you know....

U.S. airports are busier on Thursdays than any other day.

PONDERS & PRINCIPLES

"Blessed is the man who is too busy to worry
in the daytime and too sleepy to worry at night."
— Phil Marquart

-Ponder-

"Children have never been very good at listening to their elders
...but they have never failed to imitate them."

—James Baldwin

-Proverb-

"Son, pay attention to what your father and mother tell you.
Then teaching will improve your character as a handsome
turban or a necklace improves your appearance."

—Proverbs 1:8-9, Good News Bible

-Principle-

A government report in 1990 concluded that too little time with children, too little money to raise them, and overwhelming fears about their safety are tearing at the seams of family life.

It found that 88% of adults believe it is harder to be a parent today than in the past. About half of parents, regardless of income, say their neighborhoods are no longer safe. Commission chairman, Sen. John D. Rockefeller said, "What was painfully clear was that families are really trying, but it's increasingly harder for them to make ends meet and spend time with their children."

87% of parents have financial difficulties.

81% say they don't spend enough time with their kids.

33% say kids receive less love, care and attention, than they did 10 years ago.

20% of children from single parent homes had not seen their father in five years.

-Baffler-

The Western hero most often portrayed in films is _____?

Did you know....

You use 10-15 gallons of water if you leave
the tap running while you brush your teeth.

201 – A Fair Idea

-Ponder-

"A fair idea put to use is better than a good idea kept on the polishing wheel."

—Alex Osborn

-Proverb-

"If you are intelligent, you will be praised, if you
are stupid, people will look down on you."

—Proverbs 12:8, Good News Bible

-Principle-

In his book *World Horizons*, Cole D. Robinson illustrates the power of example. When Benjamin Franklin decided to interest the people of Philadelphia in street lighting, he hung a beautiful lantern on the end of a long bracket attached to the front of his house. He kept the glass brightly polished and carefully lit the wick each evening at the approach of dusk. Anyone walking on the dark street could see this light from a long way off and came under its glow.

What was the result? It wasn't long before Franklin's neighbors began placing lamps outside their homes. Soon the entire city realized the value of street lighting and followed his example with enthusiasm.

-Baffler-

Why do LifeSavers have a hole in them?

Did you know....

The shower scene in *Psycho* is probably the most famous single scene
in film history. It took seven days to shoot the 45-second scene.

-Ponder-

"It's much easier to build a child than to fix an adult."

—Bumper Sticker

-Proverb-

"You can be sure that evil men will be punished, but righteous men will escape."

—Proverbs 11:21, Good News Bible

-Principle-

Any thief knows that the easiest way to steal gas from a car is to siphon it from the other guy's tank into your own. Stick a rubber hose in his gas tank, suck on the other end of the rubber hose until you get a mouthful of gasoline, then spit it out. From then on the gasoline will flow into your tank.

A thief decided to siphon gas from Dennis Quiggley's motor home in Seattle. When Dennis, inside the motor home, heard the noises outside he investigated and discovered the thief curled up on the ground vomiting violently. It seems that the thief, instead of sucking up the contents of the gas tank, had put his hose into the wrong opening—and had sucked up the contents of the sewage tank instead. The thief, a boy of 14, will not be prosecuted—Dennis and the police agree that he has suffered enough.

-Baffler-

What is the only man-made structure you can see from outer space?

Did you know....

If you could take all of the salt out of the ocean and spread it on land, you'd have a five-hundred-foot layer of salt covering the earth's surface.

203 – Tax Dollars and Outer Space

-Ponder-

"There is just one thing I can promise you about the outer space program
...our tax dollar will go farther."

—Werner Von Braun

-Proverb-

"Poor people are the rich man's slaves.
Borrow money and you are the lender's slave."

—Proverbs 22:7, Good News Bible

-Principle-

We need to be reminded that our national debt was more than $3.5 trillion in 1991. Most of us can't relate to what a million dollars is, much less a trillion.

Here is what $1 trillion could buy:

- A 40-hour week paycheck at minimum wage for every person in the world.
- 1991-92 Harvard tuition for every person under 18 in the U.S.A.
- Two weeks at Club Med in Bora Bora, French Polynesia, for every person 18 and over in the U.S.A.
- An average-size, in-ground, concrete swimming pool for every homeowner in the U.S.A.

That certainly adds another dimension to our thinking before we step into the voting booth!

-Baffler-

What is the life expectancy of a dollar bill?

Did you know....

In the Virginia and Maryland colonies, tobacco was used as
money during the seventeenth and eighteenth centuries.

-Ponder-

"The way I see it—if you want the rainbow, you gotta put up with the rain."

—Dolly Parton

-Proverb-

"No matter how often an honest man falls, he always gets up again;
but disaster destroys the wicked."

—Proverbs 24:16, Good News Bible

-Principle-

Perseverance makes the difference. Wilma didn't get much of a head start in life. A bout with polio left her left leg crooked and her foot twisted inward so she had to wear leg braces. After seven years of painful therapy, she could walk without her braces. At age 12, Wilma tried out for a girls' basketball team, but didn't make it. Determined, she practiced with a friend every day. The next year, she made the team. When a college track coach saw her during a game, he talked her into letting him train her as a runner. By age 14 she had outrun the fastest sprinters in the United States. In 1956 Wilma made the U.S. Olympic team, but showed poorly. That bitter disappointment motivated her to work harder for the 1960 Olympics in Rome—and there Wilma Rudolph won three gold medals, the most a woman had ever won!

-Baffler-

Who is responsible when an elevator becomes overloaded?
- A. Last person to enter.
- B. Fire Dept.
- C. Elevator Mfg.
- D. Police Dept.
- E. Bldg. Owner.
- F. All the people on it.

Did you know....

Pound for pound, grasshoppers are three times as nutritious as beef!

205 – Death, Hair and Fingernails

-Ponder-

"For three days after death—hair and fingernails continue to grow
...but the phone calls taper off."

—Johnny Carson

-Proverb-

"It is better to go to a home where there is mourning than to one where there is a
party, because the living always remind themselves that death is waiting for us all."

—Ecclesiastes 7:2, Good News Bible

-Principle-

A Rumanian woman fainted recently when she opened the door and found her
husband standing there.

The Romanian weekly *Tinerama* says it all started when a man named Neagu
choked on a fish bone, stopped breathing and collapsed.

The family doctor, knowing Neagu's heart condition, didn't think twice about pro-
claiming the 71-year-old dead of a heart attack. But three days later, gravediggers at
the cemetery heard someone knock on wood.

They opened Neagu's coffin to find him surrounded by wilted flowers, but very
much alive. When Neagu arrived home his wife, fearing he was a ghost, barred him
from spending nights at home. It took Neagu three weeks to convince the authorities
to cancel his death certificate from their registers.

-Baffler-

Who, upon his death, left notes with designs for the well digger, paddle wheel
boat, sprocket chain, parachute, life jacket, helicopter, water turbine, steam gun, submarine, water pump, airplane, horseless carriage, machine gun, and plans for mass
production?

Did you know....

The average life expectancy of a left-hander is
nine years less than a right-hander.

-Ponder-

"Those who feel it is okay to tell white lies soon go color-blind."

—Unknown

-Proverb-

"When you tell the truth, justice is done, but lies lead to injustice."

—Proverbs 12:17, Good News Bible

-Principle-

Experts agree we lie—and are lied to—much more than we think.

One recent survey showed 91% of Americans lie routinely; 36% of those confess to dark, important lies.

86% of teenagers say that they lie regularly to parents, says co-author James Patterson in "The Day America Told the Truth." 75% lie to friends; 73%, to siblings; 69% to spouses. 81% lie about feelings; 43%, income; 40%, sex.

We actually encourage others to lie to us to preserve our self images, says psychiatrist Charles Ford. "We want to preserve our individual myths about ourselves," so we give others cues about what we want to hear from them, true or not. "We want to believe what we want to believe."

-Baffler-

Who has more fun, stupid people or smart people?

Did you know....

The first advertisement to discuss body odor was a 1919 ad for the deodorant "Odo-ro-no."

-Ponder-

"It is far better to give and be thanked—than to receive and be thankful."

—Ralph Vitiello

-Proverb-

"Do you want to meet an important person? Take him a gift and it will be easy."

—Proverbs 18:16, Good News Bible

-Principle-

Whom have you shown mercy lately? One night in 1935, Fiorello H. LaGuardia, Mayor of New York, showed up at night court in the poorest ward of the city. He dismissed the judge for the evening and took over the bench. One case involved an elderly woman who was caught stealing bread to feed her grandchildren. LaGuardia said, "I've got to punish you. Ten dollars or ten days in jail."

As he spoke, he threw $10 into his hat. He then fined everyone in the court room 50 cents for living in a city "where a person has to steal bread so that her grandchildren can eat." The hat was passed around, and the woman left the courtroom with her fine paid and an additional $47.50.

-Baffler-

The first vending machine was a coin operated dispenser, invented by the Greek scientist Hero, in the 1st Century B.C. What did it dispense?

Did you know....

Actor Sylvester Stallone was paid $25,000
for *Rocky*, $20 million for *Rocky V*!

-Ponder-

"Never argue with a fool…he may be doing the same thing."

—Executive Speechwriter Newsletter

-Proverb-

"When some fool starts an argument, he is asking for a beating."

—Proverbs 18:6, Good News Bible

-Principle-

How do you solve an argument? French novelist and playwright Alexandre Dumas once had a heated quarrel with a rising young politician. The argument became so intense that a duel was inevitable. Since both men were superb marksmen, they decided to draw lots, the loser agreed to shoot himself. Dumas lost. Pistol in hand, he withdrew in silent dignity to another room, closing the door behind him. The rest of the company waited in gloomy suspense for the shot that would end his career. At last the shot was heard. He friends ran to the door, opened it, and found Dumas, smoking revolver in hand. "Gentlemen, a most regrettable thing has happened," he announced. "I missed."

-Baffler-

How far does the average American travel to work,
and how long does it take?

Did you know....

Glass is considered a liquid, not a solid!

-Ponder-

"Half our life is spent trying to find something to do with
the time we have rushed through life trying to save."

—Will Rogers

-Proverb-

"There is a right time and a right way to do
everything, but we know so little."

—Ecclesiastes 8:6, Good News Bible

-Principle-

A flurry of magazine articles has probed what seems to be a growing trend among those at the top of American business. A surprising number of high-level managers, corporate presidents and chief executive officers, and Wall Street wizards are simply walking away from their positions. Their reasons? A simpler life, more time with family, less travel or stress, or the chance to follow a dream. The sudden resignation of one Wall Streeter sent shock waves all over the financial world. While most struggle to imitate these people's attainments, they have found something that outweighs the value of what they used to have.

-Baffler-

What is the windiest city in the United States?   (Hint: It isn't Chicago!)

Did you know....

According to Dr. Joyce Brothers, American women kiss
an average of 79 men before marrying.

-Ponder-

"If you think you have someone eating out of your hand,
it's still a good idea to count your fingers regularly."

—Balance Sheet

-Proverb-

"You have to hate someone to want to hurt him with lies.
Insincere talk brings nothing but rain."

—Proverbs 26:28, Good News Bible

-Principle-

There is a story about a wolf and a fox who became entrapped in a deep well. There were two containers tied at each end of a long rope. As the filled container was being drawn up, the empty one was going down.

One day a fox got into the empty container and fell deep into the well. She tried vigorously to get out, but all in vain. The wolf on top of the well heard her. "What are you fussing about, my little sister, beloved fox?"

The answer, "I'm catching fish. Come down and help me. There is plenty for you here too." "But how can I get down there?" asked the wolf. "Just get in the container that is empty up there and in no time you will be down here with me." Believing the fox, the wolf obeyed. Of course, as the wolf went down, the fox came up. The wolf was heard crying from below, "And now you leave me all alone." The fox shouted back at the wolf, "Such is the world, when one goes up, the other goes down!"

-Baffler-

When you sail from the Atlantic to the Pacific Ocean through
the Panama Canal, which direction are you traveling?

Did you know....

Only 17% of exercise bike owners use them more than once a week.

-Ponder-

"The man of character finds a special attractiveness in difficulty...since it is only by coming to grips with difficulty that he can realize his potentialities."

—Charles DeGaulle

-Proverb-

"Even a child shows what he is by what he does;
you can tell if he is honest and good."

—Proverbs 20:11, Good News Bible

-Principle-

Difficulties often cause us to soar beyond our perceived abilities.

Actor James Earl Jones is known for the richness and power of his remarkable voice. Yet from the age of nine until he was in his mid-teens, Jones stuttered so badly that he had to communicate with teachers and classmates by writing notes.

"Whenever visitors came to the house," he recalls, "I was in terror of having to say hello." Jones began to overcome his disability when a high school English teacher encouraged him to recite his own poetry in class, and he discovered that he could do so fluently.

-Baffler-

Why do bulls charge when they see red?

Did you know....

In 1960, 68% of Americans disapproved of homosexual activity.
Today, 75% disapprove.

-Ponder-

"Some people pay a compliment as if they expected a receipt."

—Kin Hubbard

-Proverb-

"If you flatter your friends, you set a trap for yourself."

—Proverbs 29:5, Good News Bible

-Principle-

Around the end of the fourth century and toward the beginning of the third century B.C., there was a famous architect by the name of Sostratos. The king of Egypt engaged Sostratos to build a famous lighthouse in order that ships might be guided safely to the port. When Sostratos finished building the lighthouse, he chiseled his own name upon a stone he used in construction. He did not allow that stone to be seen, but covered it with mud. As soon as the mud dried, he carved the king's name on it and painted it in gold in order to flatter him. Sostratos knew that sooner or later the waves would wash the mud away and the name of the king would disappear while his own name, carved in stone, would remain.

Beware of people who, on the surface, show a great deal of interest in you and flatter you. It may be just superficial. They may be just writing your name on mud while underneath all the nice words and flattery is their own name carved in stone.

-Baffler-

How far can the average aircraft carrier travel on a gallon of fuel?

Did you know....

There are still more than 300 ten-thousand-dollar bills in circulation, although they have not been printed since 1944.

-Ponder-

"People are like tea bags—you never know how strong
they'll be until they're in hot water."

—Rita Mae Brown

-Proverb-

"Hate stirs up trouble, but love forgives all offenses."

—Proverbs 10:12, Good News Bible

-Principle-

Victor Frankl, the eminent German Jewish doctor, was arrested by the Gestapo during World War II. As he was being interrogated by the Nazi secret police, Frankl was stripped of all his possessions—his clothes, his jewelry, his wedding band. His head was shaved. He was repeatedly taken from his prison cell, placed under bright lights, and questioned for hours. He underwent many savage, senseless tortures. But Frankl realized he had one thing left: "I still have the power to choose my own attitude. Bitterness or forgiveness, to give up or go on."

-Baffler-

Why should you avoid going to the hospital in June?

Did you know....

Americans use 18 billion disposable diapers every year.

-Ponder-

"Happiness is not a reward…it is consequential of how life is lived!"

—Wings of Silver

-Proverb-

"The reward for doing good is life, but sin only leads to more sin."

—Proverbs 10:16, Good News Bible

-Principle-

Sometimes we wish for wealth, fame, and power. They look so inviting and seem to hold great promise for happiness. But when we make them the goal of our existence, we take a very short-range view of life.

Secretary of State James A. Baker spoke of this at the National Prayer Breakfast. He said that the fleeting nature of political or economic power came to mind one morning as he looked down Pennsylvania Avenue. He saw a former Chief of Staff walking all alone "no reporters, no security, no adoring public, no trappings of power—just one solitary man alone with his thoughts." His power and fame had evaporated!

-Baffler-

The ark that Noah built was 300 cubits long, 50 cubits wide and 30 cubits high. How long is a cubit, and how big (in feet) was the ark?

Did you know….

Liberace's last custom-made piano was covered with 350 pounds of rhinestones.

-Ponder-

"Don't worry about what your kids are going to be when they grow up, but
…rather what they are going to be like!"

—Mitch Harrison

-Proverb-

"If you don't punish your son, you don't love him.
If you do love him, you will correct him."

—Proverbs 13:24, Good News Bible

-Principle-

A five-year-old boy was admitted into an orphanage. His parents had paid no attention to him. Some time after he came to the orphanage, those responsible realized that he was stealing little things from the other children and was hiding them away. The director of the orphanage tried to punish him through different disciplinary measures. He spoke to him, but without any visible results. One of the other workers suggested that what the child might very well need was the expression of love, an experience that he had never had with his parents at home. The suggestion was accepted by all those responsible in the orphanage. Dramatically, the child's behavior changed; he stopped stealing. Love achieved that which punishment failed to achieve.

-Baffler-

On an average day in America, 1932 children are abducted.
Of these, how many are abducted by strangers?

Did you know....

Once, while visiting Monte Carlo, Charlie Chaplin entered a "Charlie Chaplin look-alike contest." Not only didn't he win—he came in third-place!

-Ponder-

"If you are planning for one year—grow rice. If you are planning for
20 years, grow trees, but if you are planning for centuries—grow men."

—Chinese Proverb

-Proverb-

"Listen, my son, be wise and give serious thought to the way you live
...If all you do is eat and sleep you will soon be wearing rags."

—Proverbs 23:19,21, Good News Bible

-Principle-

Erma Bombeck, on the growing-up process: "I see children as kites, you spend a lifetime trying to get them off the ground. You run with them until you are both breathless. They crash...they hit the rooftop—you patch and comfort, adjust and teach. You watch them lifted by the wind and assure them that someday they'll fly. Finally, they are airborne; they need more string and you keep letting it out. But with each twist of the ball of twine, there is sadness that goes with joy. The kite becomes more distant, and you know it won't be long before that beautiful creature will snap the lifeline that binds you together and will soar as it is meant to soar, free and alone. Only then do you know that you did your job."

-Baffler-

What happens to your social security number when you die,
and how and when, if ever, is it reassigned?

Did you know....

There is evidence that counterfeiters have been practicing
their craft since about the fourth century B.C.

-Ponder-

"People are living longer than ever before, a phenomenon
undoubtedly made necessary by the 30-year mortgage."

—Doug Larson

-Proverb-

"A man may rise from poverty to become king of his country, or go from
prison to the throne, but if in his old age he is too foolish to take advice,
he is not as well off as a young man who is poor but intelligent."

—Ecclesiastes 4:13-14, Good News Bible

-Principle-

If you want to live to be 100, don't smoke or drink—and don't worry about your
diet. Hundreds of Americans 90 and older say that's what is working for them. A
lifestyle survey by the non-profit Humana Seniors Association, Louisville, KY, found:
  96% of respondents don't smoke; 89% don't drink.
  58% "eat whatever I want." Almost none are on vegetarian diets, or low-fat or
low-salt diets. But 53% eat balanced meals.
  80% exercise regularly—Top choice: walking.
  72% say the right career improved their lives.
  31% say faith in God helps them keep healthy and happy.

Humana sent surveys to 1,500 people 90 and older nationwide and got more than
375 responses. Ninety-somethings look for companionship and hobbies that will keep
them active.
  The number of people 90 and older increased 41.7% from 1980 to 1990.

-Baffler-

Why are barber poles striped?

Did you know....

The Ancient Egyptians had bowling alleys similar to ours.

-Ponder-

"If it's free, it's advice; if you pay for it, it's counseling;
if you can use either one…it's a miracle."

—Jack Adams

-Proverb-

"Get good advice and you will succeed;
don't go charging into battle without a plan."

—Proverbs 20:18, Good News Bible

-Principle-

Sometimes advice does not solve problems. In 1937 architect Frank Lloyd Wright built a house for industrialist Hibbard Johnson. One rainy evening Johnson was entertaining distinguished guests for dinner when the roof began to leak. The water seeped through directly above Johnson himself, dripping steadily onto his bald head. Irate, he called Wright in Phoenix, Arizona. "Frank," he said, "you built this beautiful house for me and we enjoy it very much. But the roof leaks, and right now I am with some friends and distinguished guests and it is leaking right on top of my head."

Wright's reply was heard by all of the guests. "Well, Hib, why don't you move your chair?"

-Baffler-

How many calories are used up in a single kiss?

Did you know….

Ice cream was invented in 1620.

-Ponder-

"Treat people as if they were what they ought to be…and you
help them to become what they are capable of being."

—Goethe

-Proverb-

"You will have to live with the consequences of everything you say."

—Proverbs 18:20, Good News Bible

-Principle-

Negative / Positive. In a survey, parents were asked to record how many negative versus positive comments they made to their children.

Results: They criticized 10 times for every favorable comment. In one Florida city, teachers were found to be 75% negative. And it was learned that it takes four positive statements from a teacher or parent to offset the effects of one negative statement to a child.

-Baffler-

We now know we use up nine calories in a single kiss (see answer to Baffler #218). If you kissed three times a day, how many pounds could you lose in a year?

Did you know....

The oldest tree in the world is the macrozamia
tree of Australia—it lives for 7,000 years.

-Ponder-

"To err is human...but when the eraser wears out
ahead of the pencil—you're overdoing it."

—J. Jenkins

-Proverb-

"When a fool is annoyed, he quickly lets it be known.
Smart people will ignore an insult."

—Proverbs 12:16, Good News Bible

-Principle-

The Army inspection was being conducted by a full colonel. Everything had gone smoothly, until the colonel stopped in front of a private. Inspecting the private from top to bottom, the colonel snapped, "Button that pocket, trooper!"

The soldier, more than a little rattled, stammered, "Right now, Sir?" "Of course, right now!" was the reply.

Whereupon the soldier very carefully reached out and buttoned the flap on the colonel's shirt pocket.

For some reason, peculiar to our human nature, it is always easier to see the unbuttoned shirt pocket of others than it is to see our own. Splinters in other people's eyes seem to be more obvious than the planks in our own eyes.

-Baffler-

Why do birds tend to stand on one foot while sleeping?

Did you know....

Bobby Darin's real name was Walden Robert Cassotto.

221 – Pushing the Wheelbarrow of Life

-Ponder-

"Most of us follow our conscience as we follow a wheelbarrow—
we push it in front of us in the direction we want it to go."

—Billy Graham

-Proverb-

"Your insight and understanding will protect you and prevent
you from doing the wrong thing. They will keep you
away from people who stir up trouble by what they say."

—Proverbs 2:11-12, Good News Bible

-Principle-

Some people need a little help to know how to act in public. Taxicab drivers in Paris came up with an idea to help their riders behave themselves. It's an electric cushion rigged to a powerful battery. If the driver notices that his passenger is about to do something unacceptable (like robbing or assaulting him), he pushes a button and zaps the rider with low-tension electricity.

That may seem like a drastic way to alert someone who is out of line, but it is a little like the monitor God has put in all of us. Each of us is equipped to receive signals to warn us when we have done wrong. It's called conscience, and it works in everyone—religious or not.

-Baffler-

What percentage of Americans flush the toilet while they're sitting on it?

Did you know....

The original Model T Ford was more expensive ($850) than a Cadillac ($750).

-Ponder-

"As you go through life, whatever be your goal…keep your eye
upon the doughnut…and not upon the hole."

—Mayflower Coffee Shop Slogan

-Proverb-

"(With wisdom and insight) You can go safely on your way
and never even stumble. You will not be afraid when you go
to bed, and you will sleep soundly through the night."

—Proverbs 3:23-24, Good News Bible

-Principle-

Roger Bannister was the first man to run a mile in four minutes. Three months later, John Landy topped his record by 1.4 seconds. Three months later, the two met for a historic race. As they moved into the last lap, the other contestants were trailing behind. Landy was ahead. It looked as if he would win, but as Landy neared the finish line, he was haunted by the question: Where is Bannister? As Landy reviewed the race for the "Time" reporter, he said, "If I hadn't looked back, I would have won the race."

Most of life's races can only be won by fixing our eyes on the prize. To look back is sure way to stumble over the present.

-Baffler-

How did the English pound get its name?

Did you know....

Scissors were invented by Leonardo da Vinci.

-Ponder-

"He who forgives first...wins!"

—William Penn

-Proverb-

"Keep your temper under control; it is foolish to harbor a grudge."

—Ecclesiastes 7:9, Good News Bible

-Principle-

In the middle of the summertime two men were out walking. Unable to restrain himself any longer, one man said, "Why is it that you are wearing your topcoat in this heat?" The friend replied, "Well, whenever I'm out like this I always run into that big man who slaps me across the chest every time I see him. This time, I'm going to get revenge. I put a stick of dynamite in my shirt pocket. The next time he slaps me on the chest he's going to get his hand blown off."

He forgot that the dynamite would also blow his own heart out. Revenge may hurt the other person, but it always blows our own heart out.

-Baffler-

Who has more hair, blondes or redheads?

Did you know....

Employees steal over $100 billion a year in goods, including pencils and paper clips, from their employers each year.

-Ponder-

"Occasional failure is the price of improvement."

—Unknown

-Proverb-

"If you get more stubborn every time you are corrected,
one day you will be crushed and never recover."

—Proverbs 29:1, Good News Bible

-Principle-

Two men were watching a Western on television. As the hero rode on horseback toward the edge of a cliff, one man said, "I bet you $50 he goes over the cliff."

"You're on," said the other man. The hero rode on, straight over the cliff. Being a sportsman, the second man handed over the money. The first man looked at it and said, "You know, I feel a bit guilty about winning this. I've seen this film before."

"So have I," said the second man, "but I didn't think he'd be stupid enough to make the same mistake again."

There is a great tragedy in making the same mistakes over and over. The challenge of life is to learn from previous mistakes, so that as many future mistakes as possible can be avoided.

-Baffler-

Why are address labels on subscription magazines usually placed upside-down?

Did you know....

The first state to let women vote was Wyoming.

PONDERS & PRINCIPLES

© 2004 Tania von Allmen for Ponders & Principles LLC

"The world is full of cactus, but we don't have to sit on it." — Will Foley

-Ponder-

"People are like stained glass windows—they sparkle and shine
when the sun is out, but when darkness sets in, true beauty
is only revealed if there's an inner light from within."

—Unknown

-Proverb-

"If a ruler pays attention to false information, all his officials will be liars."

—Proverbs 29:12, Good News Bible

-Principle-

One day a committee called on Abraham Lincoln to discuss a matter of public concern. Their case was built largely on suppositions. After listening for a while,

Mr. Lincoln asked, "How many legs would a sheep have if you called its tail a leg?" As he expected, they promptly answered, "Five!" "No!" he said, "it would only have four. Calling a tail a leg does not make it one."

Lincoln was right. Giving something a new name does not change its character. Yet we seem to think that by calling a lie a "credibility gap," it ceases to be a falsehood. A bad habit called a "shortcoming" is still a bad habit. The character of something can be dressed up, decorated, and even renamed, but it can't be changed.

-Baffler-

How many bricks are in the Empire State Building?

Did you know....

Men are 10 times more likely to be color-blind than women.

-Ponder-

"Some people are so indecisive, their favorite color is plaid."

—Unknown

-Proverb-

"Depending on an unreliable person in a crises is like trying to chew with a loose tooth or walk with a crippled foot."

—Proverbs 25:19, Good News Bible

-Principle-

When it comes to names which live in infamy, that of Pontius Pilate is certainly near the top of the list. The weak will of the Roman governor of Judea is recounted in the Easter story. But what happened to the man who gave Jesus up to his accusers? Pilate ruled until A.D. 36, when he was removed for his role in the massacre of Samaritans. Some non-biblical writings say Pilate committed suicide in Rome that year—but another work called "The Acts of Pilate" exonerates Pilate and portrays him and his wife as Christians. Amazingly, Pilate is even revered as a saint in the Coptic Church!

The key descriptive word for him seems to be: INDECISIVE. The challenge for each of us is: Where do we need to make an important decision?

-Baffler-

Why are baseball dugouts built so that they are half below ground?

Did you know....

Rembrandt, whose paintings are now valued at millions of dollars apiece, was so broke in his lifetime that in 1657 all his possessions had to be auctioned in order to pay off his debts.

-Ponder-

"You only have freedom of the seas…when you have control of the compass!"

—Zig Ziglar

-Proverb-

"Catch the foxes, the little foxes, before they ruin our vineyard in bloom."

—Song of Songs 2:15, Good News Bible

-Principle-

An old sailor, trusted and wise, was one night bringing his ship up between the coast of Wales and Ireland. He had been over the course innumerable times. This particular night, nearing port and home, with his eye on the compass and chart, he was running full steam ahead. Suddenly, with a sickening crashing sound, the ship was on the hidden rocks, resulting in loss of life and loss of ship.

Later, upon entering the pilot house, close examination revealed that someone, in seeking to clean or tamper with the compass, had slipped a thin knife blade into the compass box near the needle and the blade had broken off. That little piece of steel was enough to deflect, though only slightly, the needle by which the sailor was steering the ship. Such a little thing—such a mighty wreck.

Ask yourself the question: what has slipped into my life that could lead me off course?

-Baffler-

All the Zodiac symbols are animals, except one. Which one is that?

Did you know....

If you ate Frosted Flakes as a kid, there's a 50% chance you're still eating them.

-Ponder-

"Man can live about forty days without food or water but only about ten seconds without hope."

—Unknown

-Proverb-

"Don't be envious of sinful people; let reverence for the Lord be the concern of your life. If it is, you have a bright future."

—Proverbs 23:17-18, Good News Bible

-Principle-

If you could convince a man there was no hope, he would curse the day he was born. Hope is the indispensable quality of life.

Years ago the S-4 submarine was rammed by another ship and quickly sank. The entire crew was trapped in its prison house of death. Ships rushed to the scene of the disaster off the coast of Massachusetts. Divers were sent down to the sunken submarine and detected a tapping noise. Listening close the diver discovered that it was Morse Code and the sailor inside was tapping out slowly: "Is…there…any…hope?"

This seems to be the universal cry of humanity: "Is there any hope?" Hope is the basis of all human existence.

-Baffler-

How did the fast food restaurant *Jack in the Box* get its name?

Did you know....

The United States bought Alaska from the Soviet Union for about two cents an acre.

-Ponder-

"The measure of a man's real character is what he would
do if he knew he never would be found out."

—Thomas Babington Macaulay

-Proverb-

"Getting wisdom is the most important thing you can do.
Whatever else you get, get insight."

—Proverbs 4:7, Good News Bible

-Principle-

In the midst of election year disclosures on candidates' personal character and discoveries of "rubbergate" in Congress, one wonders if integrity might be a relic of days gone by.

When he was 24 years old, Abraham Lincoln was employed as the postmaster of New Salem, Illinois. The post office was closed in 1936, but it was several years before an agent arrived from Washington to settle accounts. At this time, Lincoln was a struggling attorney, not doing too well.

The agent informed him that there was $17 due the government. Lincoln crossed the room, opened an old trunk and took out a yellowed cotton rag bound with string.

Untying it he spread out the cloth and there was $17. "I never use any man's money but my own," he said.

-Baffler-

Where did the term "Cesarean Section" originate?

Did you know....

Howard Hughes weighed only 93 pounds when he died.

-Ponder-

"The income tax people are very nice
...they're letting me keep my own mother."

—Henny Youngman

-Proverb-

"Keep evil advisers away from the King and his
government will be known for its justice."

—Proverbs 25:5, Good News Bible

-Principle-

The sex habits of cabbage was one study done at a university. Tax money funded the study through the National Science Foundation in the amount of $32,000.

One congressman listed some wasteful programs such as $121,000 to try to find out why so many people say "ain't," and $203,000 for the city of Los Angeles to extend traveler's aid to people lost on freeways. Also $19,800 to try and find out why children fall off tricycles.

One U. S. senator reported these examples cited from the Congressional Record: $35,000 for rounding up wild boars in Pakistan; $117,000 to support a board of tea tasters; $70,000 for study of the history of comic books; $70,000 went to the study of the smell of perspiration given off by the Australian aborigines; $159,000 to teach mothers how to play with their babies.

Is it any wonder why the government deficit continues to rise so dramatically?

-Baffler-

Do you know what was Walt Disney's first full-length cartoon feature?
(Hint: It premiered in L.A. on December 21, 1937.)

Did you know....

Only one carat in every 23 tons of ore mined is a diamond.

-Ponder-

"Far better it is to dare mighty things, to win glorious triumphs,
even though checkered by failure, than to take rank with those poor
spirits who neither enjoy much nor suffer much, because they live
in the gray twilight that knows neither victory nor defeat."

—Theodore Roosevelt

-Proverb-

"Sensible people are careful to stay out of trouble,
but stupid people are careless and act too quickly."

—Proverbs 14:16, Good News Bible

-Principle-

Great accomplishments are often attempted but only occasionally reached. What is interesting (and encouraging) is that those who reach them are usually those who missed many times before. Failures are only temporary tests to prepare us for permanent triumphs!

Remember Evel Knievel and his classic fizzle, the Snake River Canyon jump? Any third grader could have told you it wouldn't work—and it didn't. But instead of sending an ambulance and a tow truck to mop up his mistake, Mr. Knievel should have sent a Brink's armored car. No one in the history of sports came off a failure with a better pocketbook.

The person who succeeds is not the one who holds back fearing failure, nor the one who never fails…but rather the one who moves on in spite of failure.

-Baffler-

All continents have deserts—except for _____.

Did you know....

The average person spends over 9 hours preparing his taxes.

-Ponder-

"Nowadays God helps those who help themselves,
and the government helps those who don't."

—Dan Bennett

-Proverb-"

When a nation sins, it will have one ruler after another. But a nation
will be strong and endure when it has intelligent, sensible leaders."

—Proverbs 28:2, Good News Bible

-Principle-

A former governor of Kansas made a statement that makes such good sense it
should be heard and read by more people.

"Had Abraham Lincoln been living today, the Rotary Club would supply him with
a set of books; the Lions Club with a good reading lamp; the Cosmopolitan Club with
writing equipment; and the Kiwanis Club with a wooden terrazzo for the cabin."

"He would have the protection of child labor insurance. A kindly philanthropist
would send him to college. A case worker would see that his father received a monthly check from the government. Abe would receive a subsidy for rail splitting, another one for raising a crop he was going to raise anyway, and still another subsidy for not
raising a crop he had no intention of raising."

"Result: There would have been no Abraham Lincoln!"

-Baffler-

What song is sung most often in America?

Did you know....

There are over 200 taste buds on each of the small bumps on your tongue.

-Ponder-

"If you want to kill time, why not try working it to death?"

—Unknown

-Proverb-

"A working man may or may not have enough to eat,
but at least he can get a good night's sleep."

—Ecclesiastes 5:12, Good News Bible

-Principle-

When Edison was a train newsboy, he'd lay over between runs in Detroit. Most of us would have gone to a ball game, to the movies, or something else to kill time, but Edison went to the library and put in time with books. Many great discoveries have been the result of a hobby, avocation, or specific need outside of the regular routine of living.

The father of photography was an army officer; of the electrical motor, a bookbinder; of the telegraph, a portrait painter. The inventor of the typewriter was a farmer; a carpenter invented the cotton gin, and the locomotive was invented by a coal miner. The telephone came from the after-school work of a school teacher, and a physician invented the pneumatic tire.

How do you use your spare time?

-Baffler-

The hamburgers McDonald's serve in a week equal
approximately how many head of cattle?

Did you know....

There are about 800 tombstones in Tombstone, Arizona.

-Ponder-

"Success is disguised. It is found in the guise of hard work
…if you avoid hard work, you will be dodging success."

—John MacCleod

-Proverb-

"If you wait until the wind and weather are just right, you will
never plant anything and you will never harvest anything."

—Ecclesiastes 11:4, Good News Bible

-Principle-

A tramp when asked about his philosophy of life replied, "I turn my back to the wind." That probably is why he was a tramp. Following the line of least resistance is what makes rivers and many people crooked. A person cannot drift into success.

In contrast to this philosophy is the statement which Captain McWhite spoke to his mate in Joseph Conrad's immortal tale of the sea "Typhoon." In the midst of a great storm, McWhite said: "Keep facing it! They may say what they like—the heaviest seas run with the wind. Always facing it! That's the way to get through!"

-Baffler-

What cartoon, introduced in 1960, was TV's first animated sitcom
…and the first prime-time cartoon show?

Did you know....

Florence Nightingale was a confirmed hypochondriac.

-Ponder-

"A man travels the world over in search of what
he needs and returns home to find it!"

—George Moore

-Proverb-

"…The best thing anyone can do is eat and drink and enjoy what he has
worked for during the short life God has given him; this is man's fate."

—Ecclesiastes 5:18, Good News Bible

-Principle-

Some years ago a London newspaper offered prizes for the best answers to this question: "Who are the happiest persons on earth?" The answers were surprising and encouraging. Here are the four answers which were adjudged the best:

"A craftsman or artist whistling over a job well done."

"A little child building sand castles."

"A mother, after a busy day, bathing her baby."

"A doctor who has finished a difficult and dangerous operation and saved a human life."

Looks as if kicks, riches, fame and rank are not rated so highly as essentials of a happy life. Plainly, the decision is that happiness is for everybody, not just a privileged few. If no one but the glamorous and the rich could be happy, then the rest of us might have real grounds for complaint.

But that doesn't seem to be the case, does it?

-Baffler-

How many commercials will the average American teenager
see by the time he or she graduates from high school?

Did you know....

Mel Blanc, the man who provided Bugs Bunny's
voice, was allergic to carrots.

-Ponder-

"Success is doing what you love and having a positive
impact on people's lives without starving to death."

—Unknown

-Proverb-

"A good man's words will benefit many people,
but you can kill yourself with stupidity."

—Proverbs 10:21, Good News Bible

-Principle-

Someone once asked Al Jolson, popular musical comedy star of the twenties, what he did when he ran into a cold audience. Al Jolson said, "Whenever I go out before an audience and don't get the response I feel that I ought to get, what do I do? I don't go back behind the scenes and say to myself, 'The audience is dead from the neck up—it's a bunch of wooden nutmegs.' No, instead I say to myself, 'Look here Al, what is wrong with you tonight? The audience is all right, but you're all wrong, Al.'"

Instead of giving up and putting on a poor show with the excuse that the audience couldn't appreciate a good one, Al tried to give the best performance of his career...he had them applauding and begging for more.

-Baffler-

What is "Spasmatomancy?"

Did you know....

The *Mona Lisa* has no eyebrows.

-Ponder-

"Happiness is a gift…you have to give it away to get it."

—Zig Ziglar

-Proverb-

"The hopes of good men lead to joy, but wicked
people can look forward to nothing."

—Proverbs 10:28, Good News Bible

-Principle-

A man over eighty years old was observed by a neighbor planting a small peach tree. "Do you expect to eat peaches from that tree?" the neighbor asked.

The elderly gentleman rested on his spade. "No," he said. "At my age I know I won't. But all my life I've enjoyed peaches—never from a tree I had planted myself. I wouldn't have had peaches if other people hadn't done what I'm doing now. I'm just trying to pay back the others who planted peach trees for me."

In practicing giving away, we both plant peach trees and eat peaches, often unconscious of the fruits of our own little thoughtlessness, and equally unconscious of the thoughtfulness others have invested for our benefit, perhaps many years ago.

Today's giving away is a blind investment in future happiness, though we can never tell when, where, or in what form this happiness will come.

-Baffler-

The most famous pardon in U.S. history occurred in
September, 1974. Who was pardoned?

Did you know....

Every year, Mexico City sinks about 10 inches.

-Ponder-

"Keep in mind the true meaning of an individual is how
he treats a person who can do him absolutely no good."

—Ann Landers

-Proverb-

"If you want to be happy, be kind to the poor; it is a sin to despise anyone."

—Proverbs 14:21, Good News Bible

-Principle-

Before William McKinley became the twenty-fifth president of the United States, he served in Congress. Going to his office one day, he boarded a streetcar and took the only seat available. Moments later a woman who appeared to be ill also boarded the car, stood in front of a fellow Congressman, who hid behind the newspaper he was reading and did not offer her a seat. McKinley walked up the aisle, tapped her on the shoulder, offered her his seat, and took her place clutching a strap.

Years later when McKinley was president, this same Congressman was recommended for the post of an ambassador to a foreign country. McKinley refused to appoint him, fearing that if the man hadn't had the common courtesy to offer his seat in a crowded streetcar, he would also lack the courtesies inherent in a man soon to become a great ambassador to a troubled nation.

-Baffler-

President Ulysses S. Grant was arrested during his term of office. Why?

Did you know....

In Helsinki, Finland, police rarely give parking tickets—they deflate the tires!

-Ponder-

"Things turn out best for the people who make
the best of the way things turn out."

—John Wooden

-Proverb-

"Above all else guard your affections.
For they influence everything else in your life."

—Proverbs 4:23, The Living Bible

-Principle-

In these days when the grip of recession is still being felt by many, we need to be reminded of a number of precepts to practice which will help us cultivate calmness.

Learn to like what does not cost much.

Learn to like reading, conversation, music.

Learn to like plain food, plain service, plain cooking.

Learn to like people, even though some of them may be very different from you.

Learn to keep your wants simple. Refuse to be owned and anchored by things and the opinions of others.

Learn to like the sunrise and the sunset, the beating of rain on the roof and windows.

Learn to like life for its own sake.

-Baffler-

What do Mark Twain, Charles Dickens, and Thomas Edison have in common?

Did you know....

It takes about 150 days for your fingernails to grow
from your cuticles to your fingertips.

-Ponder-

"If the only tool you have is a hammer,
you tend to see every problem as a nail."

—Edward E. Jones Jr.

-Proverb-

"Anyone who is determined to do right will live,
but anyone who insists on doing wrong will die."

—Proverbs 11:19, Good News Bible

-Principle-

One measure of our maturity and sense of perspective is the way we respond to our circumstances when things go wrong. If we go into depression, doubt our abilities, strike out at some innocent person, we have some growing to do.

Explorer Thomas Hearne and his party had just set out on a rigorous expedition in northern Canada to find the mouth of the Coppermine River. A few days after they left, thieves stole most of their supplies. Hearne's response to the apparent misfortune can inspire us all, for he wrote, "The weight of our baggage being lightened, our next day's journey was more swift and pleasant."

-Baffler-

Who introduced fireworks to the Western World?

Did you know....

A pair of 1969 Wheat and Rice Honeys cereal boxes featuring the
Beatles in *Yellow Submarine* once sold for $7,000!

241 – Common Sense and Plain Dealing

-Ponder-

"Nothing astonishes men so much as common sense and plain dealing."

—Executive Speechwriter Newsletter

-Proverb-

"A wicked man is trapped by his own words,
but an honest man gets himself out of trouble."

—Proverbs 11:13, Good News Bible

-Principle-

Good business leader, an Oxymoron? Not any more! Certainly there was, at the turn of the century, a proliferation of Robber Barons and burgeoning American businesses. Certainly as recently as the S & L scandals, hanky-panky in the executive suites has been spotlighted, but more than ever before our nation's top 500 corporations are being run by the Golden Rule. Dr. Charles Watson, Professor of Management at Miami University has been five years interviewing chief executive officers of our nation's most successful corporations including Dupont, 3M, Alcoa, Dow, Xerox, AT&T, and Whirlpool. In his book called, *Managing With Integrity* he concludes that successful business leaders adhere to traditional values: honesty, decency, hard work, kindness, and fair play.

-Baffler-

Do you think better in the winter or the summer?

Did you know....

The chairman of Hyundai is called "The Chairman,"
even by his wife and kids.

-Ponder-

"Character—not wealth, power, or position
...is the supreme word."

—John D. Rockefeller

-Proverb-

"The Lord hates people who use dishonest scales.
He is happy with honest weights."

—Proverbs 11:1, Good News Bible

-Principle-

A number of years ago, the Douglas Aircraft Company was competing with Boeing to sell Eastern Airlines its first big jets. War hero Eddie Rickenbacker, the head of Eastern Airlines, reportedly told Donald Douglas that the specifications and claims made by Douglas' company for the DC-8 were close to Boeing's on everything except noise suppression. Rickenbacker then gave Douglas one last chance to promise to outperform Boeing on this feature. After consulting with his engineers, Douglas reported that he didn't feel he could make that promise. Rickenbacker replied, "I know you can't, I just wanted to see if you were still honest."

-Baffler-

Where did the custom of clinking glasses after a toast come from?

Did you know....

In Albania, nodding the head means "no" and
shaking the head means "yes."

-Ponder-

"Every exit is an entry…somewhere else!"

—Tom Stoppard

-Ponder-

"Get all the advice you can, and you will succeed;
without it, you will fail."

—Proverbs 15:22, Good News Bible

-Principle-

To the millions of people who saw her in the films of the thirties, Zasu Pitts was synonymous with comedy. The world, however, might never have heard of Zasu had it not been for the understanding and compassion of her high school principal. As an adolescent, Zasu was unattractive, shy, awkward, skinny, and poor. While performing in a high school play, her words and movements brought the house down with laughter. Feeling laughed at, Zasu wanted to give up. But her principal said. "Maybe that's your mission in life. Maybe that's what God intended." Zasu dried her eyes, took a deep breath, and stepped back on stage to express what was within her.

-Baffler-

The average man shrinks a little more than one inch between the ages of 30 and 70. In the same period of time, how much does the average woman shrink?

Did you know....

A major league baseball team can break
$150,000 worth of bats in one year.

-Ponder-

"Many things are lost...for want of asking."

—English Proverb

-Proverb-

"Ask the Lord to bless your plans, and you
will be successful in carrying them out."

—Proverbs 16:3, Good News Bible

-Principle-

An elderly woman stood on a busy street corner, hesitant to cross because there was no traffic signal. As she waited, a gentleman came up beside her and asked, "May I cross over with you?" Relieved, she thanked him and took his arm.

The path they took was anything but safe. The man seemed to be confused as they dodged traffic and walked in a zig-zag pattern across the street. "You almost got us killed!" the woman exclaimed in anger when they finally reached the curb. "You walk like you're blind!" "I am," he replied. "That's why I asked if I could cross with you."

-Baffler-

What percent of American men have spent at least one night in jail?

Did you know....

There are three museums in the
world which only exhibit footwear.

245 – Give 'em Your Smile

-Ponder-

"When you see someone without a smile...give 'em yours!"

—Dolly Parton

-Proverb-

"A person's words can be a source of wisdom, deep
as the ocean, fresh as a flowing stream."

—Proverbs 18:4, Good News Bible

-Principle-

As a boy, Sir Walter Scott was left weak and lame by a severe attack of fever. Some people thought he would never amount to anything in life.

When Scott was a teenager, he visited in a home where some famous writers were being entertained. The poet Robert Burns was among them. In one room was a picture under which was written a beautiful bit of verse. Burns asked who wrote it, but no one seemed to know. Timidly, Scott gave the writer's name and quoted the rest of the poem.

Burns was impressed. Laying his hand on young Walter's head, he said, "Ah, my boy, I'm sure you'll be a great man in Scotland someday!" That brief conversation was the affirmation Walter Scott needed to set him on the road to greatness.

-Baffler-

Have you ever crossed your fingers for good luck?
Do you know where the gesture originated?

Did you know....

Disney animators drew nearly 6.5 million black
spots for the film 101 Dalmatians.

-Ponder-

"A good education is the next best thing to a pushy mother."

—Charles Schulz

-Proverb-

"Listen to your father; without him you would not exist.
When your mother is old, show her your appreciation."

—Proverbs 23:22, Good News Bible

-Principle-

A mother found under her plate one evening a bill made out by her small son, Bradley, aged eight—"Mother owes Bradley: for running errands, 25 cents; for being good, 10 cents; for taking music lessons, 15 cents; for extras, 5 cents. Total, 55 cents."

Mother smiled but made no comment. The next day Bradley found a bill under his plate along with 55 cents. Opening the bill, he read—"Bradley owes Mother: for nursing him through the chicken pox, nothing; for being good to him, nothing; for clothes, shoes and playthings, nothing; for his room, nothing; for his meals, nothing. Total: nothing."

-Baffler-

According to AT&T, on what day are the most
long-distance phone calls placed?

Did you know....

An automatic spaghetti-spinning fork was patented in 1950.

-Ponder-

"When you identify with your company's purpose, when you
experience ownership in a shared vision, you find yourself
doing your life's work…instead of just doing time."

—John Naisbitt

-Proverb-

"Wise men can see where they are going, and fools cannot."

—Ecclesiastes 2:14, Good News Bible

-Principle-

About 350 years ago a shipload of travelers landed on the northeast coast of America. The first year, they established a town site. The next year, they elected a town government. The third year, the town government planned to build a road five miles westward into the wilderness. In the fourth year, the people tried to impeach their town government because they thought it was a waste of public funds to build a road five miles westward into the wilderness. Who needed to go there anyway?

Here were people who had the vision to see three thousand miles across the ocean and overcome great hardships to get there. But in just a few short years they were not able to see even five miles out of town.

With a clear vision of what we can become, no difficulty is too great. Without it, we rarely move beyond our current boundaries.

-Baffler-

What is the British name for the game known in the U.S. as "Tic-Tac-Toe?"

Did you know....

Legendary lawman Wyatt Earp was kicked out of California for horse-stealing.

-Ponder-

"The future belongs to those who believe in the beauty of their dreams."

—Eleanor Roosevelt

-Proverb-

"So I realized that all we can do is be happy
and do the best we can while we are still alive."

—Ecclesiastes 3:12, Good News Bible

-Principle-

A group of researchers from Duke University interviewed hundreds of people in various stages of happiness, from several different walks of life. The researchers were trying to discover what it is that gives a person inner tranquility. When they finished they had a list of eight axioms.

1. An absence of suspicion and resentment.
2. Not wasting time or energy fighting conditions one cannot change.
3. Living in the present.
4. Cooperating with life rather than fighting it or running from it.
5. Forcing yourself to be outgoing with others, particularly during times of stress.
6. Refusing to pity yourself or make alibis.
7. Cultivating basic values.
8. Adjusting to one's humanity while developing a reliance on a higher power.

-Baffler-

How long is the course for a marathon race?

Did you know....

In a UCLA study, 87% of the people researchers smiled at smiled back.

-Ponder-

"Life in general; You win some…You lose some
…and some get rained out…but you gotta suit up for them all!"

—J. Askenberg

-Proverb-

"Again I looked throughout the earth and saw that the swiftest person does not always win the race, nor the strongest man the battle, and that wise men are often poor, and skillful men are not necessarily famous; but it is all by chance, by happening to be at the right place at the right time."

—Ecclesiastes 9:11, The Living Bible

-Principle-

The monuments of life are erected to all. Better known as tombstones, each has a character of its own. Napoleon's tombstone is huge. Churchill's stone is simple. The eternal flame burns over the grave of President Kennedy. The stone erected to Mozart is lost in obscurity. Each lived different lives and have different markers.

As different as each was from the other, their lives share at least one common mark—the dash between the dates. On every tombstone, be it simple or ornate, one little dash is found—a simple horizontal line recording their life story.

The character and content of our lives vary, but in the end, only one dash is chiseled.

We get one dash through life. That is it. No seconds and no restarts! Everybody finishes. Make the most of it! How can we carve out our place in life? What can we do to make our life special? That little dash can't speak. But if it could, it would teach us a few lessons.

-Baffler-

What state is known as the "Badger" state?

Did you know….

The screen on the first home television set was on 3 x 4 inches.

PONDERS & PRINCIPLES

© 2004 Tania von Allmen for Ponders & Principles LLC

"You can tell when you are on the road to success. It's uphill all the way." — Paul Harvey

-Ponder-

"We make a living by what we get…We make a life by what we give."

—Anonymous

-Proverb-

"Young people, enjoy your youth. Be happy while you are still young.
Do what you want to do, and follow your heart's desire. But remember
that God is going to judge you for whatever you do."

—Ecclesiastes 11:9, Good News Bible

-Principle-

Lou Holtz, the well-known football coach at Notre Dame, has coached at five colleges. Never once did he inherit a winner. Yet he has taken every school to a bowl game during the second season at the latest. This success was accomplished, claims Holtz, by a philosophy consisting of three simple rules:

1. *Do what is right.* You know the difference, and if you have any doubt, get out the Bible. It's right to be on time, polite, honest, to remain free from drugs.
2. *Do your best.* We do not help people at all by accepting mediocrity when they are capable of being better. Do not worry about being popular. Many times we don't encourage others to do their best because we are more concerned with our player's appraisal of our efforts than we are with them.
3. *Treat others as you would like to be treated.* I have never seen a team, a family, or a business that can't become better by emphasizing love and understanding.

-Baffler-

"Sweet Potato" is a nickname for what musical instrument?

Did you know….

"Poltergeist" literally means "noisy ghost."

-Ponder-

"It's not the day that is so important, but the God who made it!"

—Vance Havner

-Proverb-

"Trust in the Lord with all your heart.
Never rely on what you think you know."

—Proverbs 3:5, Good News Bible

-Principle-

The Wright brothers had taken their airplane by ship to Europe, and were exhibiting it in various countries. When they came to Spain, the king of that nation sent them a special command that they were to fly their plane for him the next day, which happened to be Sunday.

But Wilbur Wright, true to his early Christian training, sent back a polite but determined refusal to fly on "God's holy day"—and fly, he did not. But instead of becoming angry, the king honored them for their convictions and let Wilbur set the time when he would fly for the Spanish ruler.

-Baffler-

How many sides does a dodecagon have?

Did you know....

Giraffes can go longer without water than camels can.

-Ponder-

"Goals determine what you're going to be."

—Julius Erving

-Proverb-

"Those who plan for evil are in for a rude surprise,
but those who work for good will find happiness."

—Proverbs 12:20, Good News Bible

-Principle-

The Hopi Indians have a philosophy that gives them an inner strength to overcome life's prejudices and obstacles. They speak of the "dream catcher," a symbolic net hung in the doorways of their homes. Into this net fly their dreams, their hopes, their aspirations.

They believe that unrealistic dreams, or unattainable visions pass through the net. Only those dreams, those realizable hopes that can be achieved, remains inside.

Those dreams remain a part of them and keep them focused on their path. Once the dream has been attained, they put a feather in the dream catcher.

-Baffler-

In 1985, 5 percent of U.S. households had telephone answering machines. How many had them by 1990?

Did you know....

Rumania's capital of Bucharest has 2.5 million rats and 2 million people.

253 – Giving Away Love

-Ponder-

"Love grows by giving. The love we give away is the only love we keep.
The only way to retain love...is to give it away."

—Elbert Hubbard

-Proverb-

"Give to the poor and you will never be in need. If you close your
eyes to the poor, many people will curse you."

—Proverbs 28:27, Good News Bible

-Principle-

There was once a rabbi in a small village in Russia who vanished every Friday
morning for several hours. The devoted villagers boasted that during these hours the
rabbi ascended to heaven to talk with God. A skeptical newcomer determined to discover where the rabbi really went.

On Friday morning the newcomer hid near the rabbi's house and saw him come
out wearing the clothes of a peasant. The rabbi then took an ox and went into the
forest to chop wood, gathering the wood into a large bundle. Next the rabbi took the
wood to a shack in the poorest section of the village in which lived an elderly woman
and her son. He left them the wood which was enough for a whole week. The rabbi
then quietly returned to his own house.

From that time on, when the newcomer heard villagers say, "On Friday morning
our rabbi ascends all the way to heaven," he would add quietly, "If not higher."

-Baffler-

What is the main ingredient in "vichyssoise?"

Did you know....

Reno, Nevada is west of Los Angeles, California.

-Ponder-

"Do not follow where the path may lead…go instead
where there is no path and leave a trail."

—Unknown

-Proverb-

"Those who are good travel a road that avoids evil; so watch
where you are going—it may save your life."

—Proverbs 16:17, Good News Bible

-Principle-

The recipient of the first Nobel Peace Prize was Henri Dunant. Early in life, Dunant was a wealthy and popular Geneva banker. Dunant, later in life, witnessed first-hand the suffering of wounded soldiers on the battlefields. Out of that haunting memory he began in the 1850's a campaign to "humanize" war—to change the rules of warfare through international regulations that would ensure soldiers would not be denied medical care. His efforts paid off, and the first International Convention at Geneva was signed in 1864. From this beginning there grew the movement we know as the International Red Cross.

-Baffler-

According to *The Book of Jargon*, to what does the term "tranny" refer?

Did you know....

In 1990, Canada owned more U.S. real estate than Japan.

-Ponder-

"The best way to convince a fool that he is
wrong is to let him have his own way."

—Josh Billings

-Proverb-

"Wisdom does more for a person than ten rulers can do for a city."

—Proverbs 7:19, Good New Bible

-Principle-

There once was a village "idiot" who would be stopped every day by the towns-people and asked to pick between a nickel and a dime. The "idiot" always chose the nickel and the residents always went away saying, "There, you see what an idiot he is." Later in life the idiot explained it this way: "After all, if I kept picking the dime, they would have stopped offering it to me pretty quickly. This way I kept getting nick-els every day."

The real question is: Who was the *real* idiot?

-Baffler-

What was the origin of our word "salary?"

Did you know....

Redwood bark is fireproof, so fires in
redwood forests burn inside the trees.

-Ponder-

"Saddle your dreams before you ride 'em."

—Mary Webb

-Proverb-

"There is no one on earth who does what is right
all the time and never makes a mistake."

—Ecclesiastes 7:20, Good News Bible

-Principle-

There is a fable about a hippo who fell in love with a butterfly. He sought the advice of a wise old owl. "You must become a butterfly," the owl told the hippo, "and do it right now." The hippo was delighted. He plunged back into the jungle, only to return shortly. "How do I become a butterfly?" the hippo inquired of the owl. The bird of great wisdom responded, "That's up to you. I only set the policy. I don't implement."

-Baffler-

What city did Jack the Ripper terrorize in the 19th century?

Did you know....

In Gary, Indiana, it is illegal to attend the
theater within four hours of eating garlic.

-Ponder-

"Let us not bankrupt our todays by paying interest on the regrets of yesterday and borrowing in advance the troubles of tomorrow."

—Ralph W. Sockman

-Proverb-

"I have also learned why people work so hard to succeed; it is because they envy the things their neighbors have. But it is useless. It is like chasing the wind."

—Ecclesiastes 4:4, Good News Bible

-Principle-

"The One Who Dies With The Most Toys Wins," so say the bumper stickers. However, most Americans have little idea of the cost of consumption. The great irony in the pursuit of the most toys is that it inevitably requires the most time to get them, leaving the least time to use them. Pollster Lou Hains has found that people have an average of 32 percent less leisure time than they did a decade ago.

There are only so many hours in a day and something has to give. The dream car is parked. The country house for weekend getaways might as well be in another country. The boat hasn't been wet in months. It could be said, "Blessed are the toys for they shall inherit the dust."

-Baffler-

In the Australian song *Waltzing Matilda*, who or what is Matilda?

Did you know....

Turkeys caught in the rain have been known to look up and hold their mouths open so long that they die by drowning!

258 – In Love with a Dimple

-Ponder-

"Many a man in love with a dimple makes
the mistake of marrying the whole girl."

—Steven Leacock

-Proverb-

"How hard it is to find a capable wife!
She is worth far more than jewels!"

—Proverbs 31:10, Good News Bible

-Principle-

On July 29, 1981, Britain's Prince Charles married his Lady Diana in a grand royal ceremony. The glamorous wedding was a fairy tale of present pomp and past glory, a last gold-leaf page from the tattered book of Empire. London was a city dressed like a vast stage. Buses were painted with bows and parks bloomed with Charles' royal crest outlined in precisely painted blossoms. Some 4,500 pots of flowers lined the wedding route.

Besides the happy couple, the audience included 26 prominent clerics, a congregation of 2,500 crowding each other for space to sit under the great painted dome of St. Paul's Cathedral, more than 75 technicians manning 21 cameras, and an estimated worldwide television audience of 750 million.

Which just goes to prove that a glamorous wedding does not guarantee a great marriage.

-Baffler-

It is the only vegetable or fruit that is never sold frozen, canned, processed, cooked, or in any other form but fresh. What is it?

Did you know....

A plucked eyebrow takes about 90 days to grow back.

259 – Never Forget a Defeat

-Ponder-

"Never forget a defeat...because that is the key to victory."

—Mike Krzyzewski, Duke University Basketball Coach

-Proverb-

"They say that a man would be a fool to fold
his hands and let himself starve to death."

—Ecclesiastes 4:5, Good News Bible

-Principle-

Lena Himmel, a 16-year-old orphan, was brought from Lithuania to New York just before the turn of the century by relatives who wanted her to marry their son. But the marriage never materialized. Instead, Lena became a seamstress and married David Bryant, a Brooklyn jeweler who died two years later. Although it might have appeared she had little success, Lena saw an opportunity. She pawned a pair of diamond earrings her husband had left her and bought a sewing machine. By 1904 she had done well enough to open a store on Fifth Avenue. Seeking to provide clothing for pregnant women, she made a dress with an elasticized waistband. The first maternity dress was made and Lane Bryant, the national clothing chain, was launched.

Doors of opportunity swing open, frequently in the midst of adversity.

-Baffler-

Who suffers the most on-the-job back injuries?

Did you know....

Famous storyteller Hans Christian Anderson couldn't spell.

260 – The Enemy is No More

-Ponder-

"It is better that my enemy see good in me than I see bad in him."

—Jewish Proverb

-Proverb-

"When you please the Lord, you can make your enemies into friends."

—Proverbs 16:7, Good News Bible

-Principle-

Frederick the Great, King of Prussia for 46 years, was once in Potsdam when he encountered one of his generals who had long been in his disfavor. At their meeting, the general saluted with the greatest respect, but Frederick merely turned his back on the officer. "I am happy to see that Your Majesty is no longer angry with me," the general said.

"How so?" demanded Frederick.

"Because Your Majesty has never in his life turned his back on an enemy." It was a daring statement, but it was reported to have led to a reconciliation!

-Baffler-

In H. G. Wells' 1914 story *The World Set Free*,
he imagined a new kind of weapon. What was it?

Did you know....

According to experts, whale songs rhyme.

-Ponder-

"The most important thing a father can do
for his children is to love their mother."

—Kirk Douglas

-Proverb-

"A wise son makes his father happy. Only a fool despises his mother."

—Proverbs 15:20, Good News Bible

-Principle-

What's a Mother Worth? (circa 1990)

Sylvia Porter, a noted financial analyst, reports that 25 million full-time home-makers contribute billions to the economy each year, although their labor is not counted in the gross national product.

Porter says only the wealthiest families could pay for the services a mother provides for love. Porter calculated how much the mother added to her family's economic well-being by assigning an hourly fee for nursemaid, housekeeper, cook, dishwasher, laundress, food buyer, chauffeur, gardener, maintenance person, seamstress, dietitian, and practical nurse. She found that the labor performed by a mother would cost a family $23,580 in Greensboro, SC, $26,962 in Los Angeles and $28,735 in Chicago!

-Baffler-

What country did each of the following dishes originate?
Swiss Steak,   Russian Dressing,   Chop Suey,   Vichyssoise

Did you know....

Glen Campbell once sang backup with the Beach Boys.

-Ponder-

"Character is what you are in the dark."

—Dwight Moody

-Proverb-

"A reliable witness always tells the truth,
but an unreliable one tells nothing but lies."

—Proverbs 14:5, Good News Bible

-Principle-

One afternoon, the members of a health club assembled for a meeting on nutrition and exercise. The dietitian leading the discussion asked each member in turn to describe his or her daily routine. The first participant admitted to a number of excesses, including overeating. Others joined in agreement. But one seriously overweight member reported, "I eat healthfully and moderately, I drink moderately and I exercise frequently."

"I see," said the dietitian. "Are you sure you have nothing else to tell us?"

"Well yes," said the man. "I also lie extensively."

That comment probably brought some laughter, but it underlines an important truth: What we do in secret will eventually become evident in public.

-Baffler-

What famous North American landmark is constantly moving backward?

Did you know....

Roses cut in the afternoon last longer than roses cut in the morning.

263 – Worthwhile Achievement

-Ponder-

"The man who has achieved all that he
thinks worthwhile...has begun to die."

—E. T. Trigg

-Proverb-

"Lazy people should learn a lesson from the way ants live.
They have no leader, chief, or ruler, but they store up
their food during the summer, getting ready for winter."

—Proverbs 6:6-7, Good News Bible

-Principle-

Long term achievement must have constant motivation.

After Mickey Spillane, the writer of detective stories achieved his first success, he decided to work less and play more. He took up residence at a popular seaside resort and started having a great time. In the little time he found to work, the ideas wouldn't come. Being financially secure, he wasn't concerned. All the while, his bank account was steadily shrinking. Once, some unexpected bills came up and overnight Mickey's financial situation went from comfortable to desperate. Almost immediately, good, salable ideas began to percolate in his mind, and out of necessity he wrote one of his best stories, going on to enjoy a long and outstanding career.

Being too comfortable is a great obstacle to success.

-Baffler-

When Clint Eastwood appeared in the classic "spaghetti western,"
The Good, the Bad, and the Ugly, which role did he play?

Did you know....

37% of Americans say they are excellent drivers—
2% think other drivers are equally skilled.

-Ponder-

"The more we count the blessings we have
...the less we crave the luxuries we haven't."

—William Ward

-Proverb-

"I will make my people and their homes around my hill a blessing.
And there shall be showers of blessings..."

—Ezekiel 34:26, The Living Bible

-Principle-

During the Depression, Charles Darrow could find no work. Although he was broke and his wife was expecting a baby, he wasn't discouraged. Every evening they played a game he had devised. Remembering happy vacations in nearby Atlantic City, he laid out his own little boardwalk on a square piece of cardboard and pretended to be rich. On his "properties" he put miniature houses and hotels he had carved out of wood. The game called *Monopoly* was later marketed by Parker Brothers and ultimately made Darrow a millionaire.

Not everyone will become a millionaire. But everyone has the opportunity to survive tough situations by keeping a positive mental attitude.

-Baffler-

Approximately what percentage of American households consist of a working father, a housewife, mother and children under the age of 18?

Did you know....

Sleepwalking is hereditary.

265 – Going to the Top

-Ponder-

"I studied the lives of great men and famous women, and I found that the men and women who got to the top were those who did the jobs they had in hand with everything they had of energy, enthusiasm, and hard work!"

—Harry S. Truman

-Proverb-

"There is a right time and a right way to
do everything, but we know so little!"

—Ecclesiastes 8:6, Good News Bible

-Principle-

While touring Italy, a man visited a cathedral that had been completed on the outside only. Once inside, the traveler found an artist kneeling before an enormous wall upon which he had just begun to create a mosaic. On some tables nearby were thousands of pieces of colored ceramic. Curious, the visitor asked the artist how he would ever finish such a large project. The artist answered that he knew how much he could accomplish in one day. Each morning, he marked off an area to be completed that day and didn't worry about what remained outside that space. That was the best he could do, and if he did his best, one day the mosaic would be finished.

It is easy to become overwhelmed with the immenseness of life's challenges. To concentrate on doing the best, day after day, is the way to finish our life's mosaic.

-Baffler-

Can you name "The Three Musketeers?"

Did you know....

Americans make $500 million worth of illegal
long distance phone calls annually.

-Ponder-

"Everyone who has ever taken a shower has an idea... It's the person who gets out of the shower, dries off, and does something about it who makes the difference."

—Nolan Bushnell, Atari Founder

-Proverb-

"If you spend your time sleeping, you will be poor.
Keep busy and you will have plenty to eat."

—Proverbs 20:13, Good News Bible

-Principle-

Before the Civil War, Edmund McIlhenny operated a sugar plantation and a salt works on Avery Island, Louisiana. Yankee troops invaded the area in 1963, and McIlhenny had to flee. When he returned in 1865, his sugar fields and salt works were ruined.

One of the few things left were some hot Mexican peppers that had reseeded themselves in the kitchen garden. McIlhenny, who was living hand to mouth, started experimenting with the ground peppers to make a sauce that would liven up his dull diet. His newfound sauce is known today as Tabasco sauce. To this day, the McIlhenny Company and its Tabasco business is still run by the McIlhenny family.

-Baffler-

Lunar material was brought to earth by astronauts Armstrong, Aldrin, and Collins. What was this material named?

Did you know....

One-fifth of Americans spend their vacations at home.

267 – Impossibility

-Ponder-

"Every man is an impossibility...until he is born!"

—Ralph Waldo Emerson

-Proverb-

"Children are fortunate if they have a father
who is honest and does what is right."

—Proverbs 20:7, Good News Bible

-Principle-

Scottish novelist Sir Walter Scott first gained fame with his poems of medieval families living on the English-Scottish border. Although Scott was well-known, his son was ignorant of his father's literary fame, loving and admiring him for reasons closer to a boy's heart. Once, the younger Scott was in the company of some older people who were discussing his father's genius. "Yes," put in the boy, "He is usually first to see the rabbit." Apparently Sir Walter Scott spent a good deal of time hunting rabbits with his son. That time together meant more to young Scott than all the novels his father could ever write.

-Baffler-

What percentage of Americans claim they
would marry their spouse again?

Did you know....

In Italy, a whole year's salary is the proper
amount to pay for an engagement ring.

-Ponder-

"My wife and I have a perfect understanding. I don't try to run her life
...and I don't try to run mine!"

—Orben's Current Comedy

-Proverb-

"Better to live on the roof than share the house with a nagging wife."

—Proverbs 25:24, Good News Bible

-Principle-

Shortly after her marriage to Prince Albert, Queen Victoria had a quarrel with her
new husband. Albert walked out of the room and locked himself in his private apart-
ment. Victoria hammered furiously on the door. "Who's there?" called Albert.
"The Queen of England, and she demands to be admitted." There was no
response, and the door remained locked. Victoria hammered again.
"Who's there?" The reply was the same, and still the door remained shut. More
fruitless and furious knocking was followed by a pause. Then there was a gentle tap.
"Who's there?" Albert asked.
"Your wife, Albert," the Queen replied. The Prince opened the door at once.
When all else fails, love opens doors!

-Baffler-

What is the only game in which the ball is always in the possession of the team
on defense, and the offensive team can score without touching the ball?

Did you know....

Stevie Wonder endorses all contracts with his fingerprint.

-Ponder-

"Men grow making decisions and assuming responsibilities for them."

—Bill Marriott, Sr.

-Proverb-

"Do what is right and fair; that pleases the
Lord more than bringing him sacrifices."

—Proverbs 21:3, Good News Bible

-Principle-

In the children's fantasy "Alice in Wonderland," Alice came to a junction in the road that led in different directions and asked the Cheshire Cat for advice.

"Cheshire Puss…would you tell me please, which way I ought to go from here?"

"That depends a good deal on where you want to get to," said the Cat.

"I don't much care where," said Alice.

"Then it doesn't matter which way you go," said the Cat.

That grinning feline had it right, didn't he? If we don't know where we want to go, any fork in the road will do. Making the wrong choice in a children's story may only lead to adventure, but in real life it can lead to disaster.

-Baffler-

What bird is the only one in the world that can swim but cannot fly?

Did you know....

Garlic rubbed on the soles of your feet will be
noticeable on your breath within one hour.

270 – Take the Risk!

-Ponder-

"Take risks. You can't fall off the bottom."

—Barbra Proctor

-Proverb-

"Keep on sowing your seed, for you never know
which will grow—perhaps it all will."

—Ecclesiastes 11:6, The Living Bible

-Principle-

Academy Award-winning actor George Kennedy reached stardom only after he made a difficult decision to change the direction of his life. He was in the army and he had completed fourteen years' service—just six short of retirement—when he decided that what he really wanted was to be an actor.

His family and friends advised him not to do it. "Why give up the security of the army and sure retirement benefits for the insecurity of the actor's world? Why trade the certain for the uncertain? At your age, you're crazy to change careers. How do you know you can ever be an actor?"

"Failure didn't fit into my scheme of things," he said. He ventured to Hollywood, won an Oscar for his role in *Cool Hand Luke* and went on to star in a successful television series. He now earns more from a T.V. commercial than he did in a year in the army.

Without risk, there is no reward!

-Baffler-

What do dog breeders and trainers use for identification?

Did you know....

Approximately 80 billion beverage cans are made in the U.S. annually.

271 – Spending On the Brain

-Ponder-

"Money spent on the brain is never spent in vain."

—Joe L. Griffith

-Proverb-

"Correction and discipline are good for children. If a child has
his own way, he will make his mother ashamed of him."

—Proverbs 29:15, Good News Bible

-Principle-

Two thousand, three hundred years ago, a wise father chose the greatest scholar
of his age to tutor his young son in liberal arts. Aristotle instructed the boy in archi-
tecture, music, literature, politics, and natural sciences.

A few years later, the boy, barely in his twenties, set out to conquer the world. He
did. It took him just eleven years. He became the greatest leader, the most visionary
strategist, and the finest administrator the world has ever known. He became
Alexander the Great.

If we want to prepare leaders for tomorrow, we must give them the proper training today.

-Baffler-

Where and when was the first football stadium built?

Did you know....

Coca Cola was forced out of India in 1977
for refusing to disclose its secret formula.

272 – Stick to the Diet

-Ponder-

"Blessed are those who hunger and thirst, for they are sticking to their diets."

—Troy Ominous

-Proverb-

"When you are full, you will refuse honey, but when you are hungry, even bitter food tastes sweet."

—Proverbs 27:7, Good News Bible

-Principle-

DIET TIPS
1. If no one sees you eat it, it has no calories.
2. If you drink a diet soda with a candy bar, they cancel each other out.
3. When eating with someone else, calories don't count if you both eat the same amount.
4. Food used for medicinal purposes *never* counts, such as hot chocolate, brandy, toast and Sara Lee cheesecake.
5. If you fatten up everyone else around you...you look thinner.
6. Movie-related foods don't count because they are simply part of the entertainment experience and not a part of one's personal fuel, such as Milk Duds, popcorn with butter, Junior Mints, and Bon-Bons.

-Baffler-

What's the name of the famous clock in the tower at the Houses of Parliament in London?

Did you know....

Warning from the Canadian National Park Service: If you eat bananas, your skin will exude an odor which is very attractive to mosquitoes.

-Ponder-

"The secret of business is to know something that nobody else knows."

—Aristotle Onassis

-Proverb-

"Pay attention to what you are taught, and you will be
successful; trust in the Lord and you will be happy."

—Proverbs 16:20, Good News Bible

-Principle-

During the late 1930s, an Eastern Air Transport flight crew member entered the Marriott Hot Shoppe near Hoover Airport and asked for a quart of coffee to go.

The waitress asked, "Driving to New York?"

The young man in uniform said, "No, flying to Atlanta. We'll drink this on the way."

Soon, passengers boarding planes at Hoover began buying sandwiches, milk, coffee, fruit, and candy bars to take with them on their flights. The manager described this business to Bill Marriott. The next day, he called the people at Eastern Air Transport, and airlines have been serving in-flight meals ever since.

Opportunity is everywhere if you have an open mind.

-Baffler-

How did Confederate general Thomas "Stonewall" Jackson die?

Did you know....

Ninety-nine percent of all forms of life that
have existed on earth are now extinct.

-Ponder-

"Creativity is simply imagination with an
action to create the future you want."

—Jason R. Weckworth

-Proverb-

"Wisdom is in every thought of an intelligent man;
fools know nothing of wisdom."

—Proverbs 14:33, Good News Bible

-Principle-

A firm needed a researcher. Applicants were a scientist, an engineer, and an economist. Each was given a stone, a piece of string, and a stopwatch—and was told to determine a certain building's height. The scientist went to the rooftop, tied the stone to the string, lowered it to the ground. Then he swung it, timing each swing with the watch. With this pendulum, he estimated the height at 200 feet, give or take six inches.

The engineer threw away the string, dropped the stone from the roof, timing its fall with the watch. Applying the laws of gravity, he estimated the height at 200 feet, give or take six inches.

The economist, ignoring the string and stone, entered the building but soon returned to report the height at exactly 200 feet. How did he know? He gave the janitor the watch in exchange for the building plans. He got the job.

-Baffler-

Which raft will float fastest down a river…
a heavily loaded one, or an empty one?

Did you know....

Rain is good for wicker lawn furniture. Wicker lasts
longer if it gets wet now and then.

PONDERS & PRINCIPLES

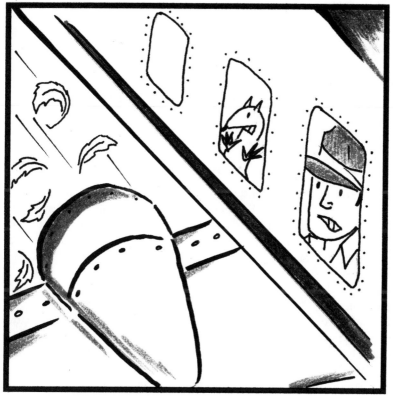

"Eagles may soar, but weasels don't get sucked into jet engines."

-Ponder-

"When we give service to others, sooner or
later it will come back to us tenfold."

—Unknown

-Proverb-

"A generous man will prosper; he who refreshes
others will himself be refreshed."

—Proverbs 11:25, New International Version

-Principle-

In the late nineteenth century, a member of the English parliament went to
Scotland to make a speech. En route, his carriage became stuck in the mud. A
Scottish farm boy came to the rescue with a team of horses that pulled the carriage
loose. Awed by the great statesman, the boy would accept nothing in return for helping him out. The grateful man asked, "Is there nothing you want to be when you
grow up?"

The boy said, "I want to be a doctor."

The man said, "Well, let me help."

True to his word, the Englishman helped make it possible for the boy to attend the
university and graduate as a doctor. A little more than fifty years later, another famous
statesman lay dangerously ill with pneumonia. Winston Churchill was given a new
wonder drug called penicillin, which had been discovered by Alexander Fleming.
Fleming was the young Scottish lad, and the man who helped sponsor his education
was Randolph Churchill...Winston's father.

-Baffler-

What is a shaddock?

Did you know....

Actress Sarah Bernhardt played the role of Juliet, in Shakespeare's
play *Romeo and Juliet*, when she was seventy years old.

276 – Work...it's the only way

-Ponder-

"Everything must degenerate into work if anything is to happen."

—Peter Drucker

-Proverb-

"The best thing we can do is enjoy what we have worked for. There is nothing else we can do. There is no way for us to know what will happen after we die."

—Ecclesiastes 3:22, Good News Bible

-Principle-

Joe Gibbs is the coach of the world champion Washington Redskins. Some call him a coaching genius, others say it's his perseverance. However, Gibbs himself credits his success to eight simple principles:

1. *Work hard*, but leave the job at the office—and take some time off. Otherwise, you'll burn out.
2. *Hire the best people* and delegate a great deal of authority to them.
3. *Set ambitious, but realistic, goals*. Don't attempt to force people to do things they can't do.
4. *Communicate well*. Let people know what you expect. But avoid hype.
5. *Be well-prepared and well-organized*. Pay great attention to details.
6. *Stay focused*. Know exactly what you are going to do and let nothing distract you.
7. *Be Flexible*. Implement major changes in strategy if conditions require them.
8. *Motivate by example and encouragement*, but don't rant and rave. And give people credit when it's due.

-Baffler-

How many times can a woodpecker peck per second?

Did you know....

Rubber bands last longer when refrigerated.

-Ponder-

"If passion drives you, let reason hold the reins."

—Benjamin Franklin

-Proverb-

"People who set traps for others get caught themselves.
People who start landslides get crushed."

—Proverbs 26:27, Good News Bible

-Principle-

A man climbing a steep mountain path saw a portion of the earth dislodge itself and come sliding down the path toward him. In an effort to divert the mudslide, he began to pick up stones and throw them at the slide. However, each stone only became imbedded in the moving projectile and made it larger and more dangerous, until at last it was so large and moving so fast, he was crushed by it. How much better it would have been for the man to get out of the way of the mudslide while it was still small instead of trying to fight it.

When hurtful things are said, it is much easier to just let them pass. Self-defensive responses and actions only feed the flame of anger and cause strife to grow until it is completely out of control.

-Baffler-

What King became President of the United States?

Did you know....

At 90 degrees(F) below zero your breath will
freeze in midair and fall to the ground.

-Ponder-

"The only way to make a man trustworthy is to trust him."

—Henry Steinson

-Proverb-

"Never let go of loyalty and faithfulness. Tie them
around your neck; write them on your heart."

—Proverbs 3:3, Good News Bible

-Principle-

Two departments in a southern textile mill were chosen for a test. New supervisors were put in charge of each department. One supervisor was told that his department had been a "problem" group and that he would have trouble getting them to produce. The other supervisor was told that he was being put in charge of the most efficient, productive department in the mill and that he could expect excellent results with them.

In reality, both departments were just about the same in every respect. Yet, because the first supervisor was deliberately misled, and because he "expected" trouble, he actually got it. Production fell off. By contrast, the second supervisor, expecting the best from his department did, in fact, get superior work.

-Baffler-

When asked to name a color, three out of five
people will say "_____" (what color)?

Did you know....

In ancient China, doctors received their fees only if their patients were kept
healthy. If their health failed, the doctor sometimes paid the patient.

-Ponder-

"Success is measured not so much by the position that one has reached in life as by the *obstacles* which he has overcome while trying to succeed."

—Booker T. Washington

-Proverb-

"Wisdom is more valuable than jewels; nothing you could want can compare with it."

—Proverbs 3:15, Good News Bible

-Principle-

Some of the world's greatest ideas came as the result of a problem.

*Leo Gerstenzang thought of Q-Tips when he saw his wife trying to clean their baby's ears with toothpicks and cotton.

*Ott Diffenbach came up with cellophane soda straws when he twisted the wrapper from a cigarette pack and saw he had created a tube.

*Oli Evinrude got angry when the ice cream in his rowboat melted before he got to his island picnic spot—so he invented the outboard motor.

*Ralph Schnieder decided to form Diners Club one night after he lost his wallet.

*Charles Strite was fuming at the burnt toast in the factory lunchroom where he worked—and thought up the automatic toaster.

-Baffler-

What is that square-topped cap worn
at graduation ceremonies called?

Did you know....

The great horned owl is the only animal that will eat a skunk.

-Ponder-

"Aim at the sun and you may not reach it…but your arrow will fly higher than if aimed at an object on a level with yourself."

—J. Hawes

-Proverb-

"If your goals are good, you will be respected, but if you are looking for trouble, that is what you will get."

—Proverbs 11:27, Good News Bible

-Principle-

Jim Marshall has been described as the most indestructible man ever to play professional football. In a sport where thirty is considered old age, he played defensive end until he was forty-two—starting in 282 consecutive games. He is what famous quarterback, Fran Tarkenton, called "the most amazing athlete I've ever known in any sport."

Jim has had his share of problems. He was once caught in a blizzard in which all his companions died. Twice he suffered from pneumonia. While cleaning a rifle, he suffered a gunshot wound. He's been in several automobile accidents and has undergone surgery.

The secret to Jim Marshall's amazing success is in his two guidelines: Find a direction and dedicate yourself to it, and remember that you can go as far as you want to go if you have a goal.

-Baffler-

When first marketed in 1924, Kleenex was called something else?
What was it called?

Did you know....

23-year-old George Armstrong Custer was the youngest man ever to become a general in the U.S. Army.

-Ponder-

"The world is full of cactus, but we don't have to sit on it."

—Will Foley

-Proverb-

"Robbery always claims the life of the robber—this is what happens to anyone who lives by violence."

—Proverbs 1:19, Good News Bible

-Principle-

A burglar broke into a house late at night. Cautiously, he made his way through the pitch-black rooms. Suddenly he heard a voice in the darkness—"Jesus is watching you." Startled, the burglar stopped for a moment, then hearing nothing more, he continued. After several seconds, again he heard the voice, "Jesus is watching you." The burglar stopped in his tracks, turned on his flashlight and in the corner of the room he saw a parrot sitting on a perch. With his light shining on the parrot, once again the parrot warned, "Jesus is watching you." The now unafraid and even disdainful burglar said sarcastically to the parrot, "Can't you say anything else?" At which point the burglar's flashlight picked up the outline of a ferocious Doberman Pincer standing next to the parrot's perch, as the parrot replied, "Sic 'em, Jesus!"

-Baffler-

At this very moment, what percentage of Americans driving on the highway are speeding?

Did you know....

It took Noah Webster twenty years to put together his first dictionary, *The American*.

-Ponder-

"It is not going out of port, but the coming in that
determines the success of the voyage."

—Henry Ward Beecher

-Proverb-

"The end of something is better than its beginning.
Patience is better than pride."

—Ecclesiastes 7:8, Good News Bible

-Principle-

A business manager who was responsible for hiring and firing personnel said, "I am more interested in what a person has finished, than in what he has started. I want a finisher."

Our country is full of people who start well but fail to finish. This has produced a spirit of quitting that is spreading in our nation. It fills the ranks of the young and old; it exists in every job market; the unemployment lines are filled with its practitioners; school dropouts stand on almost every corner; marriages and homes break up; and half-finished houses, paintings, music lessons, books and a host of other things testify to the non-finisher in our midst.

-Baffler-

What was Smokey the Bear's original name?

Did you know....

Singer Ray Charles dropped his last name, Robinson, in order to avoid confusion with boxing great Sugar Ray Robinson. (whose real name is Walker Smith)

283 – Scratch Like a Chicken

-Ponder-

"Business is never so healthy as when, like a chicken,
it must do a certain amount of scratching for what it gets."

—Henry Ford

-Proverb-

"Everyone tries to gain the favor of important people;
everyone claims the friendship of those who give out favors."

—Proverbs 19:6, Good News Bible

-Principle-

Benjamin Franklin was a master of timing. As a printer's apprentice eager to go into business for himself, he decided to become Philadelphia's leading expert in the latest printing techniques in use in London. Unable to afford the trip himself, he made an audacious suggestion to the governor of Philadelphia—that he should finance Franklin's trip.

Young Ben argued that he would then be able to provide the colony with exceptional printing services...but he was careful to make his case as persuasive as possible by approaching the governor at the most strategic moment—right after he had finished a hearty meal in the colony's best restaurant.

-Baffler-

Which hand does most of the typing?

Did you know....

After Wyatt Earp retired as marshal of Tombstone, Arizona, he moved to San Francisco and became a boxing referee.

-Ponder-

"You can tell when you are on the road to success. It's uphill all the way."

—Paul Harvey

-Proverb-

"The road the righteous travel is like the sunrise, getting
brighter and brighter until daylight has come."

—Proverbs 4:18, Good News Bible

-Principle-

A young man went from newspaper to newspaper trying to sell his cartoons. But each editor coldly and quickly suggested that he had no talent and implied that he might want to consider another line of work. But he persevered, determined to make his dream a reality.

Months and months of rejections came. Finally, he was hired by a minister to draw pictures advertising church events. The young artist was not discouraged by his unusual opportunity.

Working out of a small, mouse-infested shed owned by the church, he struggled to be creative. Ironically, this less-than-ideal working environment stimulated his most famous work. He called his character Mickey Mouse. And, of course, the man was Walt Disney.

-Baffler-

What is the capacity of an average adult's stomach (in quarts)?

Did you know....

The Tokyo Zoo in Japan is closed for two months a year to
give the animals a vacation from the visitors.

-Ponder-

"Lots of faults we think we see in others are simply the ones
we expect to find there, because we have them ourselves."

—Frank A. Clark

-Proverb-

"Everything is pure to those who are themselves pure; but nothing is pure to those who
are defiled and unbelieving, for their minds and consciences have been defiled."

—Titus 1:15, Good News Bible

-Principle-

A traveler nearing a great city asked a man seated by the wayside, "What are the
people in this city like?"

The man responded, "Well, first, tell me what the people were like in the city you
came from?"

"A terrible lot," answered the traveler. "Mean, untrustworthy, detestable in all
respects."

"Ah," said the wise old man, "you will find more of the same in the city ahead."

Scarcely was the first traveler gone when another one stopped and also inquired
about the people in the city before him. Again the old man asked about the people in
the place the traveler had left.

"They were fine people, honest, industrious and generous to a fault. I was sorry to
leave," declared the second traveler.

Responded the wise one: "So you will find the same kind in the city ahead."

Attitude is everything!

-Baffler-

What is the longest running television show?
(Hint: It's been on the air since November 20, 1947)

Did you know....

The federal withholding tax taken out of your paycheck
was enacted as a "temporary" wartime measure!

-Ponder-

"Show me a man with his head held high and I'll show
you a man who can't get used to his bifocals."

—Unknown

-Proverb-

"Wisdom will add years to your life."

—Proverbs 9:11, Good News Bible

-Principle-

When Ty Cobb was seventy years of age a reporter asked the baseball great,
"What do you think you'd hit if you were playing these days?

Cobb, who was a lifetime .367 hitter, said, "About .290, maybe .300."

The reporter said, "That's because of the travel, the night games, the artificial turf
and all the new pitches like the slider, right?"

"No," said Cobb, "it's because I'm seventy."

-Baffler-

The grandfather of Charles Lindbergh changed the family's last name.
What was the family's original last name?

Did you know....

If "beauty is only skin deep," it can't be
more than 3/16 of an inch thick.

287 – Bibles, Schools, and Prisons

-Ponder-

"Why is it that our kids can't read a Bible
in school, but they can in prison?"

—Marshall-Town Times

-Proverb-

"If you have been foolish enough to be arrogant
and plan evil, stop and think!"

—Proverbs 30:32, Good News Bible

-Principle-

What a crazy society we live in! Bibles cannot be handed out in school, but we can dispense condoms. Because we believe in the sanctity of life, we grieve over the possible execution of convicted murderers and drug pushers, while actively promoting the termination of millions of unborn children each year.

Our Bill of Rights makes it illegal to hang a Nativity scene on a government building, but guarantees that repulsive art can be hung in a gallery.

We complain about the lack of ethics and good judgment in government while continuing to re-elect the same people to office. We agonize over the outbreak of AIDS, but then do little to discourage the promiscuous behavior that spreads the disease.

If we don't wake up soon, our American dream will turn into a nightmare!

-Baffler-

What is the oldest known vegetable?

Did you know....

J. C. Penney's middle name was Cash.

-Ponder-

"A horse never runs so fast as when he has other
horses to catch up with and outpace."

—Ovid

-Proverb-

"Correct someone, and afterward he will appreciate it more than flattery."

—Proverbs 28:23, Good News Bible

-Principle-

Charles Schwab had a steel mill where the workmen were not producing their quota of work. One day Schwab asked the mill manager, "How is it that a man as capable as you cannot make this mill turn out what it should?"

"I don't know," the manager replied. "I have coaxed the men, pushed them, but nothing works. They just will not produce."

It happened to be the end of the day, just before the night shift came on. "Give me a piece of chalk," Schwab said. Then, turning to the nearest man: "How many heats did your shift make today?" "Six." Without another word Schwab chalked a big figure "6" on the floor and walked away.

When the night shift came in, they saw the "6" and asked what it meant. "The big boss was in here today," the day men said. "He asked us how many heats we made, and chalked it down on the floor." The next morning Schwab walked through the mill again. The night shift had rubbed out the "6" and had replaced it with a big "7." The day shift went about production determined to show the night shift it was not all that remarkable, and when they quit that night they left behind them an impressive "10." Shortly the mill which had been lagging way behind in production was turning out more work than any other company plant.

"The way to get things done," said Schwab, "is to stimulate competition. I do not mean in the sordid, money-getting way, but in the desire to excel."

-Baffler-

How many credit cards does the average American carry?

Did you know....

Rabbits talk to each other by thumping their feet.

-Ponder-

"Had there been a computer in 1872, it would probably have predicted that there would be so many horse drawn vehicles it would be impossible to clean up all the manure."

—Karl Kapp

-Proverb-

"Never ask, 'Oh, why were things so much better in the old days?' It's not an intelligent question."

—Ecclesiastes 7:10, Good News Bible

-Principle-

The year 1992 marked the 500th anniversary of Columbus' historic voyage. Compare the qualities of this man with the qualities of successful leaders. Consider:

1. *His persistence.* Columbus struggled for years to get an audience with Queen Isabella. Eventually, when he did get to see her and explain his need of money, ships, and supplies, the queen appointed a study committee. For five years the committee studied the proposal and finally returned with their consensus: "The idea is impossible."

Columbus persisted—A second committee was formed and after another year their consensus was the idea was "too expensive."

The lesson is—when faced with resistance, try persistence!

2. *His faith.* Columbus was a devout man of faith. He regularly prayed and sought divine guidance for his life and mission.

3. *His vision.* Columbus lived in a time when the best minds were saying that the earth was flat. However distorted their vision might have been, Columbus' clear vision gave him a vision of what can be done and how.

The lesson—vision is fragile but critical. A vision means seeing things others don't see and acting with courage.

4. *His leadership.* Columbus initiated a two hundred year period of exploration and discovery. Many would follow, but he would lead.

The lesson is—success demands that we define our activities based on a better tomorrow rather than a memory of yesterday.

-Baffler-

Men outnumber women in prison (in the U.S.) by what percentage?

Did you know....

The shell is 12 percent of the weight of the entire egg.

-Ponder-

"Live only for today…and you ruin tomorrow."

—C. Simmons

-Proverb-

"Give to others, and God will give to you. Indeed, you will receive a full measure, a generous helping, poured into your hands—all that you can hold. The measure you use for others is the one that God will use for you."

—Luke 6:38, Good News Bible

-Principle-

An unusual tree grew outside the gates of a desert city in the Middle East. It was an old tree, a landmark as a matter of fact. The tree seemed as though it had been touched by God, for it bore fruit perpetually. Despite its old age, its limbs were constantly laden with fruit. Hundreds of passersby refreshed themselves from the tree, as it never failed to give freely.

But then a greedy merchant purchased the property on which the tree grew. He saw hundreds of travelers taking the fruit of the tree and he built a fence around it. Travelers pled, "Share with us." The merchant quoted in return, "It's my tree, my fruit, bought with my money." And a strange thing happened: The old tree died! What had happened? The law of giving, as predictable as the law of gravity, had expressed its immutable principle: When a tree stops giving, it stops bearing, and it dies.

-Baffler-

What was the average life span of a cave man?

Did you know....

In Waterloo, Nebraska, it's against the law for barbers to eat onions between 7 A.M. and 7 P.M.!

-Ponder-

"Your theology is what you are when the
talking stops, and the action starts!"

—Colin Morris

-Proverb-

"God made us plain and simple, but we have
made ourselves very complicated."

—Ecclesiastes 7:29, Good News Bible

-Principle-

Ours is a mixed up society. We confuse what is real and lasting with what is fading and temporary. We look at treasure and call it trash. We look at trash and call it treasure. How so? To many, a pregnancy means inconvenience, loss of income, and extra expenses. When you realize a child is a treasure, then all the extra effort and expense is worth it.

On the other hand, when pregnancy is seen as an inconvenience, an expense, perhaps an embarrassment or a hassle, then that precious treasure is seen as only a burden.

The truth is, everyone has the opportunity to make a difference by taking a stand for what is right and moral…and worth the cause!

-Baffler-

The U.S.A.'s gold is kept at Ft. Knox, but do you
know where the country's silver is kept?

Did you know....

A termite can live thirty years.

-Ponder-

"Yesterday is a canceled check; tomorrow is a promissory note;
today is the only cash you have—so spend it wisely."

—Kay Lyons

-Proverb-

"Be grateful for every year you live. No matter how long you live, remember that
you will be dead much longer. There is nothing at all to look forward to."

—Ecclesiastes 11:8, Good News Bible

-Principle-

It has been said that some persons do not know what is happening; a few wish things would happen; some hinder things from happening; and a few make things happen. Which category are you in?

Helen Keller said: "I long to accomplish a great and noble task, but it is my chief duty to accomplish tasks as though they were great and noble. The world is moved along, not only by the mighty shoves of its heroes, but also by the aggregate of the tiny pushes of each honest worker."

These words by a great woman should encourage us to want to make things happen. The things that we make happen do not have to be great in the sight of people before they are important.

-Baffler-

In 1818, Congress reduced the number of
stripes on the U.S. Flag to (what number)?

Did you know....

The average office chair on wheels travels about eight miles per year.

-Ponder-

"A people that values its privileges above its principles soon loses both."

—Dwight D. Eisenhower

-Proverb-

"Do not abandon wisdom, and she will keep you safe."

—Proverbs 4:6, Good News Bible

-Principle-

Atop the hill in Washington D. C. stands the Capitol Building of the United States of America. The cornerstone was laid in 1793, but the crowning touch, the "Freedom Lady," was not raised into place until 1863. This stately statue, twenty feet tall, stands proudly atop the dome of the Capitol Building. Her face is framed by a crest of stars, a shield of stars and stripes in her left hand.

Sculptured in Rome, "The Lady" was brought to America aboard a sailing ship. During the trip across the Atlantic Ocean, a fierce storm developed. The captain ordered cargo thrown overboard to lighten the load. The sailors wanted to throw the heavy statue overboard, but the captain refused, shouting above the wind, "No! Never! We'll flounder before we throw 'Freedom' away!"

"Freedom" was saved. The statue was raised into place above the capitol, and there she stands today, because one man stood for "Freedom."

Regardless of the cost, some things cannot be thrown away. They must be preserved.

-Baffler-

What are you afraid of if you have "Hippophobia?"

Did you know....

Your hearing is not as sharp on a full stomach.

-Ponder-

"Confidence is the greatest asset of any enterprise—
nothing useful can survive without it."

—Albert Schweitzer

-Proverb-

"Her husband puts confidence in her, and he will never be poor."

—Proverbs 31:11, Good News Bible

-Principle-

When Nathaniel Hawthorne, a heartbroken man, went home to tell his wife that he had been fired from his job and confessed that he was a failure, she surprised him with an exclamation of joy.

She said triumphantly, "Now, you can write your book!"

He replied with a sagging confidence, "Yes, and what shall we live on while I am writing it?"

To his amazement, she opened a drawer and pulled out a substantial amount of money.

He exclaimed, "Where on earth did you get that?"

She answered, "I have always known that you were a man of genius. I knew that someday you would write a masterpiece. Every week out of the money you have given me for housekeeping, I have saved something; here is enough to last us for the whole year."

From her trust and confidence, Hawthorne was encouraged to write one of the greatest novels of American Literature—*The Scarlet Letter*.

-Baffler-

When trying out a new pen, what does the average person write?

Did you know....

The pound cake's name comes from the
pound of butter used to make it.

295 – Satisfaction at the End of the Day

-Ponder-

"Look at a day when you are supremely satisfied at the end.
It's not a day when you lounge around doing nothing.
It's when you've had everything to do, and you've done it!"

—Margaret Thatcher

-Proverb-

"Honest people will lead a full and happy life. But if you are
in a hurry to get rich, you are going to be punished."

—Proverbs 28:20, Good News Bible

-Principle-

Seventeen Secrets To Success
1. Keep your temper to yourself.
2. Give your enthusiasm to everybody.
3. Be yourself, forget yourself, become genuinely interested in the other person.
4. Be fair, honest, friendly—and you'll be admired and liked.
5. Make other people feel important.
6. Count your assets, and stamp out self-pity.
7. Meet people at their own level.
8. Put your smile power to work.
9. Keep moving.
10. Keep trying.
11. Give the gift of heart.
12. Get off to a good start in anything you do.
13. Forgive yourself if you fail.
14. Be lavish with kindness.
15. Overwhelm people with your charm, not your power.
16. Keep your promises.
17. Be an optimist.

-Baffler-

How many tiles are there in the game of Scrabble? (How many of them are blank?)

Did you know....

It is said glass is the only known substance that
gets stronger the longer it stays under water.

-Ponder-

"You have to face the music before you can lead the band."

—Barbra Johnson

-Proverb-

"He (God) provides help and protection for righteous, honest men. He protects those who treat others fairly, and guards those who are devoted to him."

—Proverbs 2:7-8, Good News Bible

-Principle-

The pages of history are filled with stories of undaunted men and women who triumphed over disabilities and adversities to demonstrate victorious spirits.

- Bury him in the snows of Valley Forge, and you have a George Washington.
- Raise him in abject poverty, and you have an Abraham Lincoln.
- Deafen a genius composer, and you have a Ludwig van Beethoven.
- Have him born of parents who survived a Nazi concentration camp, paralyze him from the waist down when he was four, and you have an incomparable concert violinist, Itzhak Perlman.
- Call him a slow learner, retarded, and write him off as uneducated, and you have an Albert Einstein.

Each one of these great men have experienced first the trial and then the triumph.

-Baffler-

In a package of M&Ms, what color will you find the most of? _____

Did you know....

No matter how low or high it flies, an airplane's
shadow appears the same size.

-Ponder-

"If all the financial experts in this country were laid
end to end...they'd still point in all directions."

—Sam Ewing

-Proverb-

"Unreliable messengers cause trouble, but those who can be trusted bring peace."

—Proverbs 13:17, Good News Bible

-Principle-

There was a man who lived by the side of the road and sold hot dogs. He was hard of hearing, so he had no radio. He had trouble with his eyes, so he read no newspapers. But he sold good hot dogs.

He stood at the side of the road and cried: "Buy a hot dog, mister?" and people bought. He increased his meat and bun orders. He bought a bigger stove to take care of his trade. He finally got his son home from college to help him out. Then something happened.

The son said, "Father, haven't you been listening to the radio? Haven't you been reading the newspapers? The European situation is terrible. The domestic situation is worse." Whereupon the father thought, "Well, my son's been to college, he reads the papers and he listens to the radio, and he ought to know." So the father cut down his meat and bun orders, took down his signs, and no longer bothered to stand out on the highway to sell his hot dogs. And his hot dog sales fell almost overnight.

The father said to the son, "You're right, son, we certainly are in the middle of a great recession."

-Baffler-

Right after World War II, Yale had the best baseball team in the East.
Who was the team's starting first baseman?

Did you know....

If you have just come down with a cold, the National Health Foundation
says you should wait at least six days before kissing someone.

-Ponder-

"Mistakes are easy, mistakes are inevitable, but there is no
mistake so great as the mistake of not going on."

—William Blake

-Proverb-

"When things are going well for you, be glad, and when trouble
comes, just remember: God sends both happiness and trouble;
you never know what is going to happen next."

—Ecclesiastes 7:14, Good News Bible

-Principle-

Success is failure overcome by persistence.

Henry Ford failed and went broke five times before he finally succeeded.

Eighteen publishers turned down Richard Bach's 10,000-word story about a "soaring" seagull, *Jonathan Livingston Seagull*, before Macmillan finally published it in 1970. By 1975, it had sold more than 7 million copies in the United States alone.

Richard Hooker worked for seven years on his humorous war novel, M*A*S*H, only to have it rejected by 21 publishers before Morrow decided to publish it. It became a runaway best-seller, spawning a blockbusting movie and a highly successful television series.

Babe Ruth, considered by sports historians to be the greatest athlete of all time and famous for setting the home-run record, also holds the record for strikeouts.

Winston Churchill did not become prime minister of England until he was 62, and then only after a lifetime of defeats and setbacks. His greatest contributions came when he was a senior citizen.

-Baffler-

"Wanted: Young, skinny, wiry fellows not over 18. Must be expert riders, willing to risk
death daily. Orphans preferred. Wages $25.00 a week.

—An advertisement for what job?

Did you know....

In New York City, the two Fridays before Christmas
are the heaviest traffic days of the year.

-Ponder-

"Giving is the most significant thing a man does."

—T. K. Thompson

-Proverb-

"Be generous and share your food with the poor.
You will be blessed for it."

—Proverbs 22:9, Good News Bible

-Principle-

About 95% of American families exchange Christmas cards—usually 60 to 70 cards per family. A staggering four billion cards are mailed during the holiday season. How did all of this get started?

Museum director Henry Cole, during the mid-19th century, used to write short notes to his friends at Christmas, wishing them a joyful holiday season. In 1843, he had no time to write and asked his artist friend John Horsely to design a printed greeting card. Inadvertently, he had invented the Christmas card.

-Baffler-

Is there *really* a Santa Claus?

Did you know....

To find out how many lights your Christmas tree needs, multiply the tree height times the tree width times three.

-Ponder-

"Peace is not something that just happens—it is created—it is constructed."

—Pope Paul VI

-Proverb-

"Better to eat a dry crust of bread with peace of mind
than have a banquet in a house full of trouble."

—Proverbs 17:l, Good News Bible

-Principle-

Christmas was first celebrated in the year 98, but it was forty years later before it was officially adopted as a Christian festival: nor was it until the fifth century that the day of its celebration became permanently fixed on the 25th of December. Up to that time it had been irregularly observed at various times of the year—in December, in April, and in May, but most frequently in January.

It is a significant fact that no great battles were fought on Christmas Day. They have occurred on the 24th and the 26th of December, but the anniversary of the advent of Peace on Earth has been observed by a cessation of hostilities.

-Baffler-

Who was the United States Ambassador to Mexico in 1828?
(You've probably referred to him, if only indirectly,
hundreds of times, especially during the holidays.)

Did you know....

You should receive at least two Christmas cards for every three
you mail out. If you don't, you are sending cards to the wrong people.

A *final challenging thought...*

"There are two ways of being happy: We may either diminish our wants or augment our means...either will do...the result is the same; and it is for each one of you to decide for yourself, and do that which happens to be the easiest.

If you are idle or sick or poor, however hard it may be to diminish your wants, it will be harder to augment your means.

If you are active or prosperous or young or in good health, it may be easier for you to augment your means than to diminish your wants.

But if you are wise, you will do both at the same time, young or old, rich or poor, sick or well: and if you are very wise you will do both in such a way as to augment the general happiness of society."

—Benjamin Franklin

PONDERS & PRINCIPLES

"A successful man is one who can lay a firm foundation with the bricks others throw at him."
— David Brinkley

Answers to Bafflers

1   Tin foil is shiny on one side because of the contact with the roller when its made. That's the only reason! Both sides retain heat equally.

2   A fly lands on a ceiling by raising the forelegs above its head, making contact with the ceiling, then brings its hind legs forward up to the ceiling…thus he lands with a flip!

3   The tooth fairy left an average of $.25 in 1950…and $1.00 in 1989. The $.25 left in 1950 was much more valuable!

4   Charlie was the second person!

5   The speed limit starts at the location of the sign!

6   Ranchers hang old boots on fence posts to keep the coyotes from killing their livestock. (Human scent keeps them away.)

7   Firehouses have Dalmatians because they (the dogs) got along well with the horses—which originally drew the water wagons. The dogs would run in front of the horses and clear the way.

8   A timber doodle is a bird.

9   The first of your five senses to develop is your smell!

10 Sherlock Holmes kept his pipe tobacco in the toe of his slipper.

11 The male praying mantis loses his head after mating…the female eats it! (What a price to pay for a night out on the town!)

12 The part of our body most commonly bitten by insects is the foot!

13 It takes seven minutes for the typical person to fall asleep.

14 The most hazardous season is summer.

15 The most talked about subject in the world is ourselves!

16 Only 1% of the earth's total water supply is drinkable.

17 The traditional drink in the Indy 500 Winners' Circle is milk!

18 The tomato is the fruit known as the "love apple."

19 The early Romans used "urine" from Portugal for mouthwash. (It was the ammonia that did the job!)

20 *Heartbreak Hotel* was Elvis Presley's first number one hit.

21 The dye for meat stamps in the supermarkets is made from grape juice.

22 The ice cap in the Antarctica is 2 miles thick and it contains 90% of the earth's fresh water.

23 A hill becomes a mountain when it's over 1,000' in height.

24 In 1985 in the city of New York, 311 people were bitten by rats, but there were 511 people bitten by people!

25 We cover our mouth when yawning because of tradition! In the ancient times it was believed that upon a giant exhalation one would lose his soul and life force, so the mouth was covered to keep it in.

26 The "cottage" in cottage cheese is a reference to where it was made. (It was originally made in cottages centuries ago.)

27 20% of the cost of supermarket food does to the packages that they come in.

28 Lightening strikes the earth 100 times a minute. During a 24-hour period lightening will strike the earth 144,000 times!

29 Sam Wilson, a meat packer (known by his employees as Uncle Sam), had a contract to

Answers to Bafflers

sell meat to the U. S. Army during the war of 1812. When the Army personnel were asked where they got the barrels of beef, they replied, "from Uncle Sam." After that the slogan "Uncle Sam" was adopted for the U. S. Government.

30 Julius Caesar always wore a laurel wreath on his head because he was bald.

31 The average person swallows 295 times during dinner.

32 50% of the books in the world are written in English.

33 People look up while thinking for two reasons: —Divine inspiration. —To help form a visual image of what they are thinking about.

34 38% of the people in America clean out their belly buttons daily.

35 "G.I." stands for "Government Issue" and thus became the nickname for U. S. service-men.

36 A group of owls is called a "clutch" and there are six in a group.

37 Four out of five people eat corn on the cob in a circle.

38 The most common street name in America is 2nd St.

39 66% of the runners think about sex while running. 8% of couples think of running while having sex.

40 The parachute was invented in 1783 to help people escape from high buildings in case of fire.

41 The "zip" in zip code stands for "zoning improvement plan."

42 To "beat the band" referred to the aim of arriving at a parade site before the band passed by.

43 The word "turnpike" originated in the days when toll collectors were armed with pikes (they used these poles with sharp iron heads to prevent travelers who refused to pay from using the road).

44 The most despised household task is washing the dishes!

45 The line in the song *Yankee Doodle* about the feather called "macaroni" refers to the Macaroni Club—a mid-18th century English Social Club of young men who wanted to bring the influence of the land to bear on their home country. (The line was intended to discredit American Revolutionaries.)

46 The number one fear of Americans is speaking before a group.

47 According to ancient legend, it was thought that the swan, silent throughout its life, sang aloud in its final minutes—thus we adopted the *Swan Song* as a farewell.

48 Public kissing is illegal in Indiana, and in Cedar Rapids, Iowa it is a crime to kiss a stranger.

49 In the heat of the day Roman soldiers wore scarves soaked in water and wrapped around the neck to cool down the body. This was the introduction of the first necktie in the 1st Century B.C.

50 The first novel ever written on a typewriter was *The Adventures of Tom Sawyer* by Mark Twain.

51 The first minimum wage set in the United States in 1938 was $.25 per hour.

52 "O.K." stands for an article in the *New York New Era*, March 23, 1884, which carried a story about the Democratic O.K. Club (initials standing for Old Kinderhook), a politi-cal organization supporting the re-election of President Martin VanBuren. During the

election "O.K." became a favorite rallying cry.

53 A person drinks about 16,000 gallons of water in a lifetime.

54 7% of the dog owners in the U.S. throw birthday parties for their dogs and invite other dogs to attend.

55 "K" in "K" ration represents the first letter of the last name of the products developer, Ancel Keys (a physiologist from Minnesota) who developed the portions of food for soldiers in World War II.

56 (7-Up) The 7 stands for the soft drink's original 7-ounce bottle, and the "Up" for the bubbles of carbonation. (It was developed in 1929 by businessman Charles L. Grigg and originally called "Biblabel Lithiated Lemon Lime Soda.")

57 Hamburger is called "hamburger" because it was named after the city where it was popularized—Hamburg, Germany.

58 Years ago there wasn't such a thing as a hot water faucet, only cold water and the faucets were placed on the right (because most people are right-handed). When hot water plumbing was introduced it made sense to keep the cold faucet on the right and place the hot faucet on the left.

59 "Watch your P's and Q's" is an English term that the wives used to tell their husbands when they were going to the pubs—"watch your pints and quarts" and don't drink too much!

60 "The apple cart" referred to is the human body. Ever since Adam was banished from Eden, man has carried the apple (original sin) within himself and so "to upset a man's apple cart" is to upset not only what he is trying to do, but the man himself.

61 The umbrella originated in Mesopotamia 3,400 years ago as an extension of the fan—for protection against the sun. (The word "umbrella" is derived from the Latin "umbra" meaning shade.)

62 The last time California went through an entire day without a traffic fatality was March 11, 1968.

63 Blue is associated with baby boys—in ancient times it was believed that evil spirits lingered over nurseries and the blue color possessed the capability to combat evil (blue associated with the sky/heaven was the most powerful color). Evil spirits weren't considered threats to girls...centuries later girls were associated with pink (since European legend professed girls were born inside of pink roses).

64 16% of the men and 41% of the women pull apart their "Oreo" cookies before they bite!

65 Twice as many women as men clean out their belly buttons daily!

66 91% of the people in America save their leftover food. (14% keep leftovers longer than a week...and 2% don't know how old their leftovers are!)

67 Dorothy's last name in the *Wizard of Oz* was Gale!

68 The typical citizen eats 80% of their daily food intake after 6:00 P.M.!

69 "007" for James Bond represented the number of seconds left until the atomic bomb was set to explode in Fort Knox when Bond shut it off in the movie *Goldfinger*.

70 The seven colors which make up the rainbow are: Red, Orange, Yellow, Green, Blue, Indigo, and Violet.

71 The most common time of the day to have a fatal heart attack is 10:00 A.M.

Answers to Bafflers

72 The least common time of the day to have a fatal heart attack is 4:00 A.M.
73 "Piggy Banks—"The name comes from a ceramic material called "Pygg" that was once used to make inexpensive decorative objects, and not because the banks were first made in the shape of pigs!
74 The average age at which most people start smoking is 13!
75 68% of the men are pleased with their appearance in the nude (compared with 22% of the women who like the way they themselves look in the nude).
76 Grooms are an average of five years older than their brides.
77 Only 25 of the 82,230 nose jobs performed in 1986 were on men!
78 "Tips" stands for "To Insure Proper Service."
79 Experts believe that the counting rhyme "Eena, Meena, Mina, Mo" used in games to select who is "it," may have originally come from an incantation used by ancient pagans in choosing human sacrifices.
80 A catfish can "taste" its prey through sense organs in its tail.
81 The state in the United States which is the world's largest produce of toothpicks is Maine.
82 You can tell a glowworm's sex by the frequency of its light flashes. Male glowworms flash every 5.8 seconds, females every 2.1 seconds.
83 In South Africa Japanese people are considered Caucasian.
84 The sulphur-bottom whale is the largest animal living today *and* the largest animal that has ever lived on the earth (they can weight over 150 tons!).
85 The most common first-name in the world is...Mohammed.
86 The most common last-name in the world is...Chan.
87 The largest organ in the human body is—the skin!
88 The smallest trees in the world are dwarf willows. They grow only two inches high on the tundra of Greenland.
89 Jai Alai, polo, and field hockey...Left-handed play is illegal in these sports because it is considered too dangerous.
90 Noel Coward, Thomas Edison, Sean O'Casey, Charles Dickens, and Mark Twain have one thing in common—none finished grade school!
91 You can tell whether someone is right or left handed by looking at the base of the nail on the thumb. On their dominant hand, the nail of the thumb is usually wider and more squared off.
92 The modern 7-inch-long lead pencil can draw a line 35 miles in length and it can write an average of 45,000 words.
93 Of the 814 Americans who enlist in the armed forces on an average day, 99 of them are women.
94 The muscles of the eye get the greatest day-to-day workout, moving some 100,000 times in any 24-hours period.
95 According to surveys, the five most universal dreams, in order of frequency, are: falling—being pursued or attacked—trying to perform a task but repeatedly failing—work and school activities—sexual experiences
96 Tests reveal that women possess slightly keener senses than men. Women display more

accuracy at identifying odors and tastes; better perception of high sound frequencies; greater sensitivity to touch; and sharper vision with a far lower incidence of color blindness than men.

97   Julius Caesar, Hannibal, and Napoleon were born with a tooth already showing. Only 1 in 2,000 infants are born with this rare occurrence.

98   The body's blood vessels would encircle the earth more than two times, if laid end-to-end.

99   The cartilage in the nose continues to grow as we age. Between the ages of 30 and 70, the nose grows a half-inch wider and longer. (The earlobes also grow a quarter-inch longer.)

100   There are approximately 10 reported UFO sightings each day.

101   Since ten gallons of gasoline will expand by nearly a quart with a temperature increase of 30 degrees F, it is most economical to fill a gas tank early in the morning.

102   A study by the National Institute on Aging found that professional singers, particularly opera singers, have the healthiest lungs in America and outlive the rest of the population by as much as 20 years.

103   Boxing is the one sport in which neither the spectators nor the participants know the score until the contest ends.

104   According to AT&T figures, the pay phone near the ticket office at the Greyhound Bus station in Downtown Chicago is the most heavily used pay phone in the U.S. An average of 270 calls are made on it a day.

105   The author of the poem *Mary Had a Little Lamb* was Sarah Hale, the woman who campaigned for the restoration of Thanksgiving as a national holiday.

106   According to a study by London's Clinical Research Center, 70 percent of the dust in your house consists of shed human skin.

107   Skim milk is heavier than whole milk or cream. (Did you forget that cream floats on top of milk?)

108   In 1919, at age 72, the already world famous Alexander Graham Bell set a world water speed record in the hydrofoil boat he created and piloted.

109   Actuarial tables show that a person in this country has the greatest chance of staying alive at nine, ten and eleven years old than any other age. These are the years with the lowest mortality rates. After eleven, it's all downhill.

110   Marie Curie, co-discoverer of radium, was the first person known to have died of radiation poisoning. Until Curie's death it was not known that radiation was dangerous.

111   Every dog except the Chow has a pink tongue: The Chow's tongue is jet black.

112   Hawaii and Arizona are the only states that have not adopted Daylight Savings Time.

113   You can tell if your water is hard or soft by looking at your ice cubes. Hard-water cubes will have a white spot in the center where minerals congregate; soft-water cubes are uniformly cloudy.

114   The Chevy Nova was not popular in Mexico because the Spanish word "No va" means "no go!"

115   You can't get a good cup of tea on the top of Mount Everest because water boils at only 158 degrees F, and this temperature is not nearly high enough to extract the best possible

flavor from tea leaves. The summit of Everest is nearly 30,000 ft high, and the atmospheric pressure there is less than one-third of the sea-level pressure, causing the boiling point of water to fall.

116   The Eiffel Tower (985 ft) is taller than the Washington Monument (555 ft).

117   The largest McDonald's in the world opened in Moscow in January, 1990.

118   From 1960 to 1990, the U. S. Post Office has raised the cost of a first-class stamp 7 times, from 4 cents to 25 cents.

119   The Treasury building is pictured on the back of the $10 bill.

120   Gillikin Country, Munchkin Country, Quadling Country, and Winkie Country can all be found in the fictional Land of Oz.

121   Plymouth rock weighs 4 tons and is about 14 feet wide and 6 feet long.

122   A "Spermologer" is a collector of trivial or unusual data.

123   Even though George Washington was called "the Father of Our Country," he had no children of his own.

124   Sleeping Beauty slept for 100 years before the handsome prince came to awaken her.

125   The vegetables used to make V-8 juice are beets, carrots, spinach, tomatoes, celery, lettuce, parsley, and watercress. Cabbage is not used.

126   "EFO's" are stamps with "errors, freaks, oddities," sometimes quite valuable.

127   The dot over the letter "i" is called a "tittle."

128   Signing "X"s for kisses began as a medieval tradition. In the Middle Ages, people who could not sign their names used an "X" instead and kissed the mark to affirm their sincerity. Eventually the kiss and the "X" became synonymous.

129   According to Dr. Whitney Smith, executive director of the Flag Research Center in Winchester, Massachusetts, the ball on top of a flagpole is purely decorative.

130   Steve Allen hosted the Tonight Show when it began in 1954.

131   According the *Harper's Index Book*, "Rover" is the most popular name for a dog in the U.S.

132   George Bush had the highest overall approval rating (76%) after one year in office over Jimmy Carter, Richard Nixon, and Ronald Reagan. John Kennedy had the best rating ever, 79%.

133   An investigation revealed that the cause of the *Mariner I* space probe failure was a single minus sign mistakenly omitted from the instructions punched into the rocket's computer.

134   Believe it or not, the only town in the US. named "Beach" is in land-locked North Dakota.

135   Houses in Tokyo are numbered according to the order in which building permits were issued, and not by location or numerical sequence. That is why finding an address in Tokyo is so difficult.

136   The *Guinness Book of World Records* got into itself in 1974 because it had set a record as the fastest-selling book in the world.

137   Do toilet seat covers protect you from anything except the thought of exposing your bare backside to the same surface area occupied by heaven knows who before you? Dr. J. Byron Gathright, Jr., the secretary of the American Society of Colon and Rectal Surgeons, confirmed what other doctors have said: "There is no scientific evidence of disease transmission from toilet seats."

Answers to Bafflers

138 The term "fall guy" means someone who takes the blame. The first people to "fall" were Adam and Eve, who fell from grace and were booted out of Eden. In England, this gave rise to the term "take a fall," meaning "to be arrested," often in conjunction with taking the rap for someone else. Someone who took the fall was known as a "fall guy."

139 Chanel No. 5 is the most popular perfume in the world.

140 Pirates thought that wearing an earring in a pierced ear improved their eyesight.

141 Elephant trunks can hold up to one and one-half gallons of liquid.

142 Your eyes and nose are the warmest parts of your body.

143 Americans' two most favorite foods are steak and potatoes.

144 20% of American women think their feet are too big.

145 On the average, a working woman spends 50 minutes a day cooking, and a working man spends 8 minutes a day cooking.

146 Most people think the Baby Ruth candy bar was inspired by baseball's Babe Ruth. Not true. Originally called Kandy Kake, it was renamed in the 1920's to honor a contemporary celebrity—ex-President Grover Cleveland's daughter, Ruth, the first child born in the White House. She was known to the public as "Baby Ruth" despite the fact she was in her late twenties.

147 We will have an average of 1,500 dreams every year.

148 The coldest place in the world is Eismitte, Greenland. The lowest recorded temperature was -85 degrees Fahrenheit.

149 The saying "raining cats and dogs" means torrential rain. In the days before garbage collection, people tossed their trash in the gutter—including deceased house pets. When it rained really hard, the garbage, including the bodies of dead cats and dogs, went floating down the street. So there had to be a lot of water for it to "rain cats and dogs."

150 California has had the most Miss Americas since the pageant began in 1921.

151 The giant squid has the largest eyes on earth, as big as pie plates.

152 Nearly half the American population never reads books!

153 The Guppy was named after R. J. Lechmere Guppy, who was a clergyman living in Trinidad.

154 When Frank Epperson found the frozen stuff he had accidentally left on his back porch the night before, he had created the first "Epsicle," later renamed "Popsicle." It was patented in 1923.

155 A *box without hinges, key or lid. Yet golden treasure inside is hid.* The answer to this riddle by J. R. R. Tolkien is an "Egg."

156 The term "Peeping Tom," referring to someone who looks in the windows of people's homes, is from the legend of Lady Godiva, who rode naked through the streets of Coventry in order to get her husband to reduce taxes. She requested that the citizens stay inside and close their shutters while she rode. Everyone did except the town tailor, Tom, who peeped through the shutters.

157 A man is likely to shave off a pound of whiskers in the course of a decade.

158 A hard rain falls at the rate of about 20 m.p.h.

159 The average person laughs 15 times a day.

160 The hands of a clock cross 12 times, including at noon and midnight.

161 You are more likely to catch a person's cold from shaking their hand than from their sneezes.

162 Your fingers and toes are the coldest parts of your body.

163 The Three Musketeers candy bars were originally made of three separate nougat sections: vanilla, chocolate and strawberry. Eventually, the strawberry and vanilla nougat sections were eliminated, leaving only chocolate nougat in each Three Musketeers bar.

164 When you are in Panama, you can see the sun rise on the Pacific and set on the Atlantic.

165 There were six dogs that played Lassie in the movies and TV series, and they were ALL males, even though Lassie was supposed to be a female.

166 *Turn-On*, was promoted by ABC as "the second coming of *Laugh-In*, a visual, comedic, sensory assault." It premiered on February 5, 1969, and it was so bad that the next day phone calls poured in from ABC affiliates all over the U.S. saying they refused to ever carry the show again. The network canceled it immediately, making it the shortest-lived primetime series in TV history.

167 *Donald Duck* comics were banned from libraries in Finland because he doesn't wear pants!

168 Michael Landon played the title role of *I Was a Teenage Werewolf* in 1957.

169 Texas is the most expensive place in the U.S. to get a divorce, and Idaho is the cheapest.

170 Over a billion people have seen *The Wizard of Oz*, the most-watched film in history.

171 According to *Playboy* magazine, 99% of cat and dog owners talk to their pets.

172 Of course money is the #1 thing that U.S. families fight about. 2nd place is kids and 3rd place, chores.

173 50% of Americans believe in UFO's.

174 "Paying through the nose" comes from Ireland. In the ninth-century they took a census (by counting noses) and levied oppressive taxes on their victims, forcing them to pay by threatening to have their noses actually slit. Paying the tax was "paying through the nose."

175 "Pantophobia" is the fear of everything!

176 39 percent of Americans think that winning a lottery is the best way to get rich.

177 More Hollywood films have been made about boxing than about any other sport.

178 There is no sun at the North Pole for 186 days of each year.

179 People live the longest in Japan. Women live 74.2 years and men live 79.7 years.

180 Julius Caesar's autograph is worth 2 million dollars.

181 An ice cream sundae will warm you more than hot chocolate because it has more calories.

182 Only three women have been commemorated by appearing on U.S. currency: Martha Washington, 1886, 1891, and 1896 $1 silver certificate; Pocahontas, 1875 $20 bill; and women's suffrage leader Susan B. Anthony, on the 1979 $1 coin.

183 The Sphinx is the only one of the Seven Wonders of the Ancient World that still exists.

184 The American slogan, "In God We Trust" was adopted in 1956.

185 The glue on postage stamps is a mixture of cassava (the source of tapioca) and corn . . . starchy, but nutritious.

186 It is said that the theme of Michael Jackson's *Beat It* is about two gangs coming together to rumble, just as is the theme for the 1961 filmed musical *West Side Story*. The first two words spoken in the film are "Beat it!"

187 Tomatoes are grown in American backyards more than another other fruit or vegetable.

188 A Ranarium is a "frog farm."

189 The average American uses 75 to 100 gallons of water every day!

190 The last Dodo Bird died in 1681.

191 Vice-President Dan Quayle's favorite movie is *Ferris Bueller's Day Off.*

192 Of the 153 movies John Wayne made, in only 11 of them was he NOT the star.

193 Ben Franklin is pictured on the $100, which is the highest denomination printed in the last 45 years. In fact, everything over $100 has been officially "retired" from circulation for 30 years.

194 Spencer Tracy was the first to win two consecutive Academy Awards for best actor in 1937 for *Captains Courageous* and 1938 for *Boys' Town.*

195 Many scholars maintain that "Mother Goose" was Elizabeth Foster Goose. In 1692, when she was 27, she married a widower with 10 children. One of her son-in-laws was a print-er and in 1719, he published a collection of her rhymes *Songs for the Nursery, or Mother Goose's Melodies.*

196 Pollsters say that 40% of dog and cat owners carry pictures of their pets in their wallets.

197 Scientists can tell your sex, age, and race from one strand of your hair.

198 60% of the cost of food is in transporting it.

199 The first gold record ever awarded went to Glenn Miller for *Chattanooga Choo-choo.*

200 The Western hero most often portrayed in films is Buffalo Bill. Second place goes to Billy the Kid.

201 In 1912 a candymaker named Clarence Crane decided to make a mint in the U.S. Until then, most mints were imported from Europe. He had the candy manufactured by a pill-maker—who discovered that his machinery would only work if it punched a hole in the middle of each candy. So Crane cleverly called the mints LifeSavers.

202 The only man-made structure you can see from outer space is the Great Wall of China.

203 The life expectancy of a dollar bill is 18 months.

204 Responsibility for an overloaded elevator rests with the building owner.

205 Upon his death, Leonardo da Vinci left notes with designs for the well digger, parachute, life jacket, helicopter, submarine, and horseless carriage, just to name a few.

206 A university study has concluded that it must be fun to be stupid. According to their findings, stupid people laugh far more than smart people; the amount of laughter is in inverse proportion to a person's intelligence.

207 The first vending machine, invented in the 1st Century B.C. by the Greek scientist, Hero, dispensed "Holy Water."

208 The average American travels 9.2 miles to work and it takes 20.4 minutes to get there.

209 The windiest city isn't Chicago, but Great Falls, Montana (with an average wind speed of 13.1 m.p.h.).

210 When you sail from the Atlantic to the Pacific through the Panama Canal you are trav-eling in an easterly direction. The canal is located at a curve in the Isthmus of Panama and the Atlantic entrance is farther west than the Pacific entrance.

211 Bulls do not charge because a cape is red. They charge because of the movement of the cape. It does not have to be red or any other bright color.

Answers to Bafflers

212 The average aircraft carrier can travel a distance of 6 inches on a gallon of fuel.

213 Avoid going to the hospital in June because that's when all the new interns start work!

214 A cubit was a unit of measurement based on a man's forearm (from the elbow to the tip of the middle finger, about 20 inches). So, Noah's ark was 500 feet long, 83 feet wide and 50 feet high. That's a big ship!

215 Of the 1,932 children abducted each day in America, only 14 are abducted by strangers!

216 Each social security number remains as unique as the individual it was first given to. When someone dies the number is retired. The first number was issued in 1936 with a capacity for one billion possible combinations. A little more than one-third of these combinations have been used since first issued over 50 years ago.

217 In the old days, barbers not only cut hair, but they performed surgery as well. When they finished, the towels used to soak up excess blood were hung outside to dry on a pole. As the wind dried them, they wrapped around the pole to make a design, so to speak, of red and white stripes. That's why we have striped barber poles today.

218 Nine calories are used up in a single kiss.

219 A person who kisses 3 times a day (using 9 calories a kiss), will lose 2-8 pounds over a year's time.

220 Birds' feet are not covered with feathers and can lose significant amounts of body heat through their feet. Birds usually try to conserve as much energy as possible, hence the habit of standing on one leg. They also stick their head under their feathers to preserve heat.

221 One-third of Americans flush the toilet while they're sitting on it.

222 Money, which was once in the form of objects that could be weighed, explains how the English pound got its name; it first referred to a load of 7,680 dried grains of wheat.

223 For some reason, redheads have less hair than other people. Blondes, on the other hand, have more hair on their heads.

224 All magazines are bound on the left-hand side. A hypothetical postal carrier, being right-handed, naturally picks up a magazine by the spine with his right hand to read the address label—the magazine is thus turned upside down. The address labels are placed upside down to accommodate the postal carrier.

225 There are more than 10 million bricks in the Empire State Building.

226 Baseball dugouts are built half below ground because if they were built any higher, the sight lines in back of the dugout would be blocked. If they were built lower, the players would not be able to see the game.

227 All the Zodiac symbols are animals, except the symbol for Libra, which is the scales.

228 There was a huge, square metal ventilation unit on the roof of Robert Peterson's restaurant. It was really ugly, but he couldn't remove it…So he covered it up instead, disguising it as a jack-in-the-box. Then he changed the name of his restaurant, making it seem as though the whole thing had been planned.

229 Julius Caesar, the Roman Emperor, was allegedly the first person delivered through his mother's abdominal wall, via "cesarean."

230 *Snow White and the Seven Dwarfs* was Walt Disney's first full-length cartoon feature. It premiered in L.A. on December 21, 1937, and received a special Academy Award—a full-size Oscar and seven little ones.

Answers to Bafflers

231 All continents have deserts—except for Europe.

232 The song sung most often in America is *Happy Birthday To You!*

233 The hamburgers McDonald's serve in a week equal approximately 16,000 head of cattle.

234 *The Flintstones* was TV's first animated sitcom, and the first prime-time cartoon show.

235 By the time the average American teenager graduates from high school, he or she will have seen 350,000 TV commercials.

236 "Spasmatomancy" is fortune-telling based upon body twitches.

237 The most famous pardon in U.S. history occurred on September 8, 1974, when Gerald Ford granted Richard Nixon a full, free, and absolute pardon for any crimes connected with the Watergate scandal.

238 President Ulysses S. Grant was arrested during his term of office for speeding on his horse!

239 Mark Twain, Charles Dickens, and Thomas Edison never graduated from high school.

240 Marco Polo introduced fireworks to the Western World.

241 According to a Yale study, you think better in the winter than in summer.

242 Nobles and knights were sometimes assassinated by enemies who'd poisoned their wine. So when they got together socially, each poured a little of his own wine into everyone else's goblet, as a precaution. Over the years, the tradition of exchanging wine has been simplified into a gesture of friendship, clinking glasses together after a toast.

243 Between the ages of 30 and 70, the average woman shrinks two inches.

244 One in five American men have spent at least one night in jail.

245 Historians suggest that crossing your fingers for good luck comes from the pre-Christian belief that a cross symbolizes perfect unity. The intersection point of the fingers was said to possess a mystical quality which would hold the wish until it was fulfilled.

246 On Mother's Day, the most long-distance phone calls are made.

247 "Noughts and Crosses" is the British name for the game known in the U.S. as "Tic-Tac-Toe."

248 The course for a marathon race is 26 miles, 385 yards.

249 Wisconsin is known as the "Badger" state.

250 "Sweet Potato" is a nickname for the "ocarina," a small wind instrument with finger holes and a mouthpiece.

251 A dodecagon has 12 sides.

252 In 1990, 31 percent of U.S. households had telephone answering machines, compared with 5 percent in 1985.

253 The main ingredient in "vichyssoise," a thick soup, is potatoes.

254 According to *The Book of Jargon*, the term "tranny" refers to a car's "gearbox."

255 Salt was given to Roman soldiers as wages. That was their "salarium," which is the origin of our word "salary."

256 In the 19th century Jack the Ripper terrorized the city of London.

257 "Matilda," in the Australian song *Waltzing Matilda* is Australian slang for a knapsack.

258 Lettuce is the only vegetable that has never been sold in any other form but fresh.

259 Garbage collectors and warehouse workers suffer the most on-the-job back injuries.

260 H. G. Wells imagined a new kind of weapon in his 1914 story *The World Set Free*. He called the fictional device an "atomic bomb!"

Answers to Bafflers

261 Swiss Steak, Russian Dressing, Chop Suey, and Vichyssoise all originated in the United States.

262 The rim of Niagara Falls is being worn down by the millions of gallons of water that rush over it every minute, and the falls recede about two and a half feet a year.

263 In the classic "spaghetti western," *The Good, the Bad, and the Ugly,* Clint Eastwood played the role of the "Good."

264 Only about 10 percent of American households consist of a working father, a housewife mother and children under the age of 18.

265 "The Three Musketeers"—Aramis, Athos, and Porthos.

266 Lunar material was brought to earth by astronauts Armstrong, Aldrin, and Collins, and has been named Black Armalcolite in their honor.

267 94 percent of Americans claim they would marry their spouse again.

268 Baseball is the only game in which the ball is always in the possession of the team on defense, and the offensive team can score without touching the ball.

269 The penguin is the only bird in the world that can swim but not fly.

270 Breeders and trainers take nose prints from dogs and keep them on file for identification purposes.

271 The first stadium built especially for football was at Harvard in 1903.

272 The name of the clock in the tower at the Houses of Parliament in London is not "Big Ben" but the "Tower Clock." "Big Ben" is the name of the thirteen-ton bell which rings the hours in the clock.

273 Confederate general Thomas "Stonewall" Jackson died after being shot accidentally by his own troops in 1863.

274 A heavily loaded raft will move faster down a river than an empty raft because it lies deeper in the water.

275 A "shaddock" is a grapefruit.

276 A woodpecker can peck twenty times a second.

277 When Leslie King's parents were divorced, he was adopted by his stepfather and given a new name, Gerald Ford.

278 When asked to name a color, three out of five people will say "red."

279 The square-topped cap worn at graduation ceremonies is called a "mortarboard."

280 Kleenex was called "Celluwipes" when first marketed in 1924.

281 At this moment, 70% of Americans driving on the highway are speeding.

282 Smokey the Bear's original name was "Hot Foot Teddy."

283 A person's left hand does 56 percent of the typing.

284 The capacity of the average adult's stomach is about two quarts.

285 The longest running television show is *Meet The Press,* which first aired on November 20, 1947.

286 The grandfather of Charles Lindbergh changed the family's last name from Manson. If he hadn't, our high flying hero would have been known as Charles Manson.

287 The oldest known vegetable is the pea, used by the Chinese as far back as 2,000 B.C.

288 The average American carries four credit cards.

289 Men outnumber women in prison in the U.S. by 25 to 1.

290 A cave man's life span was only 18 years.
291 The U.S.A.'s gold is kept at Ft. Knox and the country's silver is kept at West Point.
292 In 1818, Congress reduced the number of stripes on the U.S. Flag from 15 to 13, which was the original number of stripes. They had been increased to 15 after 2 states had been added.
293 "Hippophobia" is a fear of horses.
294 Four out of five people who try out a new pen will write their own name.
295 There are 100 tiles, 98 letters and 2 blanks, in the game of Scrabble.
296 You'll find more brown M&M's than any other color in a package of that candy.
297 In 1948, George H. W. Bush, as first baseman, was named captain of Yale's NCAA champion baseball team.
298 "Wanted: Young, skinny, wiry fellows not over 18. Must be expert riders, willing to risk death daily. Orphans preferred. Wages $25.00 a week." If you fit this mid-1800's help wanted ad, you'd have been a perfect candidate for the Pony Express.
299 Yes, there really was a Santa Claus, which is another name for St. Nicholas, the 4th-century Bishop of Myra, in Asia Minor. He was known as the giver of gifts. The English and Dutch combined the St. Nicholas and Christmas traditions; and when many Dutch emigrated to America, they brought St. Nicholas with them as part of the Christmas gift-giving custom.
300 Dr. Joel R. Poinsett was the United States Ambassador to Mexico in 1828. He is responsible for bringing the beautiful blooming plant we now call the poinsettia to this country. In Mexico it is known as the *Flower of the Holy Night*, and has been a favorite symbol of the holidays long before it was brought here.

MORE TO PONDER

Visit www.ponders.biz for additional products and services

Ponders.biz – Visit our web portal for a dose of daily inspiration. Learn about our new products and services including branded relationship building tools, PonderNotes, Ponder Mugs, Ponder Cookies and more. Join our emailing list to receive free Ponders of the Week. Suggest favorite quotes for us to include in future publications.

Branded Relationship Mailer Service –
A proven "high touch" method to build and solidify relationships with current customers and prospects. This is essentially the same concept Rodney Weckworth used to help grow his company to multi-millions in sales. You provide us with an initial mailing list and we will take care of the rest.

Branded Permission Email Program – Our service allows you to automatically send your branded emails to clients and prospects on a weekly basis. You simply log into our website, set up an account and enter or upload the names and email address of those people you wish to stay in touch with on a weekly basis. Our systems do the rest. We send out emails on a weekly basis to arrive at your customers' inbox each Monday morning.

Ponders Web Feed Service – Need a tool to encourage visitors to revisit your site? Consider placing our inspirational quote feed on your website front page. Have your webmaster or us insert a piece of code in your site and a new quote will appear there daily. You may even find people using your site as their home page.

www.ponders.biz

Thank you for your recent note and enclosed copy of Rod's Ponders. I wanted you to know how much I appreciate them.

—Alan Greenspan, Chairman of Federal Reserve System

Thank you for your recent note and the copy of "Rod's Thoughts to Ponder" - week of September 24, 1990. I did enjoy reading them. It was most thoughtful of you to add me to your list of weekly recipients.

—Colin L. Powell, Chairman Joint Chiefs of Staff

I just wanted to let you know how much I appreciate receiving Rod's Ponders each week! I pass it around to each member of my staff and even fax it to a few close friends and family.

—Sammy F. Cemo, Cemo, Inc.

We have already gotten a number of positive responses from our Ponders recipients, and we look forward to expanding our Ponders mailing list soon.

—Alan Gunn Steal, Business Development - Tom Hopkins Construction

Today I received your first Thoughts to Ponder, and I'm already looking forward to next week's thoughts.

—Mary Lou Watts, Associate Editor - Daily Pacific Builder

They (Ponders) are always a welcome sight as they arrive at my desk. They have often been just the boost I have needed to recommit the energy required to engage the challenges of my personal life and the daily rigors of operating a small business. They are much appreciated.

—Rick Carlile, Principal Architect - Arktegraf

My wife and I enjoy your...efforts in putting out "Rod's Ponders." Ponders and Principlas are frequently put on the refrigerator door for our children and grandchildren alike to peruse. They make a lot of sense and can certainly contribute to a better attitude on life and everyday relationships.

—J.C, Roseville, CA

I would like to send my thanks for your helpful thoughts to ponder.

—Pete Wilson, United States Senate

On behalf of President Bush, thank you for your thoughtful message.

—Shirley M. Green, The White House , Washington D.C.